Refusing Sustainability

Refusing Sustainability

Race and Environmentalism in a Changing Europe

Elana Resnick

STANFORD UNIVERSITY PRESS
Stanford, California

Stanford University Press
Stanford, California

© 2025 by Elana Resnick. All rights reserved.

No part of this book may be reproduced or transmitted in any form or by any means, electronic or mechanical, including photocopying and recording, or in any information storage or retrieval system, without the prior written permission of Stanford University Press.

Library of Congress Cataloging-in-Publication Data
Names: Resnick, Elana, author.
Title: Refusing sustainability : race and environmentalism in a changing
    Europe / Elana Resnick.
Description: Stanford, California : Stanford University Press, [2025] |
    Includes bibliographical references and index.
Identifiers: LCCN 2024042785 (print) | LCCN 2024042786 (ebook) | ISBN
    9781503635425 (cloth) | ISBN 9781503641259 (paperback) | ISBN
    9781503641266 (ebook)
Subjects: LCSH: Romanies–Bulgaria–Social conditions. | Racism against
    Romanies–Bulgaria. | Refuse and refuse disposal–Bulgaria–Employees. |
    Sustainability–Social aspects–Bulgaria. | Environmental policy–Social
    aspects–Bulgaria. | Bulgaria–Race relations.
Classification: LCC DX221.5 .R47 2025 (print) | LCC DX221.5 (ebook) | DDC
    305.8914/970499–dc23/eng/20241228
LC record available at https://lccn.loc.gov/2024042785
LC ebook record available at https://lccn.loc.gov/2024042786

Cover design: Lindy Kasler
Cover art: lzabela Ivanova, *Heart of the City*, 2024, digital illustration,
Sofia, Bulgaria.
Typeset by Newgen in Latino URW Regular 9.75/14

The authorized representative in the EU for product safety and compliance is: Mare Nostrum Group B.V. | Mauritskade 21D | 1091 GC Amsterdam | The Netherlands | Email address: gpsr@mare-nostrum.co.uk | KVK chamber of commerce number: 96249943

*To Will, Ezra, and Ares, who are the
best part of every day.*

CONTENTS

Acknowledgments		ix
Note on Language and Terminology		xix
Note on Illustrations		xxiii
	Introduction	1
1	Waste and Race	33
2	Recycling	66
3	Surveillance	93
4	Voting	123
5	Friendship	151
	Conclusion: Running Water in the Land of Spitting Dragons	179
	Notes	201
	References	235
	Index	261

ACKNOWLEDGMENTS

This book has seen a lot of life and death along its path. A book, I've realized, is a testament to how time passes and what we make in its midst.

My deepest thanks go to the people in Bulgaria who shared their time with me. Without them, this project would not be possible. Since so many of them need to remain anonymous, I cannot thank them individually here, but I hope they know how much they mean to both this book and my life.

Fortunately, there are some people I can name. Kalinka Vassileva and Orhan Tahir, you have been my steadfast friends, brilliant colleagues, and co-theorists since you first welcomed me to Bulgaria in 2003. I can never thank you enough. You have taught me a way of thinking, including the power of finding humor, even in dark times, that is the foundation for this project. Without your generosity, I never would have started my PhD or written this book. The Vassilevi family entered my life when I was nineteen and have been part of every life cycle event since. I only hope I have absorbed some of the infectious joy and dedication to adventure they bring to the world. Orhan, your wisdom, wit, intellectual courage, and critical analyses have taught me more than any famous social theorist ever could. Our conversations keep me energized and grounded, and I just wish we could talk more. Biserka Yotova and the entire Yotovi

ACKNOWLEDGMENTS

family made Bulgaria, especially Fakulteta, a home. Your faith in me, strength, and love for life inspired me to keep this project going. Some of my warmest memories are in your kitchen on the holidays, and some of the most fun I had in Bulgaria involved driving in the car with you, music blaring and windows open, on our way to do just about anything.

The street sweepers in this book, who remain anonymous, showed me what adult friendships between women could be, something that is hard to come by wherever one is. They accepted me and my terrible sweeping skills, taught me about so much more than just work, and listened to my daily ups and downs with empathy. They saw the best in me and this project, and I hope I have at least come close to writing something that lives up to what powerful, brave, and wonderfully tenacious people they are. Their experiences of working motherhood are something I still reflect on, in awe, nearly every day. Baka, your generosity and fearless humor inspire me and this book in countless ways. I hope you see your contributions to all its pages.

I started this project with activists in the NGO sector, Romani media, and other human rights and civil society organizations in Bulgaria. Over the years they welcomed me, my questions, and my presence in a variety of spaces. I feel lucky to also call you my friends: Tano Bechev, Zarko Chankov, Vassil Chaprazov, Tony Chinkov, Emil Cohen, Emiliya Dancheva, Aneliya Dudinova, Dimitar Georgiev, Mihail Georgiev, Gancho Iliev, Milena Ilieva, Ognyan Isaev, Angel Ivanov, Krassimir Kanev, Anton Karagyozov, Asen Karagyozov, Toshka Kocheva, Deyan Kolev, Stela Kosteva, Lilyana Kovacheva, Krasimir Krasimirov, Hristo Kyuchukov, Valeri Lekov, Emil Metodiev, Maria Metodieva, Spaska Mihaylova, Daniela Mihaylova, Milen Milanov, Violeta Bogdanova Monteban Naydenova, Dimitrina Petrova, Silvia Petrova, Pepa Puncheva, Asen Radev, Tossan Ramar, Rumyan Russinov, Silvia Slavcheva, Snezhina Slaveva, Antoaneta Stefanova, Maya Stel, Atanas Stoyanov, Tashko Tanov, Mira Tchileva, Galya Traykova, Nataliya Tsekova, Yuksel Yasharov, Miglena Yordanova, and Ludmila Zhivkova.

On issues related to waste, infrastructure, and environmentalism in Bulgaria, I am honored to have an incredible group of people to turn to: Milen Atanasov, Rosalina Babourkova, Biliana Boneva-Atanasova, Diana Dimitrova, Ivaylo Hlebarov, Nina Ilieva, Genady Kondarev, Petko Kovachev, Malina Krumova, Velislava Petrova, Julian Popov, Borislav Sandov, Nikolay Sidjimov, Albena Simeonova, Stefan Stefanov, Evgenia

ACKNOWLEDGMENTS

Tasheva, Elka Vasileva, Nikola Venkov, Danita Zarichinova, Nikolay Zhelev, and Teodora Zheleva.

On topics related to just about everything else in Bulgaria, I have had the pleasure of discussions with and feedback from Matthew Brunwasser, Ivaylo Dinev, Tsvetelina Hristova, Mariya Ivancheva, Veneta Ivanova, Rada Kaneva, Dimiter Kenarov, Stefan Krastev, Anna Krasteva, Robert Levy, Natalia Miteva, Irina Nedeva, Proshko Proshkov, Angela Rodel, Louisa Slavkova, Ruslan Stefanov, Chuck Sudetic, Evgeni Todorov, and Martin Vladimirov. I also wish to thank my friends and colleagues in Bulgaria who always made time for me and reminded me that sometimes I could stop taking notes: Kamelia Atanasova, Daniel Bensen, Pavlina Borisova-Bensen, Sarah Perrine Chandra, David Djambazov, Joseph Herr, Evgeni Kirilov, Mihail Kossev, Mladen Minev, Valentina Nikolova, Zhoro Penchev, Mariana Pencheva, Maria Petrova, Nevena Petrova, Kiril Radulov, Andrew David Ridgway, Desislava Sarbinovska, Tsvetan Sarbinovski, Anna Stoeva, Hristina Tahchieva, Ana Todorcheva, George Tsonev, and Elitsa Yakimov. Iliana Dimitrova, Stana Iliev, and Sophia Kleinsasser—for more than a decade you have been there for the small things and the big events (including the end of my twenties!), and you keep reminding me that there are always more good times ahead.

I never could have done this project without the many friends and interlocutors who served as informal language teachers, helping me learn as I go. But I also need to thank my incredibly patient and committed expert language teachers, for both Bulgarian and Romanes: Stefka Bachvarova, Kristina Bumbarova, Vassil Chaprazov, Hristo Kyuchukov, and Radost Sabeva.

This book has taken many paths, some of which are still in flux. One is a performance-based collaboration with Christina Freeman that helped me see the power in the present when all I was doing was documentation. I also developed an interest in film along the way, in great thanks to a project developed with Bojina Panayotova. Bojina then introduced me to Rayna Teneva, who has helped me understand more about filmmaking and collective creation than I had ever hoped. Brian George's artistic expertise helped me see my work in new ways.

This book is the product of so much labor, including, in Bulgaria, the research assistance of Dimiter Angelov, Gergana Chinovska, Emil Dimitrov, Nina Dyakova, Iliana Gyulcheva-Bobova, Hristo Hristov, Rositsa Hristova Milkova, Filipa Kirilova, Alexandra Markova,

xii ACKNOWLEDGMENTS

Veronica Martinova, Adrian Nikolov, Kalin Radulov, Denitsa Spasova, Nicoleta Stefanova, and Silvia Slavcheva. Denitsa Stoimenova and I worked together at all hours through the end—I am incredibly grateful for Deni's unwavering support of this project and her careful attention to the smallest details. At the University of California, Santa Barbara (UCSB), I have benefited from working with brilliant graduate students: Gehad Abaza, Patrick Hunnicut, Heather Prentice-Walz, and Ramsha Usman.

This book comes out of many conversations with and thoughtful feedback from Chloe Ahmann, Sarah Bakker Kellogg, Ethel Brooks, Melissa Caldwell, Cécile Canut, Emily Channell-Justice, Ioanida Costache, Sarah Craycraft, Gerald Creed, Carl Dahlman, Eric De Sena, Theodora Dragostinova, Ger Duijzings, Martin Fotta, Severin Fowles, Rosalind Fredericks, Susan Gal, Ilana Gershon, Kristen Ghodsee, David Boarder Giles, Zsuzsa Gille, Donna Goldstein, Kathryn Graber, Krista Harper, Krista Hegburg, Michael Herzfeld, Max Holleran, Anikó Imre, Yuson Jung, Roy Kimmey, Neringa Klumbytė, Angéla Kóczé, Martha Lampland, Siv Lie, Eran Livni, Paul Manning, Nikolay Marinov, Kathleen Millar, Robin Nagle, Mary Neuburger, Steve Norris, Damani Partridge, Eda Pepi, Joshua Reno, Sunnie Rucker-Chang, Carol Silverman, Michael Silverstein, Marisa Solomon, Daniel Sosna, Sophia Stamatopoulou-Robbins, Zara Torlone, Chelsi West Ohueri, and Amy Zhang. Bruce Grant, an unofficial advisor on most things, read this work in its entirety over his summer vacation and provided extensive and incredibly incisive feedback. His level of generosity is unobtainable but a goal to strive for.

These conversations formalized in a book workshop in January 2021 sponsored by the University of California Humanities Research Institute. Neda Atanasoski, Catherine Fennell, Mayanthi Fernando, Jessica Greenberg, Anand Pandian, Savannah Shange, and Deborah Thomas took two days to turn this book into something I'm proud of. Their collective push to take my time and stop hedging subsequently emboldened me in ways that are revealed in these pages and beyond.

To my friends-who-are-now-family spread across the United States and beyond, who remained patient enough to wait for me while I was in the throes of writing (and forgetting to text them back), and who continue to remind me how much lifelong friendships matter, I thank you: Rebecca Aronauer, Christina Freeman, Sarah Greene, Jacqueline Novello, and Niloufer Siddiqui.

ACKNOWLEDGMENTS

This project began at Haverford College in the summer of 2003 when the Center for Peace and Global Citizenship sponsored my first trip to Bulgaria. I had taken a class on endangered languages and read about the role of Romani language in school-based discrimination in Europe, and I decided to work on educational issues facing Roma in Eastern Europe. I sent an email to a human rights mailing list about wanting to volunteer on the topic and got dozens of responses. It was serendipitous, or perhaps an act of fate, that I landed on the Equal Access Foundation, the organization led by Kalinka Vassileva in Sofia, Bulgaria. I returned to Haverford in the fall of 2003 committed to Romani activism, and I thank the faculty there at that time for helping me find concrete ways to investigate what moved me: Kimberly Benston, Jenny Godley, Laurie Kain Hart, Martin Hébert, Laura McGrane, Zolani Ngwane, Jennifer Patico, Gus Stadler, and Christina Zwarg.

University of Michigan is where this book took shape. Alaina Lemon was the best advisor I could have ever imagined. She empowered me to take the space to develop the project in my own way and never stopped asking her amazingly insightful questions. Her trust in me and the project gave me the confidence I needed to see it through. Krisztina Fehérváry's approach to postsocialism and materiality has had a lasting influence on my work. After taking my first course with her, I could never see anything the same way again. I appreciate her ongoing support and sage advice. Gillian Feeley-Harnik's office hours were meditative. Her reminders about my responsibility to the people in this book, as my primary audience, is something I return to at each fork in the road. Pamela Ballinger helped so much in the final stages at the University of Michigan and enabled me to see the work in a new way. Damani Partridge asked the question I keep on asking: "What are the stakes?" I start my own graduate seminars with those same words, which keep us all as grounded as we can be. Webb Keane's courses sparked so much thought and I know now that it is hard to replicate those kinds of neural firings on a regular basis. Matthew Hull fundamentally changed this project when he asked me if there was something material to focus on, beyond a politics of Romani identity. That marked the moment when waste moved from my peripheral vision into the foreground. Jason De León's feedback along the way, both waste-related and not, have made this a better book. What Stuart Kirsch taught me about collaboration and engaged anthropology runs through my

xiv ACKNOWLEDGMENTS

ethnography and writing at each step. John Fine, Dario Gaggio, Judith Irvine, Rudy Linder, Bruce Mannheim, Barbara Meek, Erik Mueggler, and Jennifer Robertson helped me figure out academia and my contributions to it. I entered into a four-field cohort in Michigan of nearly forty students. I had fun in graduate school thanks to the collective spirit of the group and some key friends whose support and friendship still keep me afloat: Meghanne Barker, Nick Emlen, Lavrentia Karamaniola, Scott MacLochlainn, Shana Melnysyn, Luciana Nemțanu, Bruno Renero-Hannan, Jessica Robbins-Panko. Vanessa Díaz and Jane Lynch, you have helped me stay true to what drives my research and me as a person—I am so grateful.

UCSB gave me the job security, time, and support to write this book. When I felt lost in Santa Barbara's freeway traffic and strangely warm winters, Write-On-Site for faculty in the UCSB library provided solace. One of my favorite ways to make friends, I've discovered, is writing in silence next to them for months, only to later figure out they are great to talk with, too: Summer Gray, Rebecca Powers, Martha Sprigge, and Heather Steffen. The relationships I have built in Santa Barbara, at UCSB and beyond, have made California feel like home: Elizabeth Ackert, Jean Beaman, Cristina Bentley, Alicia Boswell, Inés Casillas, Jia-Ching Chen, Rachel Cohen, Mona Damluji, Esmé Deprez, Raine Hahn, Charles Hale, Hahrie Han, Ben Levy, Megan Mahdavi, Matto Mildenberger, Samantha Narang, David Pellow, Swati Rana, Dana Ullmann Rosenkrantz, Vineeta Singh, Leah Stokes, and Lisa Sun-Hee Park. My colleagues in the Department of Anthropology and their time, support, and generosity have made this project immeasurably better, especially the sociocultural faculty: Mary Hancock, Barbara Harthorn, Jeffrey Hoelle, Mohamad Jarada, Raquel Pacheco, and Casey Walsh. Barbara and Lisa, your mentorship has provided me much strength in the face of everything.

Research and writing was made possible with support from the American Councils Title VIII Research Scholar Program, the American Research Center in Sofia, Central European University's Institute for Advanced Study, the Council for European Studies/Andrew Mellon Foundation, the Fulbright Program, the Havighurst Center for East European, Russian and Eurasian Studies, the School for Advanced Research, the University of California at Santa Barbara, the University of California Humanities Research Institute, the University of Michigan, and the Wenner-Gren Foundation. The UCSB Academic Senate provided a subvention award that offset production costs and made it possible to share this book widely by making it open access.

I am grateful to all who provided feedback at presentations and workshops along the way: Central European University Romani Studies Program, Columbia University Department of Anthropology, the Czech Academy of Sciences Institute of Ethnology, the Discard Studies Collective, EASA Linguistic Anthropology Network (ELAN) Reading Group, Miami University Havighurst Center for East European, Russian and Eurasian Studies, New Bulgarian University Department of Anthropology, Oberlin College Center for Russian, East European, and Central Asian Studies, the Ohio State University Mershon Center for International Security Studies, the UCSB Mellon Sawyer Seminar on Race, Precarity, and Privilege, the School for Advanced Research in Santa Fe, Sofia University Department of Theory and History of Culture, the United States Holocaust Memorial Museum, the University of Connecticut Human Rights Institute, the University of Illinois Urbana-Champaign Midwaste Symposium, the University of Massachusetts Amherst Department of Anthropology, the University of Michigan Center for Russian, East European, and Eurasian Studies, the University of North Texas Department of Anthropology, the Institute of East and Southeast European Studies (IOS) in Regensburg, the University of Southern California Department of Anthropology, and Washington University in St. Louis Department of Anthropology.

I also want to express gratitude to the editors and reviewers at *American Anthropologist*, *American Ethnologist*, *Cultural Anthropology*, and *Public Culture*, where pieces of this book have trickled out over the years. I thank the editors and the anonymous reviewers for their excellent feedback and for the permission to reprint selections. Parts of Chapter 2 appeared in "Sustaining Containability: Zero Waste and White Space," *Cultural Anthropology* 39, no. 2 (2024): 216–245. An earlier version of sections from Chapter 5 appeared as "The Intimacy of Labor: Street Sweeping and the Pleasures of Anything Else," *Public Culture* 35, no. 2 (2023): 233–254.

At Stanford University Press, Dylan Kung-lim White acquired this book with so much enthusiasm that it made me excited about the book again. His kindness, creativity, and editorial skills are unmatched, and I feel fortunate to have the chance to work with him. The two anonymous reviewers who read the manuscript helped shape it into something infinitely more readable, interesting, and emotionally honest. Amy Benson Brown coached me through a pandemic, helping me to keep writing, and

ACKNOWLEDGMENTS

to keep finding peace in it, while the world felt like it was falling apart. Megan Pugh saw beauty where I saw only words; her developmental editing is art. Micha Rahder fine-tuned this manuscript into something publishable and clear while retaining my vision. Caryn O'Connell, you have been there when I needed help most and have repeatedly turned my mess of words into cogent sentences. Finally, Izabela Krasimirova Ivanova created the book's cover and illustrations. Izabela, I am so lucky to learn from you and your commitment to representing empowered Romani womanhood. You made this book come to life visually by giving a beautiful and playful answer to the questions of how to preserve anonymity without having to blur faces.

I could not have written this book without the community that cared for my children while I was tending to the research and the writing. My deepest thanks goes to Sophia Maranon, a superhero of a person who cared for our children while attending UCSB and figuring out life as a twentysomething during a pandemic. I also thank all the childcare providers in the United States, Greece, and Bulgaria that shared in raising my two children.

My father, Paul Resnick, died not long before I completed my PhD. His sense of humor, courage, and fearlessness, I now realize, probably inspired much of my approach. My mother, Adrienne Resnick, has always supported my ideas and plans, allowing me to give life to what I desire most. Molly Starkman, my grandmother who helped take care of me as a child, passed away in 2021. Her love of music, me, and the small things in life reverberate. Martin Starkman's strength and dedication live on through this. George Nomikos's enthusiasm and support for this project and our family helped at each stage. Andriana Vellis was a uniquely generous force of nature, who also took off from work whenever we went to Bulgaria to help take care of us all.

Ezra and Ares, you are in each page of this book. Ezra shared his COVID toddler years with my deadlines; playing with him was the best distraction from my writing and would remind me of all the joys that exist beyond the text. Ezra has been my constant research companion and question-asker since, and I will never stop appreciating his excitement about spending his precious childhood summers in Bulgaria. I went into labor with Ares while bouncing on a yoga ball and proofreading an application for a fellowship to give me the time to finish this book. Thanks to his staunch persistence, I submitted that file fast, got off the

ACKNOWLEDGMENTS xvii

yoga ball, and reached the hospital right before he came earthside. I finished the first version of this manuscript during his morning naptimes (a writing practice, emblematic of the pressures of academia, that I don't recommend to anyone). I thank him for sleeping long enough to allow this book to happen.

That leads me to thank my partner in all things, Will Nomikos, who wore Ares in a baby carrier and bounced him for hours while he wrote his own book, so I could get out of the house to write mine. His dedication to our family and my research makes everything possible. I never thought I would love anything as much as I love my work in Bulgaria until I met him. Will, you have helped me realize how I can be a partner, mother, scholar, friend, and human, in the fullest way.

NOTE ON LANGUAGE AND TERMINOLOGY

Pseudonyms

I have struggled with pseudonyms in this book. I have fully anonymized anyone whom I was unable to reach for consent in making their name public in the book, to err on the side of privacy protection. However, there are others in this book who told me they were fine with being anonymized, or not. In those cases, I have kept them anonymous in order to allow them to choose on their own how they will represent their role in the book when it is published and to allow them to change their choices later. Baka made it clear she wanted to be known by her name, which I have included here along with her photo.

Most organizations and neighborhoods in the book, including where I worked as a sweeper and NGO volunteer, have been anonymized to preserve the privacy of those with whom I worked. Anyone who passed away over the course of the book writing has also been anonymized because although their next of kin might be able to consent, they no longer can, and I want to respect that for the sake of their memory. Public figures, except when noted otherwise, are not anonymized. Large Romani neighborhoods, like Fakulteta and Filipovtsi, are not anonymized due their size.

xix

Terminology and Capitalization

In line with Romani scholars like Ioanida Costache,[1] I omit the first "y" from "G*psy" throughout this book because the term is used as a racial slur, and I don't want to inflict harm on readers or replicate this racist terminology in my own work. I have also replaced the "a" in the Bulgarian derogatory slur (m*ngal) for the same reason. I have maintained all original spellings in the reference list, however.

I capitalize "Black" throughout the book when referring to positionality or racial identity but have decided not to capitalize it when it's used (in Bulgarian [m. cheren/f. cherna/pl. cherni] or Romani [m. kalo/f. kali/pl. kale]) as a descriptor term. My choice to leave "white" uncapitalized does not indicate that whiteness is any sort of standard, unmarked, nonracial category.

Language

I conducted my research predominantly in Bulgarian but also in Romani. My interlocutors tended to use Bulgarian when I was actively transcribing, and therefore, when transliterations appear, the default language is Bulgarian. When one is working with people day after day, the boundaries between collegiality, friendship, and ethnography blur. For that reason, I decided to only write down what sweepers explicitly noted I should, which was often indicated by their pointed use of Bulgarian. To allow for some workplace privacy, I witnessed and took part in but rarely documented conversations between sweepers that were in Romani unless directly told to do so. However, there were times when they used the Romani terms for things and indicated they wanted those documented, so I made sure to write those down. I have noted that throughout. Most translations are my own.

Transliteration

I transliterate the Bulgarian Cyrillic alphabet into Latin letters throughout this text. I base this transliteration on a combination of the US Library of Congress transliteration system, the Bulgarian Transliteration Law, and what is most commonly used to represent the sound of spoken Bulgarian characters.[2]

NOTE ON LANGUAGE AND TERMINOLOGY

I transliterate the characters as follows:

Cyrillic Bulgarian uppercase/lowercase	*Latinized Bulgarian uppercase/lowercase*
А/а	A/a
Б/б	B/b
В/в	V/v
Г/г	G/g
Д/д	D/d
Е/е	E/e
Ж/ж	Zh/zh
З/з	Z/z
И/и	I/i
Й/й	Y/y
К/к	K/k
Л/л	L/l
М/м	M/m
Н/н	N/n
О/о	O/o
П/п	P/p
Р/р	R/r
С/с	S/s
Т/т	T/t
У/у	U/u
Ф/ф	F/f
Х/х	H/h
Ц/ц	Ts/ts
Ч/ч	Ch/ch
Ш/ш	Sh/sh
Щ/щ	Sht/sht
Ъ/ъ	A/a
Ь/ь	Y, y
Ю/ю	Yu/yu
Я/я	Ya/ya[3]

NOTE ON ILLUSTRATIONS

All illustrations were created for this book by Bulgarian Romani artist Izabela Ivanova. The illustrations in this book have been used in two ways: 1) to preserve anonymity of those photographed in the book and 2) to replace images that were originally in low, unusable quality. Izabela used photographs I had taken as the starting point for each one.

Izabela Ivanova also created the cover for this book based on our discussions about images and excerpts from the book. The cover represents Sofia, a city in flux, and the empowerment of the people that make it what it is—the waste workers. The statue in the foreground is a take on the towering downtown statue of Saint Sofia (*Sveta Sofiya*), the patron saint of the city. In front of the statue is the illustrator's representation of Sofia's iconic landmark, the Largo (*Largoto*), an architectural ensemble of three socialist-built edifices in central Sofia that were designed and erected in the 1950s with the intention of becoming the city's new socialist center. In all likelihood, to build the Largo, Romani homes in the vicinity were displaced and destroyed.[1]

The Largo is now revered as a prime example of socialist classicism architecture: In the center, one can see the former Bulgaria Communist Party House (now used as the seat of the National Assembly of Bulgaria).

NOTE ON ILLUSTRATIONS

On one side (not pictured) is an edifice accommodating the socialist-era, still-working TSUM department store and the Bulgarian Council of Ministers. On the other side (also not pictured) is a building currently occupied by the President's Office, the Ministry of Education, and the Sheraton Sofia Hotel Balkan (the site of the protest in Chapter 3). The statue's garment is imaginatively depicted as red, the same color as the uniforms of the workers around her and the waste workers in this book, highlighting the wisdom and importance of the people that sustain Sofia as a "European" city.

The cover image links the urban environmentalism happening in Sofia all around the city's patron saint, with signs of European Union (EU) progress set against both the grandiose socialist classicist buildings and socialist-built prefabricated apartment buildings (*panelki*) and vegetable stalls (*sergii*). Saint Sofia is overlooking all of it with a distinguished crown on her head (like the sweepers of Chapter 5) and the owl of wisdom on her arm. The reader can also see the recycling bins, horse carts, street sweepers, garbage collectors, and Sofia's EU-era emblems like the new metro station, recycling bins, the Inter Expo Center (of Chapter 2), and an eminent skyscraper.

Introduction

I had just finished eating an entire birthday cake on the side of a busy road with my good friend, Baka.

We had finished her rounds collecting discarded items from city streetside dumpsters in Sofia, Bulgaria, when we came upon one of her favorite spots for a quick rest. The cake had been discarded fresh from Nedelya, one of Sofia's nicer cake shops. As we passed the store that October morning, Baka had sweetly asked its young clerk if anything had been recently thrown out; it was getting hot, and she did not want us to eat cream that had gone bad. He greeted her, smiled, and exaggeratedly threw out a big, beautiful, white-frosted cake right in front of us, so that we would know it was safe to eat.

We took the cake and sat on the cool concrete curb between two parked cars. Baka reminded me, laughing, that we were not far from where, working together a few weeks earlier, I had discovered a dead mouse in a metal dumpster and screamed so loudly it made her jump.

We washed our hands with water from a plastic bottle I carried with me, wiped them on the inside of our shirts, and ate the sugary vanilla cream and strawberry cake until we felt sick. "Life is good to me," Baka announced as we walked away, fingers sticky. "It's not easy, but it's good.

———

Baka, a sixtysomething Romani widow, had worked as an office cleaner earlier in her life, under state socialism. Now, she supplemented her insufficient pension by collecting other people's trash from dumpsters for resale. She went on foot each morning, carrying her tools: a metal stick and a magnet made of tiny, connected balls. Baka used her stick to move things around inside dumpsters, protecting her hands from used diapers, stray needles, and broken bottles. It was her first line of defense against the potential harms of unknowable discarded items. The magnet was important for figuring out if something was iron and therefore worth keeping to sell as raw material or if it was aluminum and not worth lugging around. The price of scrap metal depends on the international waste market, and Baka was acutely aware of its daily fluctuations.

Baka was small and wry, with sparkling blue eyes that made her look quick to laugh, which she was. She was well-liked by many who lived and worked in the area she traversed—a white, non-Romani, and therefore, in local parlance, "Bulgarian" neighborhood—and she told me that the

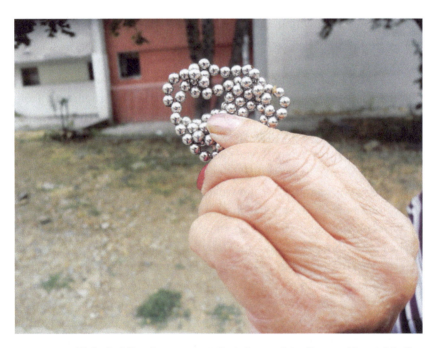

FIGURE 0.1 Baka holding her magnet that she used to discern if metal is ferrous (containing iron) and magnetic or not. She painted her fingernails different colors as a kind of walking advertisement to display the cosmetics she found in the dumpsters that she would resell. Photo by the author.

FIGURE 0.2 Baka working, picking out which items to resell. Illustration by Izabela Ivanova.

police never stopped her.[1] Still, she always kept her state-issued ID ready in the front pocket of her homemade uniform, a blue-and-white cotton smock that hung loosely on top of her clothing, "just in case."[2]

As we moved along Baka's route, we ran into a middle-aged couple from Fakulteta, the Romani neighborhood (*mahala*) where she lived, who were on foot like us. Baka asked why they were not working from a horse cart, as they typically did. They explained that they had been in the cart a few days earlier when a man with a knife stopped his car at a traffic light, got out, and attempted to stab them. They referred to the man as a "skinhead" (*skinar*), but it was not clear to me if he had been dressed in neo-Nazi paraphernalia, as had become common among Sofia youth, or if they categorized him as such based on the attack. The husband took a small rusting pocketknife out of his shirt pocket to show me that he would have protection if it happened again. His wife snickered, muttering under her breath with affectionate exasperation that he would never be fast enough to use it. Being on foot, she explained, made it easier to avoid attention. Baka nodded knowingly.

After we walked away from the couple, Baka recounted the time a few years back when she had been collecting from dumpsters with her daughter, Aneliya. A young man accosted them on the street, yelling slurs, and attempted to beat them. The worst part, she explained matter-of-factly as she took a drag from the single Marlboro cigarette she had purchased from a nearby convenience store, was that it had happened in the middle of the day on a crowded street, and everyone looked on in silence. Nobody did a thing. "It's okay," she explained when she saw the pained look on my face. "I already knew that there is only misery here. We are going to die of something, probably hunger. But it is convenient for us Roma because the cemeteries are nearby."

FIGURE 0.3 Men collecting trash with a horse cart, outside of Fakulteta. They are passing a storage shed with the word for social "trash" (*boklutsi*) written in Bulgarian next to a graffitied swastika. Photo by the author.

INTRODUCTION

Baka's morbid joke referred to the fact that many of Sofia's Romani neighborhoods border large cemeteries. This is a material outcome of a long history of Bulgarian urbanization projects in which Romani communities have been moved farther and farther from city centers to end up near undesirable spaces, including where dead bodies are buried.[3] It is an irony often noted in my Romani interlocutors' descriptions of there being "no life" (*nyama zhivot*) left for them in Bulgaria—even their neighbors were dead. This understanding of "no life" functions across multiple registers. I came to understand the phrase as referring to the landscapes of death amid which Roma are forced to live, to the everyday violence they encounter while working on the streets of Bulgaria's capital city, and to the so-called progressive EU policies that both subjugate and rely on them.[4]

Baka laughed, hitting me on the arm to make sure I laughed too, and we kept walking to finish our work before the noonday heat. We moved quickly from dumpster to dumpster, weaving down major roads where she repeatedly held my hand to cross the street, outstretching her other arm across my chest to protect me as we ran through traffic. She continuously commented on things she found in the trash: "Look at these uncultured Bulgarians, they don't even eat what they buy."

She had just found a full box of expensive, individually foil-wrapped Merci chocolates, not yet melted. It could make her some money if she sold it as is, so we did not open it. "It's Europe now, here, but they're not European." Upon discovering a complete, ripe, unblemished watermelon in the trash, she explained that discarding usable things like this signaled that their former owners, who would have been white Bulgarians (based on where we were in the city), had no sense of "culture." "They don't even know how to socialize. Just look at them."

At that, Baka looked up at a man wearing only a skimpy blue bathing suit on a balcony in a fancy high-rise above us, gesturing and speaking so loudly on his cell phone that we could hear his conversation six floors below. "Is that Europe? Is that culture?" I shook my head. I had heard so many different invocations of Europe—as a geographic place, a fanciful aspiration, a proxy for whiteness—that I did not know what the word meant anymore.[5] Baka recounted the time that one of her cousins, while collecting waste in Germany, found a kilo of gold in the pointy toe of a discarded boot. It was a take on an urban legend I had heard many times before, circulating among waste workers and allowing them to imagine

FIGURE 0.4 Baka at home. Photo by the author.

the possibility that their daily labor would one day pay off. "That's what we've become. Europe. *They* throw out gold and we eat cake from the trash. But isn't it delicious?"

The midmorning cake break was a temporary moment of shared respite, one of many I documented: the intimate yet communal kinds of life-making that take place amid decaying infrastructures, strenuous waste labor, and a political system unable and unwilling to remedy the entrenched racism that threatens the lives of Bulgarian Roma. In this book, drawing on fieldwork with both official and less-regulated waste labor practices at multiple scales, I show how Bulgarian Roma, and particularly Romani women, are conflated with the trash they collect.[6] In other words, they are often made out to be less than human despite the increasing significance of the work they do for international environmental policy standards.[7] However, even the fact that their work's importance has to be pointed out is part of the problem: For centuries, Roma have tried, in myriad ways, to assert the value of their humanity to society, which still deems them disposable. But these newer attempts to claim humanity based on recognition of their environmentalist contributions are also subject to their critique. As my interlocutors throughout this book point out, it is impossible for Roma to achieve respect using the

INTRODUCTION

same frameworks of value that racialize them in the first place. And so, they play with these terms of engagement, diagnosing them as absurd while still acknowledging their life-and-death consequences.

My Romani interlocutors recognize that "progressive" European environmental mandates, for things like waste management and recycling, rely on their racialized disposability and could never be achieved without their labor.[8] I call this phenomenon "racial sustainability," drawing attention to how environmentalist projects both depend upon and generate racialized power.[9] When implemented in Bulgaria, EU programs, like many international environmental sustainability efforts designed in the face of climate crises, end up sustaining an urban landscape structured by racial hierarchy. Yet, even as Romani people understand their environment as speeding toward a destruction that will kill them (before their white neighbors), and their labor as necessary for slowing that process (at least hypothetically), their knowledge does not change the fact that they still have to live in these worsening conditions. Racial sustainability thus necessitates redefining, collectively, what it means to sustain life amid environmental harm and the racializing effects of the top-down progressive projects aimed at alleviating it.

While Baka worked independently to recuperate other people's trash, typically in quickly built, 1990s-chic wealthy suburban neighborhoods, much of Sofia's daily municipal trash collection and street cleaning is done by teams of Romani women. These teams wear brightly colored red and orange uniforms and reflective vests, making them especially visible on city streets.

Over the course of my research, I worked with Baka on and off for three years. I also served as an employee of a municipally contracted street-sweeping team for nearly a year. White Bulgarian passersby would throw trash at the feet of my Romani colleagues, put out lit cigarettes inches from their flammable uniforms, and at times even throw buckets of water on them from the balconies overhead. These were acute manifestations of anti-Roma sentiment, blatant forms of the pervasive racism that has become part of everyday Romani life.

Before 2007, most Bulgarians equated joining the European Union (EU) with hope for positive transformation, including economic growth, anti-corruption measures, environmental protection, minority integration efforts, and an end to the political stasis that had plagued the country since the end of socialism in 1989.[10] Since Bulgaria joined the EU in

FIGURE 0.5 A woman sweeping in downtown Sofia, Bulgaria. Photo by the author.

2007, waste labor like Baka's has been critical to Bulgaria's ability to meet EU-era environmental mandates and reflects a deep-rooted desire to become "European." The racial logics that exclude Romani people from full personhood by positioning them as "social waste" (*boklutsi*), common and coded racial terminology in Bulgaria, also sustain Bulgarian efforts to realize EU sustainability requirements.[11] These requirements mandate that increasing percentages of waste be recycled each year and that decreasing amounts of waste end up at landfills.[12] Since official recycling programs do not work well in Bulgaria, due to lasting legacies of compulsory socialist-era waste recycling and a deep cynicism among the public, the unrecognized labor of predominantly Romani waste workers fulfills pressing EU mandates.

Something Else

This book explores how environmental sustainability initiatives, which are critical to the contemporary project of European expansion, both reinforce enduring racial orders and establish new ones. It also takes up a corollary question: What does it mean for people living among, working with, and seen as waste to keep on living amid conditions that they call "no life"? Even as Roma are conflated with waste, they create possibilities for what they call "something else" (*neshto drugo*)—ways of living and making life amid conditions of racial sustainability.[13]

Under conditions of racial sustainability, as the following pages recount, new forms of racialization materialize through written and unwritten contracts of debt entrapment, decaying water pipes, election-period speed bumps, neighborhood barricades, and even the construction of plastic recycling bins. By "racialization," I refer to the processes of hierarchically categorizing people, using "a conglomerate of sociopolitical relations that discipline humanity into full humans, not-quite-humans, and nonhumans."[14] The materialities of racialization I address have a particular importance in the Eastern European context, where race has long been something of an absent presence, "rejected and rendered inapplicable" by those living in, writing about, and creating policy for the region.[15]

As Bulgaria strives toward Europeanization, it brings together particularly postsocialist denials of race with longstanding European postcolonial modes of "color-blind racism."[16] The term "sustainability" helps us to see how the status quo takes shape within different spheres—environmental, human, political—and invites questions of why and how certain things and people are discarded to enable the endurance of others. The frame of racial sustainability helps us better understand the materiality of contemporary racialization and its connections to liberal environmentalist projects.

In bringing postsocialist and postcolonial thought to present-day Europe-making projects, I show how processes of "modernization"—whether born of colonial, socialist, or EU accession endeavors—naturalize race as a core system of social relations.[17] Modernity writ large creates conditions for the hierarchization of people along the lines of humanness and nonhumanness that epitomize the racial project. In Bulgaria today, modernity takes the shape not of settler colonialism or nonsettler imperialism, as it has for centuries throughout Europe and the rest of the world, but of political Europeanization via European Union expansion.[18]

Contemporary Europeanization manifests through laws and policies, working to "remedy" newly accessed states of their socialist pasts by harmonizing their national policies with Western European mandates.[19]

One major way that EU-era Europeanization has worked to confirm its antisocialist modernity is with programs for environmentalism. As greening has become a vacuous rhetorical strategy for environmental development worldwide, European Union policy has turned to focus on "improving" the material afterlives of socialism. In the EU imaginary, this means addressing socialism's iconic decay, pollution, and ruins through the cure-all of environmental reform. Yet, as this ethnography shows, those very EU policies also perpetuate a race regime in which Roma are fundamentally at the bottom of a racialized, and racializing, social hierarchy.

Situating Race in Bulgaria

Quantitative and qualitative analyses from international organizations like the World Bank and European Union Agency for Fundamental Rights make clear that Bulgarian Roma have significantly higher poverty and unemployment rates than non-Roma.[20] Bulgarian Roma have higher child mortality rates and an average life expectancy ten years shorter than non-Roma, even when living at a similar economic level.[21] This is the result of systemic racialization rooted in long histories of oppression and bolstered by contemporary policies that rely on this oppression to meet EU mandates. While some hoped that EU integration efforts might mitigate the situation, that has not come to pass: These statistics did not improve with Bulgaria's EU accession in 2007 but, in many cases, stayed the same or worsened.[22] Roma are still racialized as less-than-human waste and continue to work and be associated with trash.

Bulgarian society generally claims to be raceless, but Bulgaria is a multiracial, multiethnic nation that comprises many ethnicities, religions, and languages. Roma are thought to make up approximately 10% of the Bulgarian population, although census information is notoriously inaccurate.[23] And Roma are racialized differently from other minorities in Bulgaria, which include Turks, Pomaks, Jews, and more recent immigrants and refugees from both the Middle East and Ukraine. While Turkish Bulgarians have had a particularly painful history in Bulgaria, including being imprisoned, deported, and killed as recently as the 1980s (during the socialist "total assimilation" [*palna asimilatsiya*] policy that forced anyone with a Turkish name to change it), Roma are now generally the first to be scapegoated. In casual conversation, many older white Bulgarians would tell me, sometimes referencing popular Turkish television shows or films, that Turks still have a sense of family, like "how we, Bulgarians, used to be." This romanticization does not hold for Roma, who are perpetually discussed by Bulgarians in nearly all walks of life as outside of a glorified Bulgarian past and antithetical to a European future.[24]

Race, although often understood to be about skin color, is actually about power and positionality. As Jonathan Rosa explains, the workings of race are "historically and institutionally constituted subject formations that are rooted in the rearticulation of colonial distinctions between normative Europeanness and Othered non-Europeanness."[25] Thinking about race in Bulgaria in terms of Europeanness helps us to see that the racialization of Roma has changed over time, in concert with global flows of racial thought. Although not its origin, one can look back to transnational eugenics movements in the 1920s and 1930s as a critical moment in this trajectory.[26] During this time, as part of efforts to assert Bulgaria's place within a white European framework, Roma were racialized as nonwhite outsiders.[27] This path continued during the socialist period through various reforms designed to assimilate Muslim and Romani (and Muslim Romani) populations into a Bulgarian working class, including the forced removal of Roma from city centers, the relocation of Roma into "Bulgarian" apartment buildings, and the forced placement of Romani children in boarding schools to limit the influence of their families.[28]

In Bulgaria and much of the broader global imaginary, Roma have represented Eastern foreignness against which others can define themselves as white and European.[29] While the articulations of racial difference I witnessed in Bulgaria (as in other locales) involved terms that might seem reducible to skin color (e.g., "black," "white"), they are actually rooted in other associations having to do with occupation, accent, material proximities, immigration status, religious affiliation, and names.[30] Racialization in Bulgaria is predicated on white European formulations of what humanness and nonhumanness mean, rooted in liberal European epistemologies, as well as a particular socialist history in which humanness was racialized as white and linked to the ideal "Soviet Man."[31] Within this framework, Roma were seen as quintessentially "non-Europeans whose backwardness and stagnation defied the very premise and promise of socialism and communism" and treated as an "ideological and political threat that had to be managed, controlled, and eliminated."[32]

A major part of Bulgarian Roma's contemporary racialization as non-white, disposable, and less than human comes down to how the ruling majority associate them with waste work. Throughout my research, I heard their bosses compare Romani workers to animals and machines. The white Bulgarian boss of the street-sweeping crew I joined often reminded workers, "Even animals need a break." For their part, workers worried that they would be replaced by the expensive machines that they had learned were essentially the waste workers throughout much of Western Europe. If that happened, Romani waste laborers feared that they would become even more discardable.

The racialization of Roma as waste takes shape not only through interpersonal interactions but through governance infrastructures and the institutionalized discursive strategies of politicians, business owners, and ordinary people who are ordinarily racist. But while scapegoating Roma helps racialize non-Romani (and non-Turkish) Bulgarians as white within a local social hierarchy, a pan-European framework puts those same non-Romani Bulgarians' white Europeanness into question.[33] This includes institutionalized issues, like Bulgaria being blocked, until March 31, 2024, from joining the esteemed Schengen Zone, which permits passportless travel and virtually no border control between included countries, on the basis of "security concerns" about Bulgaria's ability to manage its external (non-EU) borders.[34] White Bulgarians struggle with being perceived as not quite European when traveling to places like Germany and England, with consequences for how they see themselves within local racial hierarchies.[35] They imagine themselves as victims of a series of external empires (Ottoman, Soviet, now European Union) and thus understand their whiteness as safely "outside of colonial processes" for which they themselves are not responsible.[36] While many white Bulgarians regard their not-quite-European status as a core reason why they cannot be racist, it often results in their assertion of hyperwhiteness in Bulgaria, particularly in relation to Bulgarian minority groups like Roma.

For the Romani men and women whose voices are at the heart of this ethnography, these local contours of racialization shape how they make life amid circumstances designed to break them down. Their day-to-day practices can be boldly disruptive, political, and funny, and serve as the basis for life-making humor—the kind of sensing, being, feeling, and laughing that sustains life in enduringly dire times.

INTRODUCTION

The Waste-Race Nexus and Racial Sustainability

As many scholars have made clear, systemically marginalized people and communities of color face disproportionate environmental harms from pollution, toxic exposures, and climate change.[37] In this book, however, I address a different relationship: one between waste and race that illuminates how efforts to alleviate environmental degradation can also fall hardest on marginalized groups. The EU's liberal policy programs emphasize environmental, political, and social sustainability, but these efforts are drastically racialized.[38] In what I term the "waste-race nexus," discarded things and discardable people come to constitute each other. I argue that we should understand this dynamic within the framework of racial sustainability. Relying on the logics of the waste-race nexus, international sustainability efforts in Bulgaria end up sustaining an environment structured on anti-Roma racism and postsocialist racial capitalism.[39]

EU sustainability initiatives are a key mode of contemporary Europeanization because they focus on well-accepted approaches to greening, appealing to most in the EU, while also solidifying racial hierarchies by preserving an aspirationally European status quo that I argue is, by definition, white. As the following chapters demonstrate, sustainability in Bulgaria encompasses not only EU environmental regulations but also Romani civil society and Bulgarian political life. In this framing, sustainability is a tool for maintaining European imperialist logics, albeit in progressivist guise.[40] In the realm of waste, capitalist sustainable development is often about finding a "sink" (or dump, or unregulated Romani neighborhood) where waste can go.[41] Environmental sustainability, or sustainable development, encompasses a tension between enabling a modern, greener future to take shape and maintaining a present racialized status quo.

Bulgaria's National Waste Management Programme, the guiding EU-approved document for the waste sector in Bulgaria, promotes what Max Liboiron would term a colonial project of transforming "Land into Resource."[42] The document states: "Sustainable development in the waste management field means use of the natural resources without destroying or harming them and by a manner that does not restrict the possibilities for their use by the future generations."[43] Sustainability, in this framing, entails creating conditions in which the present can persist into the future. This is racial sustainability in that it actively seeks to maintain the differentiated and hierarchizing status quo for generations to come. To be clear, waste sector officials and employees in Bulgaria rarely focus on what kind of world they want to sustain or what they want to change. Instead of musing ideologically, they work to meet whatever pressing European Union standards are set out for them, bullet point by bullet point. And, in attempting to meet these standards, they sustain the current racial order by propagating institutionalized and systemic conditions of racialized power in the name of progressive environmentalist endeavors.

In attending to the contours of Europeanization's racial sustainability projects, this book is about both Romani life-making and what it means to reshape the material impacts of power. As such, the book is an account of social change, both intended and unintended. It shows how some actors attempt to remake themselves—Bulgarians into Europeans, for example— and how others work to remake, and sometimes refuse, the categories into which they have been placed: human, nonhuman, disposable.[44] These projects at times align and at other times conflict, depending on the constellations of power operating at each moment. But a steady lode-star in these constellations has been Romani efforts to denaturalize and thus help diagnose both European modernization and their own racial categorization as fundamentally absurd (*absurd*).

Absurdity has long been a well-documented part of Bulgarian life.[45] Many of my interlocutors jokingly referred to Bulgaria as "Absurdistan," signaling both an "etymological connection to the border republics" of the former Soviet Union and the "recognition of just how tragically comic life had become."[46] Bulgaria's escalating attempts to conform with EU environmental standards reanimate socialist-era efforts to deal with life in a system that seems to make no sense. The postsocialist EU-era system also relies on a logic of differentiation, as it rejects a socialist past in order to remake its environmental and urban landscape as new and modern. Despite its attempts to reconstitute urban space as "green," this system re-invigorates longstanding absurdities that come into friction with newer, liberal capitalist ones.[47]

The Romani women and men throughout this book frequently diagnose the absurdity of their so-called modern condition and point to their place within its hierarchy, like Baka critiquing the façade of European-ness performed by white Bulgarians who discard still-valuable items.

INTRODUCTION 15

Although they attempt to dislodge themselves from such absurdity by mocking it and calling it out, they also know that their labor upholds the conflicted and contradictory programs upon which Bulgarian Europeanization relies. Living within an absurd system that they cannot fully overturn and upon which they still depend, waste workers, neighborhood communities, and activists engage the status quo and flout it in a host of ways: through practices of resistance, refusal, public critique, intimate solidarities, political disengagement, protest, and play.

Refusing Sustainability demonstrates how politics, or "contestation[s] over the form and distribution of authority and accountability," can grow out of experiences of racialized labor and environmental racism.[48] These practices of contestation make room for more kinds of life, beyond a death or less-than-human paradigm. For decades, resistive politics in Bulgaria, especially in Romani communities, has not typically involved explicit protest because of fear of retribution and the expectation that it won't do anything. Instead, resistance in Bulgaria has a long history of taking on furtive forms, of subverting the state in quiet, even routine ways.[49]

Romani activists in Bulgaria do not regularly demonstrate publicly. And Romani street sweepers, who have far less cultural capital to stage a formal protest than activists, disrupt their status quo on their own terms. They joke in insubordinate ways, support one another materially and emotionally, and creatively repurpose their material world.[50] But Romani activists and waste workers share two important understandings: one, that their state-sanctioned oppression legitimates Europeanization projects (and vice versa), and two, that there are alternatives to life under state-sponsored civil society initiatives and supposedly transformative EU frameworks.

Racialized Cleaning and Racial Cleansing

Bulgaria's history of environmental transformation and racialization is part of a larger Europeanization project with its own unique contours. The European Union deploys a rhetoric of freedom and equality that has shifted from advancing a human rights agenda in the 1990s, in tandem with an emphasis on "cultural diversity" as crucial to European identity, to a focus, in the 2000s, on minority employment and economic contributions.[51] Yet racism is still part of the European project; in fact, it is constitutive of it.[52] As Robin D. G. Kelley points out, the project of racialization itself arose in Europe: "The first European proletarians were *racial* subjects (Irish, Jews, Roma or G*psies, Slavs, etc.) and they were victims of dispossession (enclosure), colonialism, and slavery *within Europe*."[53] Since then, people have been dehumanized, objectified, and treated as expendable in colonial projects around the world, in chattel slavery and its aftermaths, in settler-colonial systems, in conditions of genocide, and as part of liberal infrastructure projects.[54]

As long as the European project has been subjugating people as inferior, esteeming the category of human and deeming some as less-than-human both inside and outside Europe, Roma have lived and been dehumanized within European territories. In other words, racial capitalism and what might be called racial socialism have involved racialized value extraction processes in which Roma are considered surplus.[55] In this sense, Roma are seen as extra—effectively the leftover waste within a system of efficiency and profit. However, most Roma know that they are not waste but are instead critical to maintaining the white ruling class's status because, as many of my Romani interlocutors told me, the ruling class needs the (nonwhite) working class to sustain itself. This can be witnessed in international programs with titles like "Roma Inclusion is Smart Economics" that position Roma as valuable so long as they are contributors to the capitalist system, albeit typically on the lowest rungs of the labor ladder.[56]

Despite vacillations around how Roma might fit within capitalist models, across Europe Roma are still considered other to Europeanness despite their legal status as EU citizens and their ongoing labor that helps build Europe's symbolic and material landscape. In working to understand how racialization intersects with environmentalism in Bulgaria, I have been inspired by the work of scholars who consider racial regimes and power in Bulgaria, throughout Europe, and across the globe.[57] I bring these approaches into conversation with a growing body of Romani feminist scholarship, which also draws on critical race and Black feminist epistemologies, in order to highlight the interrelated global flows of capital, waste, and "progressive" policies in Europe and beyond.[58] My approach emphasizes the long-lasting impacts of imperial formations of Europe that have been analyzed by both Romani and Black feminist scholars and that continue to scaffold EU sustainability regimes.[59]

Roma, who are widely believed to have migrated from current-day India, have been in Europe at least since the fourteenth century and most likely even earlier. According to the Romanian Romani feminist Nico-

INTRODUCTION   17

leta Biṭu, "We were most probably living in the Byzantine Empire—the territory of what is today's Greece—before 1200, and there is consistent written evidence of our presence on European soil dating back to 1400, which is in fact when the first accounts of our deportations and expulsions appeared."[60] Starting in the second half of the fifteenth century and continuing for another five hundred years, Roma were enslaved in current-day Romania. In other parts of what is now Eastern Europe— occupied variously by the Ottoman, Russian, Austro-Hungarian, and Holy Roman empires—Roma, though not formally enslaved, were generally at the bottom of the social hierarchy.

Historians surmise that, while under Ottoman rule, Roma in what is now Bulgaria were categorized as a distinct group from both Muslims and Christians and were generally low in the Ottoman hierarchy. Muslim Roma, as well as some Roma who served in the Ottoman army, did receive tax benefits, but most Roma were employed either independently in low-paying positions (as metalworkers, gardeners, etc.) or in other stigmatized sectors like waste collection and well digging.[61] When the Ottoman Empire started to decline in the 1870s, Roma were further marginalized. The government rescinded tax privileges that it had formerly provided to army-serving Roma, and an 1874 governmental report effectively rewrote history, declaring that Roma had never served in the Ottoman army.[62]

After 1878, in the wake of the Ottoman Empire's collapse, during what is known as both Bulgaria's liberation period and the age of de-Ottomization, Bulgarians "simultaneously discovered and constructed their own Europeanness."[63] In the new capital city of Sofia, this quest for Europeanness entailed modernization of the built environment, often undertaken with Romani labor, as well as the widespread political scapegoating of Roma (along with Turks and other Muslim groups) for the problems Bulgaria faced in terms of urban development.[64] The government retracted many citizenship rights to which Roma had previously been entitled, including, from 1901 to 1905, Muslim Roma voting rights.[65] The government also razed Romani neighborhoods, and the Sofia Municipal Council shunted residents from the city center to the outskirts of the city. Today, most of Sofia's Romani residents still live in those outskirts, which include the neighborhoods of Konyovitsa, Konstantin Velichkov, and Fakulteta, where I conducted much of my research.[66]

In this post-Ottoman landscape, amid anti-Roma campaigns and newspaper accounts suggesting that Roma were vectors of disease and urban contagion, a Romani cultural movement and civil society sector developed.[67] Romani schools, civic organizations, and newspapers sought to serve a public the government had largely abandoned, fighting for equal rights and cultural and political representation. Many of these efforts were led by Romani writer and activist Shakir Pashov. However, when Kimon Georgiev came to power as Bulgarian prime minister through a right-wing coup in 1934, he quickly banned Pashov's work.[68] This ban did not stop Pashov and others from campaigning against continued efforts to evict Roma from their homes and push them into segregated neighborhoods under the pretense of preventing the spread of illnesses.[69]

The rise of fascism, and particularly the Nazi Party, made the late 1930s through the end of World War II a tragic period for most Roma in Europe.[70] Romani children were removed from their parents. Romani women were forcibly sterilized. And entire Romani communities were violently murdered in concentration camps, mass shootings, and through "scientific" testing on children by doctors, so-called race scientists, and anthropologists.[71] However, Roma did engage in anti-fascist resistance. On May 16, 1944, in a celebrated act of Romani resistance, more than six hundred Roma imprisoned at the Nazi death camp Auschwitz-Birkenau refused to come out for roll call. They knew that the Nazis were planning their execution, and so they barricaded themselves in their sleeping quarters with homemade weapons. This resulted in a successful delay of their execution. Starting in 2005, under the leadership of the French Roma civil society organization La Voix des Rroms, Romani communities and organizations across the world, as well as EU bodies, have marked May 16 as the International Day of Romani Resistance.

Bulgaria prides itself on having "rescued its Jews" during the Holocaust, since it did not, for the most part, deport Jewish or, for that matter, Romani citizens living inside the boundaries of the Bulgarian state to concentration camps. But this nationalist framing conceals other forms of violence. Bulgaria deported Jews and Roma living in occupied Bulgarian territories (current-day Macedonia and Greece), put both Jews and Roma into labor camps within Bulgarian borders, and enacted both de facto and de jure discrimination against both groups.[72]

INTRODUCTION 19

According to the Council of Europe Roma Genocide Fact Sheet, during World War II, Bulgarian Roma "were denied access to the central parts of Sofia, forbidden to use public transportation and were given smaller food rations than the rest of the population."[73] In some places, they were forced to convert to Christianity, subjected to state-sanctioned compulsory labor, and banned from marrying non-Romani citizens. Notably, while Bulgaria takes pride in having "rescued" its Jewish citizenry, it has never acknowledged any sort of Roma rescue as part of its nationalistic wartime narrative. In fact, in 2002, Bulgaria declared March 10 the "Day of the Holocaust and Rescue of the Bulgarian Jews," with no mention of Roma.

In September 1944, the Bulgarian Communist Party, supported by the Soviet Red Army, overtook the government of what it renamed the People's Republic of Bulgaria. Following the coup, the Bulgarian Communist Party began to institute widespread mass arrests, executions, and confiscations of property belonging to "enemies of the people." Between 1949 and 1951, the state expelled hundreds of thousands of Turks across the border until Turkey refused to accept them, even as Bulgarian schools promoted Turkish language instruction in the name of ethnic appreciation.[74] Under a parallel logic in line with the Soviet nationalities policy, the Bulgarian state both marginalized and recognized the Roma as a distinct ethnic group, allowing the publication of Romani-language periodicals until 1949, when Georgi Dimitrov died and Vuko Chervenkov took over as the Communist Party leader.[75] Chervenkov called for the repression of Romani culture and language to advance a "pure Bulgarian nation."[76] This "purity" was understood as white, Christian, European, and definitively anti-Ottoman.[77] Anyone who was Turkish-speaking and/or Muslim was considered a threat due to the proximity of non-Soviet Turkey, and this included many Roma.[78]

The racialization of Roma was shaped by and overlapped with that of Muslim Turks and, under the leadership of Todor Zhivkov from 1954 through the end of socialism in 1989, Muslim Roma were subjected to particular scrutiny. Before Zhivkov came to power, in the interwar and early socialist periods, Roma were prevented from accessing properties designated for Muslim Confessional Organizations (MCOs). In public letters and complaints, Muslim community leaders discussed Roma in terms of fear of their "infiltration" into property systems based on intergenerational Muslim community land inheritance.[79] Beyond these divisions between Turks and Turkish-speaking Muslim Roma, the state also imposed a set of mandates targeting Roma based on a fear of their perceived desire to "become Turks" in light of their precarious identity position.[80] For example, nearly a decade into Zhivkov's leadership in 1962, a Bulgarian Communist Party resolution to "limit certain expressions of Turkish influence among Bulgarian Muslims, G*psies, and Tatars" segregated schools and army organizations accordingly.[81] It also encouraged minorities with Turkish names to change them to "Bulgarian names."[82]

By the 1980s, name changes for Muslim Bulgarians became compulsory as part of the "total assimilation" policy, or, as the socialist government named it, the "Revival Process" (*Vazroditelen Protses*). Under the guise of promoting socialist "equality," the state forcibly assimilated and violently repressed Muslim Turks, Muslim Roma, and Pomaks ("Bulgarian-speaking Muslims") as well as Jews, Catholics, and other religious minorities.[83] The government instituted race-based laws barring "non-Bulgarians" (including Romani, Turkish, Pomak, and Jewish people) from practicing their customs, removed Roma from public and political positions, forcibly resettled any nonsettled Romani groups, and erected concrete walls to divide Romani neighborhoods from adjacent white neighborhoods throughout the country. Between May and August 1989, during an ethnic cleansing campaign euphemized as "The Great Excursion" (*Golyamata Ekskurziya*), over three hundred thousand Turks were forcibly displaced from Bulgaria to Turkey.[84] By then, changes to the census had already created the impression that there were "no minorities" in Bulgaria. While the 1975 census collected information on ethnic affiliation and nationality, results were "declared a state secret" and were never published.[85] In 1985, the last communist census collected no information about ethnicity whatsoever in an effort to statistically "confirm" that the entire population was "composed of ethnic Bulgarians."[86]

Throughout the socialist period, Roma were steadily employed at the lower rungs of the labor hierarchy: as cleaners, construction workers, and sewer diggers. However, some had better jobs working in textile factories, for example. As Sofia's population increased, the Bulgarian state socialist cleaning firm, Chistota, shifted from recruiting nearby villagers to hiring urban Roma. This shift was intended both to assist large-scale urban cleaning endeavors and to provide Romani citizens

INTRODUCTION 21

with work so that they would not organize and revolt, as the socialists feared might happen.[87] As Roma took over much of Sofia's waste management, their work was valued more highly and paid better than it is now, due to state socialism's commitment to adequate compensation for all workers and to the state-run economics of the waste sector at that time.

Internal Chistota documents suggest that waste labor was seen as important to re-educating its workers to become more serious and diligent socialist citizens.[88] Chistota tried to boost workplace productivity by hosting regular trainings and providing material support in the form of higher salaries and food, clothing, and housing for workers. Company documents make clear that the job became more racialized over time and served as a labor-based way to assimilate minority populations: "We also need to mention the fact that a large number of the workers are from the minorities—G*psies, Turkish...most of them have a lot of children, they live in bad hygiene conditions, which also has a bad impact on their productivity."[89] Chistota expressed concern about workers becoming ill and provided them with winter clothing, but noted that "the worst part is that a large portion of the workers, especially the women, don't wear the clothes given to them and give the shoes to their children or sell them."[90] A 1967 Sofia report in the state socialist security archives praised Chistota for having eradicated "wandering" among Bulgarian Roma via stable employment.[91] In 1973, state security forces praised the fact that "around 80% of the g*psies of working age are employed. We could say that the inclusion of the g*psies in work activities will gradually lead to core changes in their life and mentality."[92]

———

When the Bulgarian socialist state collapsed in November 1989, Bulgaria's established practice of racial disavowal did not. Bulgaria's first postsocialist constitution was created from the total assimilationist legacy, so ethnic and racial groups did not officially exist—on paper, in census forms, or in legislative documents. Today, the government still refuses to systematically publish disaggregated demographic data, so it is nearly impossible to know accurate statistics for Romani communities. When anti-Roma racism does appear, the Bulgarian government often dismisses it as an invention coming from elsewhere. And when anti-Roma racism is addressed in public forums or other venues, it is

22   INTRODUCTION

typically disregarded as a blunt Americanization of more nuanced local issues. Many Bulgarians view places like the United States as imperial nations that impose a "black-white" race ideology on Bulgaria, denying that Bulgaria has racial hierarchies or racism in the first place.

However, when Bulgaria started preparing for EU accession in the 1990s, a goal that was achieved in 2007, Europeanization came with its own discourse pertaining to minorities, including Roma. Even documents about "integration" focused on target groups not through a language of racism but through bureaucratically coded language like "vulnerable people" or "marginalized populations."[93] Such projects reinforce public anxieties about Romani demographic growth, while the language of vulnerability creates a practical loophole for Bulgarian politicians to siphon European Union funds toward other groups—whomever they want to fit the criteria. The result is that very few EU funds ever reach Romani communities.

In Romani neighborhoods and in the workplace, however, Roma use a very different language to discuss their positionality. I had become accustomed to hearing my Romani friends and colleagues calling others, and calling themselves, racial terms. Romani communities have discussed racial categorization in terms that include but cannot be reduced to axes of Blackness and whiteness since long before EU accession was on the table.[94] In practice, these usages intersected with global systems of racialization. Throughout Bulgarian history, as many interlocutors told me, Romani people with dark skin have been referred to (and refer to themselves) with terms like "dark" (*tamni*), "swarthy" (*murgavi*), and "black" (*cherni* in Bulgarian, *kale* in Romani, pl.), while those with light skin who could pass as non-Romani Bulgarians were lauded as "white" (*beli* in Bulgarian, *parne* in Romani, pl.). This discourse of colorization is just one aspect of racialization and links up with widespread racial hierarchies in Bulgaria that, during the socialist period, encompassed, among others, nonsocialist Western Europeans, Turkish Bulgarians, guest workers from Vietnam, and students from Ghana and Angola.[95]

I heard stories of how Vietnamese guest workers in Sofia, mostly men living in dormitories at the edges of Fakulteta were the butt of racist jokes but also coveted as acquaintances because they could buy goods (like white jeans) at hard currency shops, reserved for foreigner use.[96] African students in Bulgaria, many of whom were from Ghana and Angola, moved to Sofia to study as part of internationalist socialist agendas, but

INTRODUCTION   23

left en masse in 1963 in response to racism that culminated in police violence against members of the African Students' Union.[97]

In the early postsocialist years, as Bulgaria aspired to official European status, international notions of Blackness intersected with local terminologies to become part of transnational policy frameworks for Roma integration. American-sponsored initiatives strategically compared contemporary Romani issues to Black American civil rights struggles of the 1950s, and such analogies became commonplace in the NGO sector.[98] When my Romani interlocutors referred to themselves as "black," they did so for different reasons at different times. Some did so to refuse Bulgaria's longstanding politics of racial disavowal, which, they noted to me, ended up being a way for Bulgarians to deny the fact of institutional racism within their country (Resnick 2024a). When reading my field notes, I am struck by how often terms about Blackness came up in discussions of Romani communities' role in EU sustainability and integration initiatives. For example, one of my good friends, Maria, often recounted her analysis of the Roma's role in EU accession policy: "Of course we are expected to just take it, to help the Bulgarians meet these EU standards—we are black after all."

Blackness has resonances among Romani activists in Bulgaria that differ from the colorization tropes used by nonactivist Roma.[99] Beyond this context, "Blackness" (in English) also has other, less nuanced resonances in white Bulgarian space. Throughout my time in Bulgaria, I would see posters for "Black Parties," which meant clubs would be playing hip-hop music. Other times, "Black" was used as a pun, as with the "Black Energy" drink advertising that gained prominence across the region and was plastered across Bulgarian supermarket windows, featuring a picture of Mike Tyson in a white suit holding a black can with the English words "That's How Black Works." While white Bulgarians' blunted and commodified stereotypes reveal their exoticizing fascination with what they imagine to be Black culture abroad, Romani communities engage Blackness for political and other affiliations.[100] They connect their own lives, including both struggles and possibilities of mobilization, to those of other Black communities globally as a way to sustain life amid the liberal sustainability regimes that contribute to this oppression.

In Bulgaria, Roma navigate a waste-race nexus that positions them as racially inferior, or less than human. Or, as a middle-aged Romani woman at Bitaka, Sofia's largest outdoor flea market, told me, "Here, we are like trash. They give more respect to dogs than to us G*psies."[101] White

24 INTRODUCTION

Bulgarians echoed this sentiment throughout my fieldwork; the CEO of a waste firm I worked for told me, "Where there is trash, the G*psies are near." Many of my interlocutors made fun of Bulgaria as "backward," the joke—and the "trash"—of Europe. White Bulgarians would go further, trying to explain the situation by providing equivalencies: "If we are the trash of Europe, Roma are the trash of Bulgaria."[102]

Attempting to shake off its reputation as the trash of Europe, Bulgaria depends on Romani labor to accomplish its progressive environmental goals, further propagating both the persecution of Roma and their dehumanizing associations with waste. I saw this both in the early 2000s, when Roma integration was critical to Bulgaria's hopes of EU accession, and in my later fieldwork (2010–2014), when underpaid Romani labor enabled Bulgaria to meet its EU-imposed recycling quotas and avoid costly sanctions.[103] Indeed, waste management companies are currently the largest employers of Roma in Bulgaria, and oral histories show that some workers still hold the same positions they had under socialism, even as uniform colors, pay scales, and company names have shifted.[104] Waste labor of the past was certainly racialized, but it was also more highly valued as part of socialist development than it is under contemporary EU policy.[105]

European minority integration initiatives have focused on education rather than repairing decaying Romani neighborhoods and their infrastructures, remedying Roma overrepresentation in stigmatized and underpaid labor sectors, or addressing the racial capitalist logics that undergird social life. Although EU policies aim to integrate young Roma into mainstream public schools, many of their parents remain illiterate and unemployed. Without other job prospects, even young, high school–educated Roma turn to waste work as one of the only sectors where they can find employment.

There were some flickers of potential change in the early 2000s.[106] While Bulgaria's objective to join the EU hinged on market development and economic privatization, other key criteria included social inclusion, public health, antidiscrimination, nuclear energy and safety, and environmental conservation.[107] Bulgaria was required to reform its waste system, and while the language of this directive never acknowledged the racialization of waste work, the country was also instructed to integrate the "vulnerable" Romani population. A robust local NGO landscape could, and did, reliably depend on external funds for Roma-supporting endeavors. But after Bulgaria joined the EU in 2007, both pre-accession EU funding and private-donor grants dried up, sending Romani civil

INTRODUCTION 25

society into flux. As the early EU-accession period shifted into a European status quo, it became clear that the EU requirements for Bulgaria to (1) integrate the Roma and (2) reform its waste management system were inextricably connected. EU environmental sustainability quotas are only met because of racialized Romani waste labor, both formal and informal.[108]

As Roma work to clean up Bulgaria, they do so under municipal regulations that adhere to an aesthetic Europeanness. These aesthetics of Europeanness were described to me by both my waste-collecting colleagues and non-Romani interlocutors in terms of "order," "cleanliness," "beauty," and, cumulatively, whiteness.[109] For most Bulgarians, Europe remains a kind of imaginary, aspired to but unreachable. Long after Bulgaria joined the EU, a sign at Sofia's central station still pointed to "Buses to Europe."[110] Europe remains elsewhere, both westward and existentially far away.

Throughout my research, many white Bulgarians would romantically reference a short period of Bulgarian imperialism in the ninth and tenth centuries—an expansive "Bulgaria on three seas" (the Black Sea, Adriatic Sea, and Aegean Sea)—expressing aspiration to "return" to this unquestionable power. At the same time, they would reckon with Bulgaria's subjugation under multiple imperialisms, Ottoman, Soviet, and European Union, through the lens of victimhood, relating that it was impossible to think of a Bulgaria that was not a pawn of larger empires. Both sides of this coin, aspirations toward empire and assertions of perpetual victimhood, bolster white supremacist politics in Bulgaria (Imre 2005; Resnick 2024a).

The European Union has not conquered its member countries in the same manner as earlier European imperialisms, but Europeanization, as the case of Bulgaria makes clear, maintains longstanding imperial categorizations of who and what are considered European—or not. To many white Bulgarians today, just as in the post-Ottoman era, becoming European involves othering and subjugating Roma, while still relying on their underpaid labor.

The walls built during state socialism to barricade Roma from public view remain standing in Europeanizing Bulgaria. In some places, municipal projects added art to these walls, but racist graffiti subsequently covered it up. This sort of hate graffiti is ubiquitous throughout Bulgaria. The invocation of white power and swastika symbolism are highly visible manifestations of longstanding racisms. The sentiment is old, but the use of English is new, invoking Bulgaria's place in white supremacy's "global reverberations."[111]

FIGURE 0.6 Wall outside of a Romani neighborhood in Kazanlak; the graffiti reads: "Bulgaria without G*psies, kill the G*psies!" Photo by the author.

FIGURE 0.7 "White Power" graffiti near the edge of Fakulteta. Photo by the author.

Positionality and Multi-Scalar Methods

Although this book attends to the life-and-death stakes of European expansion, racialization, and white supremacy, my fieldwork on waste and with waste workers in Bulgaria has been filled with joy, humor, and empowered refusal to uphold the kind of relations upon which Europeanization's racial sustainability depends. When I first worked through my field notes and recordings, I wondered how I could write a book that documented the high stakes of systemic, institutionalized racism while also attending to the play and pleasure of daily life. I considered the work of others who have dealt with similar predicaments, thinking through humor as a discursive space of possibility and "one of the fugitive forms of insubordination."[112] When my friends in Bulgaria generously explained the nature of their work and shared their analyses of liberal Europeanization, their humor held a space of possibility too—not always as insubordination, but certainly as a critical theory of European expansion, however indirect, and as an ongoing diagnosis of the absurd status quo.

Their attitudes bolstered my commitment to write against what Tuck and Yang characterize as a "fetish for pain narratives" among scholars.[113] They suggest that it is better to be "working inside a more complex and dynamic understanding of what one, or a community, comes to know in (a) lived life."[114] When I describe the lives of the people I met and worked alongside, my aim is neither to prove Romani abjection nor to justify their humanity. Neither do I seek to "reveal" Romani life, using an ethnographic voice to fetishize poverty or locate redemption through naturalized resilience.[115] Instead, I focus on how my Romani friends and interlocutors work to create vibrant lives in which they both push against conditions of their own discardability and, with humor and disruptiveness, live within them while working toward creating something else.[116]

I avoid reiterating European Union progressive political language as it pertains to Roma; this means I reject the unexamined language of integration, inclusion, vulnerability, and human rights. These concepts, as many scholars have shown, bolster the institutional racism that they claim to reject.[117] Instead, I explore how Romani life is formed amid EU waste policy and practices—sometimes in relation to EU interventions, sometimes despite them, and sometimes without even acknowledging them.

I am humbled by and grateful to those who made space for me and welcomed me into their homes, lives, families, and work. As I write this from the comfort of my tenure-track job on the West Coast of the United States, I want to make clear that I was and remain a visitor, a friend, and an ally, one deeply enmeshed in the racial power hierarchies about which I write. I am a white, American, non-Romani woman—*gadji*.[118] I hope that this book helps shift attention away from Romani social issues to focus on "white privilege/*gadjo*-ness" and its role in creating and sustaining racial hierarchies.[119] I will likely fall short along the way. After all, the racialization processes and projects of white supremacy that I write about in these pages have also been involved in the production of my own being, my privilege, my educational and employment capital, and anthropology itself. The structures of white supremacy I address extend from the streets of Sofia, Bulgaria, to my kitchen table where I write this in Goleta, California.

The research for this book spans twenty years, with repeated travel to Bulgaria from 2003 through 2024, including three consecutive years of fieldwork (October 2010–January 2014). Much of my work took place in Sofia's urban center and the Romani neighborhoods at its peripheries. As Brian Larkin writes, "urban space is comprised of the historical layering of networks connected by infrastructures."[120] In this sense, waste is also enmeshed in spatial networks within and beyond the sites where I physically spent my time. The book's scope therefore extends to landfills throughout the countryside, waste management corporate offices, and the EU's headquarters in Brussels, where the environmental regulations Bulgaria follows are made.

Over the years, I have worked at Romani civil society and educational organizations, shadowed waste company CEOs and employees, engaged politicians in municipal and national politics, and held a three-month internship at Bulgaria's Ministry of the Environment and Water. The largest component of my fieldwork, however, entailed working as a contracted street sweeper for eleven months. I was paid for twenty-four hours of work per week, as mandated by Bulgarian law, but often worked more or fewer hours as I attended to other research meetings, interviews, and trips back to my home in New York. My ability to move in and out of different spaces was critical to the development of this project. Within a single day, I might travel from meetings with international human rights leaders in US embassy compounds to homes without running water in

Sofia's segregated Romani neighborhoods. I was a guest in all of these spaces. Almost everyone with whom I spent time knew about the other facets of my life and work, thanks in part to the smallness of Sofia life and to occasional news coverage of my research. My sweeping work was televised, and I was interviewed as a modern-day marvel/lunatic: "A white American from luxurious New York sweeping Sofia's streets," the Bulgarian TV announcer proclaimed while Lenny Kravitz's "American Woman" was playing in the background. My sweeping colleagues and their children followed my Facebook feed, paid attention to my trips home, and brought up my ability to traverse so many social spaces. In other words, my privilege as a white American woman was lost on nobody.

I did not originally intend to work on waste management. I first went to Bulgaria in 2003 to work in the then-burgeoning activist NGO sector. I posted my desire to volunteer for educational desegregation on a listserv and received dozens of responses, choosing an organization run by three Romani activists who invited me to help with their English-language website. When I returned to Bulgaria in 2008, hoping to work with these NGOs for my dissertation research, I soon realized that most of the organizations I had met with previously had effectively "died" in the wake of European Union accession. EU accession meant that direct donors and relatively accessible pre-accession funding were replaced with EU structural funds, which are filtered through EU member state governments. As a result, grassroots Roma organizations were defunded in favor of "expert"-run professional organizations aligned with anti-Roma national governments. I found myself without a project and with a lot of time on my hands during this transition period. Each morning, I would leave the house to read novels on my favorite park bench in Sofia's City Garden. During one of these outings, I realized that one of the last vestiges of public, collective Romani presence was as waste workers on city streets. This project stems from that realization.

When I worked with Romani women on the streets, sweeping or collecting waste, I was regularly misrecognized by passersby as a "really white G*psy," driving home the racialization of the uniform and the job.[121] When my sweeping colleagues introduced me to friends, family, and new coworkers, they would explain that I "was writing the book of how much they suffered." This was usually said with a smirk, followed by "she can joke" and "she's not a spy...at least we don't think so." Their joking suggested that they never could be sure, but the colleagues with whom I worked regularly would explain that, given how badly the bosses treated me, there was no way I could be secretly working for them. It was true that the bosses pushed my limits, like asking me to get on hands and knees and pick up cigarette butts with my fingers. But this was work that other sweepers also did, and unlike them, I was never on the receiving end of slurs or threatened with job loss. I had been hired by someone much higher up than my day-to-day bosses, so my job security was unrelated to my work performance. At the same time, my direct managers knew I would not leave if they pushed me physically. I had too much at stake.

It was not until I had been sweeping for eleven months, and had begun working with a French–Bulgarian filmmaker who hoped to document my research, that the bosses casually told me, after I picked up my paycheck, that I could bring my uniform to the office tomorrow.

This was the euphemism used when sweepers were fired, under austerity measures and when winter constraints on cleaning meant fewer workers were needed. As the seasons changed, one worker was fired each day until the team was reduced to the size that municipal funding could support. I will never know exactly why I was fired that day, but I suspect the company was uneasy with their work being closely documented, despite having agreed to allow us to film. (Most of the sweepers, however, told me that they wanted to be in the film.) When my colleagues learned

FIGURE 0.8 On the way to work. Still image from film footage by Bojina Panayotova.

INTRODUCTION   31

what had happened, they repeated what they told other sweepers who were fired without warning: Not to worry, it would be okay. Their kindness threw into relief the fact that, unlike them, I had taken the job as one that I could easily leave without material losses.

———

As I was reminded during a 2019 visit to Sofia, refusals of the status quo must be continually made and remade over time. One morning after attending a wedding in Fakulteta, I was heading back to the apartment I was renting downtown with my family when I saw Baka's daughter-in-law, Tanya, at a bus stop in front of the supermarket just outside the neighborhood's edge. We boarded the bus together and stood holding on to the same cold metal handrail as the bus rocked along the uneven pavement.

As we caught up on the time that had lapsed since we last saw each other, she pulled a watch out of her small backpack. The band was hard, made of blue-green marbled resin, and she told me that the watch just needed a battery to work, but that it was more of a jewelry piece anyway. I loved it, and I told her so. She showed me that she had another one in an orangish red in her bag and asked me which I wanted. I told her I wanted her to sell them. She could make good money. But she insisted that she wanted me to have something from her to take back to the United States. I held them both up to the light to see which would go better with the outfit I had on. Suddenly, a blond woman in big black sunglasses sitting beside us screamed, shaking the slumbering passengers into attention: "Stop taking advantage of the foreigner! This is not Bitaka; this is not the flea market. This is public transport on a Sunday morning. Put away your stolen trash!"

I was familiar with this kind of scene from my earlier fieldwork. Jolted out of my hungover contemplation, and without thinking, I shouted back in Bulgarian about my close relationship to Tanya: "This is my friend, my family...!" I yelled, feeling my face redden and trailing off as the rest of the bus fell into silence.

Tanya grabbed my hand and patted it. "Elanka, let's get off."

The woman continued to harass Tanya as the bus came to a stop: "You don't even have a ticket—get off this bus!" Tanya grabbed her bag and pulled my arm, and we hopped off a few stops too soon, but close enough to our final destination.

On the street, in the quiet early morning sun, Tanya finally spoke: "See, this is what it is like in downtown Sofia. I can't give a gift without people telling me to be quiet, that I'm stealing, that I'm dealing trash." She paused, lighting a cigarette she had pulled out from behind her ear and inhaling slowly. "Now, write this down. This is Bulgaria."

ONE

Waste and Race

I recognized the logo on the booth from the back of street-sweeper uniforms I had seen throughout the city. The booth was one of hundreds lining a packed showroom in Sofia's newest convention center for the 2011 International Waste Expo. I approached and asked one of the men staffing it if I could volunteer as a sweeper. It was for my dissertation research, I explained in Bulgarian.

He stared back as if he did not understand me, so I repeated myself in Bulgarian and then again in English. This time he laughed, motioning to his colleagues to join him in witnessing this. I waited patiently and went through my explanation again. He finally exclaimed in English, "You're not black!" I looked at him in stunned silence. He continued, "You are white." His coworkers laughed and asked me where the hidden camera was located.

It was nearly a year later, in October 2012, when I was finally hired as a contracted and paid part-time street sweeper. I had approached the job from multiple angles, asking first if I could volunteer or shadow workers. Ultimately, I was told by a contact at one of Sofia's largest waste management companies that they could not offer me any position unless it was paid. Only by accepting compensation, and by signing waivers to take responsibility in case I was injured on the job, was I hired as a part-time (twenty-four hours per week) street sweeper.

CHAPTER ONE

Waste work in Bulgaria is so racialized that most waste company bosses I encountered thought it nearly impossible that a non-Romani person, let alone a white American, could do street-sweeping labor.[1] In Bulgaria, a clear racial hierarchy emerges in discussions of who can and should do waste work.[2] "Blackness" is equated with the ability to do hard manual labor, while "whiteness" is entirely excluded, except for the sector's better-paid driver, managerial, and office positions. While waste company bosses are white, non-Romani Bulgarians, street cleaners are almost exclusively Roma (and mostly women), a group widely seen as intrinsically expendable that performs labor vital to Bulgaria's development of a "European" urban aesthetic.

Street sweepers work in extremely difficult emotional, financial, and physical conditions within a system that rejects their humanity. Anyone wearing a waste uniform is assumed to be Roma. They are humiliated on city streets by residents and passersby. They become trapped in cycles of intergenerational debt and suffer physically because of their labor. All of this contributes to their paradoxically essential disposability, which is part of the waste-race nexus upon which Bulgaria's European environmental sustainability project depends. In the waste-race nexus, Romani sweepers are made both essential and expendable through their labor while also dehumanized as a stereotype.

In the Introduction, I described how, through the logics of the waste-race nexus, discarded things and "discardable" people come to constitute each other. This chapter develops that coupling. It argues that Bulgaria's uptake of EU initiatives makes waste work environmentally sustainable in the sense that it sustains an environment structured on anti-Roma racism and postsocialist racial capitalism. Understanding the waste-race nexus in Bulgaria requires understanding how waste work is racialized. To do so, I draw on my experiences as a sweeper from October 2012 through August 2013. Although street cleaning has long been racialized labor in Bulgaria, this chapter shows how that racialization has changed over time and through different political and economic regimes.

Sweeping Fundamentals

Along with visiting booths at waste expos, in my quest to be hired as a street sweeper, I sent emails, made phone calls, and honed my personal connections. It wasn't until someone I knew at a well-established donor organization invited me to meet Boyan, a waste firm manager, that I found my "in."

I later found out that Boyan, unbeknownst to most of his colleagues, was the father of an upper executive at one of Sofia's largest waste conglomerates, anonymized here as Wonder Clean Sofia (WCS). One morning, Boyan invited us to accompany him on his work rounds conducted from the inside of an old Jeep. I had a sense that he held an important position but couldn't pinpoint exactly what it was. Later, I learned that he had held internationally significant governmental positions during socialism, but in an effort to ward off the boredom of his retirement and to help the company function better, he was now tasked with surveilling the company's sweeping work and generally keeping an eye on workers.

I sat in the backseat of the Jeep and stayed quiet for most of the meeting, knowing I was invited as a favor and that this was a critical moment in the trajectory of my research. At the end of our drive, Boyan told me to call him in a month, after he had surgery and was recovered. When I called him a month later, he answered and curtly agreed to meet with me the following week at the metro station nearest to where the team gathered before they started sweeping each day. When I arrived, he invited me to sit with him in his Jeep while he surveilled the workers. I did so for about a week, watching him do crossword puzzles and taking notes when he would pause to discuss the budgetary constraints and municipal issues the firm faced. Then, one day, he took me to the company's fleet garage, where waste vehicles were parked next to a set of offices on the outskirts of the city.

The garage served as the local headquarters of WCS, which coordinated with the regional branch of the Sofia municipality inspectorate in charge of city cleanliness and responded to national standards stemming from European Union mandates. Upon entering, I sat down at a massive wooden desk and spoke to someone in a suit that Boyan described as "the boss." I explained the work I needed to do for my PhD, and then, quickly, Boyan ushered me to another room to meet the office assistants and fill out some paperwork I was too nervous to read.

Upon leaving the garage, without my realizing where we were going, Boyan stopped his Jeep in a parking lot where a colleague pulled a plastic bag out of his trunk and asked my size. "Women's medium?" I answered doubtfully. He rummaged through the bag and handed me an orange uniform. I held it up against my body. "It works." It wasn't the red that the other sweepers wore because I came aboard outside the usual hiring cycle, and it was the only uniform available. Boyan told me to go home and rest because I would start work as a sweeper the next morning at 6 a.m. I tried to play it cool, to not smile in relief.

―――――

When I first started sweeping, I did not choose who to work with but was assigned by the bosses based at first on who was "calmest"—as though I needed protection—and then, later, based on who needed an extra set of hands. I soon learned through practice how sweeping is done and its annual rhythms.

Throughout the year, Sofia's minimum-wage street cleaners sweep up cigarette butts, dirt, and plant litter from curbs, handpick garbage items from streets and sidewalks, and dispose of any dead rats, birds, or squirrels they encounter.[3] But street-sweeping responsibilities also change with the seasons and the weather. In the spring and summer, a truck with a brush attachment sweeps up most of the heavy dust and debris that accumulate along the gritty edge of the curb where the sidewalk meets the street, and manual sweepers follow up with brooms and dustpans. In late fall and winter, however, when the streets are covered with leaves or snow, the sweeping truck stops its rounds. The dense debris makes the truck's brushes ineffective and can damage the machinery. As a result, on one dreaded day each autumn, sweeping shifts from hybrid to purely manual labor. After this shift, on top of their regular duties, sweepers are also responsible for cleaning fallen leaves from city streets and sidewalks.

In the deep winter months, the work occurs in fits and spurts. Although sweepers are tasked with cleaning snow and ice from bus and tram stops and with salting sidewalks, there are days when it is just too snowy to sweep, and they can rest indoors after the morning commuter rush. Trucks first plow the streets, then drive through again with someone sitting in the back atop a huge pile of coarse salt, shoveling mounds onto the slippery sidewalks, what they jokingly call "being Santa Claus for the day." Sweepers then pass through with hand-hauled bags of salt to cover any remaining icy spots.

During the winter, sweepers still work with brooms but are also equipped with other tools, including a metal shovel and an ice pick. Sometimes, on the coldest winter days, their work entails using all their

WASTE AND RACE

FIGURE 1.1 Sweeping work. Photo by the author.

strength to break up fully iced sidewalks. When their tools fail, they use whatever they can. They jump on the ice, throw rocks down, or pour water onto the frozen sidewalk—anything to break the ice enough to remove it. When winter ends, sweepers return their shovels and ice picks to their bosses. If they lose or misplace their equipment, their pay is severely docked to recoup the item's cost (and then some).

In the spring, they sweep up leftover salt and pull the weeds that grow through cracks in the sidewalks, bending to pick the plants from the root. They also collect fallen tree debris. In addition to being responsible for street sweeping, cleaning companies in Sofia collect garbage from large metal street bins and from the smaller garbage pails near bus and tram stops, then transport that waste to the local landfill or waste depot. Under socialism, this work was done by Chistota, the state-owned street cleaning and waste management firm. Postsocialist legislation called for the privatization of waste work, but this process was not fully realized until the late 1990s, bolstered by strict anti-monopoly laws put into place in the early 2000s.

Today, a number of private cleaning companies operate in Sofia, although many are still under the umbrella of a single firm, WCS, that

FIGURE 1.2   Fallen plums on the street, to be swept up during the rain. Photo by the author.

employs many of the same staff and maintains the same practices as socialist-era Chistota.[4] All garbage collected while sweeping is disposed of in the company's large street bins, then collected by garbage trucks each evening. These bins are placed into cutouts or engineered "pockets" (*dzhobove*) in the sidewalk, and most are on wheels to allow for easy movement. The trucks lift them by hooking onto the sides with the assistance of the two men, almost always Romani, hanging off the back of the truck.

These large bins are placed at seemingly haphazard intervals along Sofia's streets, usually with two or three placed side by side at each location. The bins are typically metal, but some have been constructed from hard black plastic since 2006 both because, as waste officials told me, metal was being stolen and sold as scrap, and because the plastic ones are cheaper to produce. Plastic bins, while less expensive to produce, tend to catch fire when citizens use them to dispose of still-hot coals, which they use along with wood for heat, since much of the city lacks a public heating grid.

To get rid of daily domestic trash, people tie up waste in a small plastic grocery-store bag and drop it in one of these bins on their way to work or the market. In some parts of Europe, including Swedish and German

FIGURE 1.3 Metal mixed-waste dumpsters, located in a streetside cutout, or "pocket," in downtown Sofia. Photo by the author.

cities, waste taxes are calculated on the amount of waste each household discards; in Sweden, residents use an electronic key card that tracks their discarded waste. Sofia's waste tax, however, is based wholly on the size of an apartment or home. There is no monitoring of how much waste individual residents discard, since everyone, including local businesses, which are supposed to dispose of waste through separate contracts, throws their waste in the city's streetside bins. EU environmental consultants explained to me that this practice makes it impossible to impose fines on households that produce abundant trash, a measure that might reduce waste.

In public forums, like the Sofia City Council's Environmental Protection Commission meetings I attended, people often complained about the structure of the waste tax in highly racialized—albeit coded—terms. At one meeting, for example, a centrist municipal representative explained that the tax unfairly burdened single pensioners living alone in large Soviet-style apartments who paid according to the square meterage of their homes. But "large families with lots of kids," she exclaimed, did not pay such high taxes, "if they paid at all." She never used the word Roma, but she did not need to. Listeners knew the stereotype of Romani families gaming and draining the system by having "too many" children. "Poor pensioners," on the other hand, were understood to have paid into a system that now fails them, and thus needs systemic reform. Notably, public concern seemed to revolve more around perceived inequity in tax burdens than in reducing waste.

FIGURE 1.4 Black plastic mixed-waste bin on fire in downtown Sofia. Photo by the author.

Even if the tax structure did change—and with it, the amount of waste left in streetside bins—it's not clear that Romani waste workers' situations would. They remain ensnared in a waste-race nexus with labor relations characterized by economic precarity. Waste workers are seen as interchangeable and disposable. Employers are opaque about when payday will come each month, and sweepers often take on high-interest debt to survive. These conditions are normalized, even justified, to many white Bulgarians. Due to the racialization of waste labor as Romani work, it seems inconceivable that white Bulgarians could undertake it at all.

—————

Each winter, Sofia's municipality cuts funding to its private street-cleaning contractors. Shoveling snow and laying salt is body-breaking work, but fewer people are needed to do it since this work only focuses on public transportation stops. Sweepers know the routine. Every autumn, the bosses would first fire the oldest and slowest among them. My colleagues warned me that someone would be publicly fired at the end of each autumn day, so they all needed to perform hard-working dedication to keep their jobs. Mistaking my look of outrage for fear when they first told me their plan, they reminded me that I could not be fired: "You aren't one of us, you started with the orange uniform." They recalled how mine had been a different color at the start and bore the name of another subsidiary company owned by WCS.

To my coworkers, the uniform was a visual reminder that I was subject to different rules. "The bosses like you, you're American. You won't get cut." I knew that, I reassured them. While I was in fact anxious about them, I tried not to show my concern, following their lead. I knew that they too worried about not having work in the hardest and most expensive months of the year, though they rarely showed it in public. Instead, they led with bravado. They insisted that it would be all right, that they would get their unemployment benefits and be hired again when the weather changed. They reassured me that they could use a much-needed break.

In autumn, I became nervous at the end of each workday, knowing what was to come. As we gathered to be dismissed one day in November, Ani, one of the team's immediate supervisors, began calling out our names. As she moved through the list, those who hadn't heard their names started to pace and smoke their cigarettes a bit faster. Finally, she got to the last name—an old man on the team. "Georgi, bring your uniform tomorrow." That's how he was fired. The women yelled to him in Romani to reassure him: "You'll get unemployment!" "Better to stay home with the grandkids!" "It's fine, you'll get paid for watching TV!" These expressions of sympathy papered over the likely reality: Georgi had worked enough months to be eligible for unemployment benefits, but these were not enough to live on and often difficult for sweepers to obtain.[5] Nobody *wanted* to be fired.

Street sweepers were fundamentally replaceable, and they knew it. This replaceability secures the waste-race nexus. Bosses often reminded the team that "at least five women" were waiting to take any of their positions. And workers feared that, in the future, automation would take their jobs. Some had seen sweeping machines firsthand—not the big ones they already worked alongside, but smaller ones that could potentially replace their detailed manual labor—and others had learned of their ubiquity from relatives who traveled to Western Europe. They described machines in Germany that cleaned the street so quickly that their own work could not compare.

FIGURE 1.5 Donka and Rada talking to the driver of a mechanized sweeping truck. Photo by the author.

Perhaps machines were simply the inevitable future of Bulgaria's Europeanization, a future that would render their labor obsolete.[6] Others on the team argued that machines could never do what humans could, like getting under parked cars and between sidewalk crevices. Jesus, one of the few men on the sweeping team and the son of one of the sweepers, pointed out that machines cost a lot more than Romani workers. "They cannot even pay us [on time]," he emphasized, "but machines cost real money." The future of automation in Bulgaria looked uncertain, but the present precarity was real. If workers did not do their jobs, they knew that in the short term they could be replaced by other, low-wage Romani workers.

Workers tried different strategies to prevent their own obsolescence. They would often hide before the end of the official workday to make sure it looked like their work took the entire day to complete. During autumn months this was not hard, because they would barely finish by the end of the day. But during other months, they needed to ensure that the work did not appear "too easy" or like it could be done by a smaller number of employees or by machines. Working to protect their jobs also prevented the social breakdown that losing work entailed. To lose one's job or be replaced would sever the social and economic connections that keep Romani women and their families alive amid systemic racialized disposability.

Loans and Racialist Capitalist Entrapment

To lose one's job also cut off the possibility of getting loans, which were crucial for survival. Most sweepers lived off high-interest loans, some formal, from banks, and some informal, from loan brokers or neighbors. When their electricity was about to be cut off or they were threatened by credit bureaus, they often resorted to taking any loans accessible to them, typically with extremely high interest rates. I cannot attest to the exact rates of different loans, since when sweepers explained the compounding interest rates on their multiple loans, they talked quickly and with so many detailed mathematical computations that I could not write it all down. But it was clear that the rates were exorbitant. What I could exactly surmise is that two weeks of late payment would easily turn into years of accumulated debt. Many sweepers had credit scores so low that they had no way to obtain official loans, even from a high-interest credit company. Debt scared them, but it also helped them provide for their families while working minimum-wage jobs with uncertain pay cycles. The company often failed to pay on schedule and was cryptic about if or when that would change. Sofka, one of the most outspoken longtime members of the sweeping team, asked me, "How can I ask [to borrow] ten leva if I don't know when I'll be paid and return it?"

Sweepers told me that their last resort was to take out a loan with Zlatna, a fellow sweeper who was known to be relatively wealthy, and whose primary reason for working as a sweeper was to gain access to the team as an informal loan lender. Her loans required no paperwork, but the interest rates were so high that if a debtor missed a single payment, their debt would multiply so rapidly they would never be able to pay it back. None of the women with whom I worked had defaulted on a loan, but all of them had fretted about it.[7] Rada, one of the sweepers I worked with often, described the experience of being in so much debt that each paycheck was already spoken for before it arrived: "Tomorrow [there will be] money, and then, here and there, debt (*borchove*), and then again, nothing."

Although many Roma now rely on high-interest loans, this was not always the case. In the first half of the twentieth century and through the 1970s, many Romani communities had *londzha* systems, which functioned like local mutual aid credit unions.[8] People entered into them through long-term trust relationships and were able to take out low- or no-interest loans from the money amassed by the group. The socialist state outlawed these organizations in 1976 because they provided an avenue for Romani economic sovereignty. In the state's view, economic freedom could lead to "nationalistic" Romani self-determination.[9] State security archives reveal that the government was concerned that, without needing to rely on banks, Roma could organize "like the Turks" and threaten Bulgarian state power. Yet it was difficult for Roma to get bank loans at the time.[10] Ultimately, the socialist state assessed that it would be more advantageous to provide loans directly from the Bulgarian National Bank to Roma rather than to allow them to sustain their own systems of economic solidarity and extra-state sovereignty.

The sweepers I knew understood that their economic entrapment was invisible to most white Bulgarians, except those who depended on the loans they issued them for income. In this way, it was similar to their work: The better they cleaned, they told me, the less anyone cared—it was only when they missed something that they were noticed. As one woman put it, "Look, we are going to work to sweep nicely. That's it, and nobody is going to know if we are hungry." Yet if they did not sweep, and did not take out loans, they would be hungrier still.

One of the younger workers in her early twenties, Maya, pulled me aside one afternoon. Maya would reach out to me often, likely because I was closer in age to her than most of the other sweepers. While the older women had assured her that I could not be fired, she recommended that I take out a loan with our other white Bulgarian boss, Mimi, to ensure my position. Mimi worked with Ani to surveil the sweepers' labor. She also moonlighted as a high-interest loan company representative. Maya told me, "If you take out a loan with her, just a few hundred, she can't fire you. If you have an outstanding loan with Mimi, she is responsible for you paying it back.... She can't fire you then because her ass is on the line for you if you lose your income and can't repay the loan." The rates were as high as Zlatna's, but you had longer to pay it back, and it came with the benefit of informal job security. I felt touched that she was looking out for me, and a bit guilty as I reminded her that my case was different. I reminded her of the uniform I wore when we started. She understood but still looked concerned. I promised her that I was not subject to the same kind of job insecurity as her and our other colleagues; my hiring and firing operated according to a different rationale.

Maya was a young mother, and she worked hard to keep her children well fed and dressed. One cold morning in December, during our fifteen-minute sweeping break, she explained that she needed to pay off a leased washing machine and had just received word that there was a new company offering 3,000 leva (about 1,660 dollars) loans to sweepers. To apply, you needed an ID card, proof of steady employment, and a bank account. She relayed the information to the rest of the team and, immediately, my colleagues called their husbands at home to bring them the necessary documents. Maya insisted I apply as well. At first, I refused, since I was a foreigner and did not have the necessary paperwork. But Maya worked to convince me. I relented because I wanted to see how it worked—and Maya was excited to show me. She told me it should be fine but that I would need a debit card to access the funds, were I to be approved.

I explained to Maya that I had a Bulgarian bank account but not a debit card. "Don't worry, we can open a new one, easy," she said with confidence. She led me to the nearest branch of the bank. We walked in with our bulky uniform jackets tied around our waists and sat down with a white Bulgarian clerk. Maya told me to speak with the clerk, who swiftly took my Bulgarian ID card to photocopy it as the first step. As we waited, Maya explained how the debit card system worked and told me some funny stories about her children to pass the time. I began to laugh loudly, and to my surprise she admonished me, looking around at the clientele: "Elanka! Shhhhh, we are in public! And in uniform." She smirked, "We need to be demure (*skromni*) women here."

With her help, I opened a bank account with a debit card that cost five leva (about three dollars) and a monthly fee, both of which I would be able to pay later since I did not have cash with me. Then we went to a nearby park where colleagues had already gathered around the credit agency representative who was sitting on a bench with clipboards and paperwork strewn about. Maya pushed me forward, but the agency representative quickly denied my request for a credit line on account of my foreigner status. Soon after, I forgot about the bank account I had opened that day, remembering it only eight months later as I prepared to leave Bulgaria for a trip home. I went to the bank and found that my five-leva fee had accumulated interest and was now over forty leva. It was a basic, if relatively benign, indicator of how debt could accumulate. I was lucky to be able to pay it off, but the debt entrapment into which sweepers necessarily enter as they try to survive the waste-race nexus was far more destabilizing.

Most of my colleagues were the sole income earners for their households and often negotiated between loan brokers, relatives, husbands asking for money, and children in need of clothing, toys, and school supplies. Rada, for example, tended to worry about paying her bills each month. Her husband had previously worked in construction in Sofia but, after not being paid for months, moved to the Czech Republic to lay cobblestones. Despite promises from the friends who had invited him, he was not getting paid regularly there either—and he and Rada had three children at home. I sometimes offered to loan her money, but Rada said she didn't want to depend on anyone else's help and repeatedly assured me that she would manage somehow. I eventually convinced her to let me loan her ninety leva (fifty dollars) so she could pay the minimal amount to get her electricity turned back on, and she promised to pay me back as soon as payday came around.

Each morning since I had started sweeping, Rada and Donka, who met at work but had become like sisters, asked the bosses to include me on their team and would pull me into their intimate and boisterous conversations. Rada regularly invited me to eat a meal at her home on paydays before we traveled together by bus to the company's garage to get paid. But when payday came a few weeks after I gave her the loan, she avoided me and started going out of her way to keep from working alongside me. It was clear that she didn't have the money to pay me back and was too embarrassed to tell me. Our relationship changed significantly for a time. Eventually she relaxed, explaining that she had thought of the money she owed every time she talked to me. She felt bad about the debt and not being able to pay me back, and she couldn't escape either of those facts. I reassured her that it was okay, I understood. I had loaned it to her without expectation of repayment, as I knew how precarious her situation was, but I had not wanted to tell her that out of fear of changing our dynamic. She looked down as she admitted, "I never wanted to be like this."

One day in March, when we went to the garage to collect our pay after a three-week delay, I noticed a group of men in leather jackets surrounding the parking lot, leaning on parked cars that ranged from modest sedans to high-end SUVs. Rada explained that they were with Marko, a half-Romani pawnshop owner whose primary business was providing loans to street sweepers. His pawnshop was in downtown Sofia but easily accessible via public transport from the neighborhood where most sweepers lived. Knowing when payday was, he ensured that sweepers would repay him by waiting in the garage parking lot. This also ensured that they would pay him before returning to their husbands, families, and household obligations that would inevitably drain their newly acquired funds.

Unlike bank loans or even high-interest credit company loans, informal loans like Marko's came without a credit check. The interest rate was also much higher than that of a bank loan. Rada had taken out a three-month loan of 300 leva and had to pay back 160 leva each month, accumulating a total interest payment of 180 leva. She insisted that it wasn't so bad, but she still couldn't afford electricity. She had run lines to her husband's uncle's house so that she and her children could watch TV in the evenings. Although she lived in Filipovtsi, the home of many sweepers on the team, she would regularly send her children with bags of clothing for her mother to wash in Fakulteta, not far down the ring road that encircled Sofia.

Knowing that Mimi provided legal high-interest loans through a credit company, I asked Rada why she didn't take out a loan with her. Rada told me that she would never take out a loan with Mimi "because the percent of interest she asks for is very large. For example, if you borrow four hundred leva, you have to return eight hundred." Rada also explained that she was ineligible for further bank loans because she had an outstanding one, taken out for her husband's sister, who needed money to travel abroad for work, that she would never be able to repay. Instead of borrowing from Mimi, she preferred to work odd jobs on her days off. "I will start a second job, and we will deal with it somehow," she told me. "I mean, the problem is not that my husband is without work, but just that he hasn't been paid yet. And we have so much electricity to pay! We will go today to the place where we pay our bills, to ask if we can gradually start making payments so they can start our electricity up again."

Middle managers at the firm like Mimi tried to suggest that they suffered just as much as workers. When sweepers complained about payment delays, I heard Mimi say, "I'm hungry too. Don't you see that all I eat is pretzels?" It was true that their payments were also delayed, but their income provided a buffer that sweepers lacked. Sofka told me that, according to her estimations, middle managers made one thousand leva a month (about 250% of what sweepers made); Ani and Mimi's nearest boss made at least two thousand leva a month, and sweepers estimated that the women working in the firm's administrative office made that amount or more. Nearly all of these bosses, as well as garbage truck drivers—who were paid much more than sweepers and back-of-truck workers—were white, a difference so obvious to all involved that it didn't need to be noted.

The cleaning company's opacity about payday timing led sweepers to generate their own explanations. They knew that there was a link between the municipal budget and the private firm that paid them, but the nature of that relationship remained obscure. Most were certain that they were being kept in the dark on purpose to make it easier for the company to pay them late, which happened often. When pay was late, the bosses would usually claim that the company didn't receive its funding from the municipality. Although I could not substantiate their claims, many of my other interlocutors, some involved in politics, and some not, shared that deliberate obfuscation was a useful capitalist strategy in the postsocialist EU era. One city official explained that it was often hard to tell if people obscured facts strategically to skirt the laws, like those for privatization, or if it came down to incompetence and people just didn't know the policies and procedures.

Veronika, an elderly and devoutly Christian Romani sweeper with whom I regularly worked, offered her theory: "The inspectorate gives the money to the big boss of our company, he pays himself and then distributes the rest of the money elsewhere, and now he doesn't have any more. He could have paid us, but he gave it away." She continued, "In other countries, it isn't this way. But here, there is no work, so we tolerate it." In the absence of regularity, everyone looked for signs indicating when payday would come. One time when pay was late, Rada told me she had good news: "My hands are itching, tomorrow there will be money." This struck me as an astute articulation of the absurdity of payday's inconsistency—an attempt at levity, perhaps, to cope with the darker absurdity of sweepers' life circumstances. Absent a logical narrative, my colleagues would invent one, enjoying their creative capacity to find humor in the midst of the very precarity they diagnosed.

When I started sweeping, the workers' uniforms were red for the first time in years. They joked, "See, we are red communists again now!" Many sweepers on the team had collected uniforms over multiple decades, noting that with every political or corporate change, for them, nothing changed except the color of their uniform. Rada explained to our team that the uniforms were made red to match the national football (soccer) team that was owned by the "big boss" of our company. Even though paydays were never regular and could even be many months late, she rationalized: "When they win, the boss is happy and we get paid. It's all connected." Referring to how her uniform was the same color as the communist flag and team uniform, while also punning on the sweepers' debt, she declared, "See, we're all in the red." Everyone laughed. Later, during a long period of work without pay, another sweeper raised the idea again: "Maybe if the team wins, we get paid. We are, like them, all in uniform, aren't we?"

Jokes could only provide so much solace, however, and my colleagues knew they were fundamentally disempowered in the face of the workplace hierarchy and the racial capitalist logics that comprise its foundation. Sofka told me that the big boss was only "playing with us. We are his players, we are the football players. But football players have everything, they get free coffee, free meals, and we don't have anything to eat." As each month ended, workers whispered among themselves: "When are we getting paid?" "Did you hear that we aren't getting paid till after the fifth?" "What am I going to do with my creditor who won't stop calling?" As the days went on without pay, this would quickly escalate to panic: "What if we don't get paid and they turn off my electricity?" "How can I buy Christmas presents for my kids without a paycheck?" "How will we eat?" "We're hungry, where should we get food from?" "We're going to bed with empty stomachs. That's a shame." "Now when I get paid, I will have to give it [to creditors] right away, and what will I eat with after that?" Sweepers often told me about their elevated blood pressure due to financial stress and hunger. Most workers were silent when we met with the bosses each morning but quickly joined angry discussions with other workers once they were out of the bosses' earshot.

One day, while waiting for the bus home, Sofka pulled me aside. She wanted me to know that the late payments were a relatively recent development. "I've worked this job for so many years. Fifteen years I'm here and I'm seeing this for the first time. This cleaning company is fucked up." "Before," she explained, "we were working, and it was such a miracle. We got advances, salaries, parties...so that we can work calmly, and now we are with this company for three or four years, and it's always like this. Here we never get money." She took a drag of her cigarette. "You know, before, we used to be people."

I understood Sofka to be commenting on what it means to be a person, and to call that status into question when workers are dehumanized by the capitalist logics of the workplace.[11] This was the result of both the racialization of Roma—as nonwhite, and, in a way, nonhuman—and the degrading conditions of undervalued contemporary waste labor.[12] Indeed, she explained, it wasn't just this company that had changed. Street sweeping had been better under socialism, both in terms of its physical demands and its compensation.[13] Many colleagues told me the same thing. Before capitalism, they said, sweepers worked until their assigned streets were cleaned and then could return home to take care of their families, rather than being hemmed in by a rigid eight-hour workday. This allowed them to work outside the home for income and be at home for their children when they came back from school. Bosses had valued the cleanliness both of the streets and of the workers themselves. No one was allowed

WASTE AND RACE

to wear a dirty uniform or to relax in the entryway of a building. This was a kind of surveillance, but it was associated with pride because the state celebrated cleaning as a political good. Waste workers were part of most official events—including marches, holiday parades, and urban development celebrations—and were esteemed as critical to the public and international face of socialist development. Today, as Bulgaria seeks to define itself as fully European, sweeping is still linked to narratives of development. But now this connection does not celebrate sweepers. Rather, it ensures that, insofar as they are racialized and poorly compensated, they remain an exploitable labor force used to develop Bulgaria within the ongoing project of Europeanization.

In March 2013, paychecks were weeks overdue, and a large group of sweepers convened after morning roll call in a nearby café. They were supposed to be cleaning, but it was still dark out, so they invited me to gather with them in a hidden spot, knowing that they could take some time to talk before the bosses found them.[14] As my colleagues laughed, bantered with the café owner, and drank their sweet Nescafé coffees, I suggested that they strike. I didn't know the word in Bulgarian, but I mimed holding up a sign while marching and chanting, provoking laughter until they eventually admitted they understood what I meant. Angel, the husband of a sweeper, who was also temporarily sweeping while waiting for a position on the back of a truck, was standing nearby, apart from the table reserved for the women. Overhearing us, he said that if we went for it—and we should—we should make clear how widespread the problems were: "Tell them that the men are this way too. We're looking for our money. Yesterday the bills came, and just the electricity is 220 leva [about 122 dollars]." But my colleagues laughed at the idea, insisting that I was naive. They explained that they wouldn't protest or strike because they needed their jobs. They had children who relied on them. They knew that if they went on strike, they would be easily replaced, probably within the same day.

I asked Sofka, who was leading the conversation, why they would stay with this company when I had heard of other companies that paid regularly. At the time, there were two firms (with many subsidiaries in name only) that fully controlled sweeping in Sofia, one that paid cash and one that paid via direct deposit. The direct deposit companies were known to pay regularly and even provide food vouchers for workers. My colleagues explained that sweepers with bank debt did not want to be paid by direct deposit: It would be garnished directly upon hitting their accounts. Cash was safer, even if it was late and less certain.

Sometimes the sweepers did seem to consider striking, asking each other in Romani to avoid the bosses from listening in, "Can't we look out for our rights?" One afternoon, when the workers had once again gone without pay for months, Sofka told Ani, "We won't come to work at all or sweep the streets." Sofka's sister-in-law, Kalina, chimed in, "Sofka is right, everyone is hungry." Ani responded, "Okay, only, you know, I can't stop you. I can't tell you that I will pay you until I hear from the higher-ups. You're right. I will ask Boyan again today to see what's going on, and I will tell him that you're uprising. So, they should make their calculations." But Ani seemed to know that striking would never happen, even though late payment remained a crushing hardship.

Animals, Bodies, Machines

One early spring morning, after everyone was finally paid, Ani told us, "I can make you sweep the sand on all the streets every single day. But I don't, because you are people; you are not animals. When you work with animals, after a whole day of work you need to leave the poor animal to relax. Even animals need a rest in the shade." No one objected, but Ani's analogy struck me as tellingly conflicted. She had begun by asserting that workers are people but went on to equate them with hard-laboring animals. It was consistent with the naturalized dehumanization of waste workers, which my colleagues told me took a toll on them, both mentally and physically.

The work was especially difficult at that time. The company had not yet hired new workers, so the thin winter staffing levels were still in place. Yet the workload was growing, and they needed to sweep away the accumulated sand from the winter snow cleaning. Most workers had back pain, and paychecks were delayed again. Ani explained that it was about to get worse. "I want you all to gather the salt and sand you can find, all of you. There will be no street-cleaning machine on Saturday, Sunday, or Monday."

Veronika interjected, "I can't even remember the last time the street-cleaning machine was actually out cleaning." The rest of the women nodded. Sofka announced, "I think I saw it for a minute yesterday." Ani explained, "There are some streets that it can't go down." Some streets were too narrow for the machine to pass through, and others had illegally parked cars blocking the way. "Saturday, Sunday, and Monday there will be no machines, people, so you had better prepare yourself for some work."

Ani moved on to other matters: We must—as she said nearly every day—work in harmony and not fight among ourselves. Maya nodded. "Yes, that's no way to work. We are here to work, not argue." I heard Sofka laugh. Ani often yelled at the sweepers and punished them based on how they reacted when she scolded them. But Maya explained her approach to me later that day: "You need Ani to like you. It doesn't matter what you say anyway. Just let her yell and get it out."

My colleagues had a variety of such coping strategies to manage the stress of the job, which was both emotionally and physically taxing. Their bodies ached, and their mental health suffered due to chronic uncertainty and worry, but they needed to keep working if they were going to get paid. Labor turned the body into a tool and wore it down, so that they sometimes experienced themselves not as full beings but as discrete pieces—blood and organs, aching muscles, taut nerves.[15]

Sweepers explained that their feet swelled during the long workday and, after years on the job, their veins enlarged. Like many of my other Romani women friends, they were especially concerned with blood pressure as the physical manifestation of their fraying emotional nerves coupled with long days on their feet. Among sweepers, they explained, blood pressure could be raised by hunger, too much coffee, and too many cigarettes. It could also be raised by stress or anger. Blood pressure served as the interface between the material, the emotional, and the somatic. Blood, no longer associated with life force, threatened to pool and swell, or to move at a speed matching their high levels of stress. The body thus materializes the emotional, financial, and physical experiences of racialization as it is pressured and shaped by its status as essential and expendable.

Many sweepers preferred to work outdoors because it was better for their nerves. Working inside buildings like malls was more highly esteemed work for sweepers, who told me matter-of-factly that "they only hire the white, blond ones," whereas "black G*psies work outdoors." Yet these same women told me that they would go crazy inside; the pressure of life was so intense that "you can explode," and outdoor work helped them find relief.[16] They would explain that, unlike me, who lived alone, they could never "take it easy" at home. This was not only because people constantly needed them—kids, parents, in-laws, neighbors—but also because they found it hard to rest even in moments when they could. Despite problems with varicose veins and high blood pressure, they could not just sit. Even if rest might help their veins, their nerves would "explode" without work. Hearing this refrain so many times, I asked if they had thought of other ways to deal with nerves. Sofka shook her head. "My nerves are shot, I'm always anxious, there's nothing to do. This is who I have become." In other words, the conditions of her racialized labor, coupled with the demands placed on her at home, had become so deeply somaticized that she has given up hope of changing them. Instead, she accepts her body's struggle, as is, and manages its flare-ups through more work.

Some workers had small blood pressure readers at home, and nearly all older Romani women I met had been diagnosed with high blood pressure. Nadka, a sweeper who lived in Fakulteta, shared her increasing concern after taking her mother to the hospital only to be scolded by the doctor for not having brought her in earlier. Nadka lamented that she would have to go all the way home to wash up after work before she could visit her mother in the hospital. She also worried that she was next in line. Her mother was suffering the same way her grandmother previously had. Their stress was intergenerational and embodied. One day, when I asked Donka, usually boisterous and irreverent, why she was so quiet, she too brought up high blood pressure. She acknowledged that she was angry at her bosses and the other sweepers. She told me that because Maya helps Mimi find more loan clients, she gets to work less, leaving Donka with more to do. But Rada had told her to stay silent so as "to not get angry, to not raise [her] blood pressure."

Not "exploding" required serious effort when work was unjust, pay was late, and sweepers carried the responsibility of their households' financial and emotional needs on their backs. Sometimes this included worrying about children who were at home sick, or secretly bringing sick children to work so as not to miss a day on the job and risk losing the position altogether. Sweepers also bore the pain of deceased family members, including children, sick parents, or, like Rada, distance from husbands working abroad without enough pay to come home. Nadka's firstborn son, she revealed to me a few months into sweeping together, had died as a small child. She told me that her team member, Petya, had a teenage son who had recently died, and they discussed this during the workday. Petya worried about her surviving children a great deal and told me, gratefully, that her colleagues like Nadka gave her immense emotional support. They calmly and consistently reminded her to take care of herself and said things like, "Don't cry, don't be angry. Look at you, you'll get sick." She knew that she needed not to be angry. Anger would raise her blood pressure.

Both Romani waste workers and white Bulgarians repeatedly told me that only Roma, and not white Bulgarians, have the capacity for such taxing labor. They did not mean quite the same thing, though. Sweepers would tell me that they had watched white Bulgarians—often villagers coming from the countryside to seek work in Sofia—cycle in and out of the workplace. When a white Bulgarian woman was hired while I was on the team, the bosses didn't invest in a full uniform for her because they assumed she wouldn't last. She wore her own clothing with a borrowed fluorescent vest on top and disappeared after her second day at work. I asked the bosses what had happened to her, since I had never seen someone join the team and leave so quickly. Ani explained that she could not do the work and that this was typical of the white Bulgarian women they hired. She noted that the work was very difficult and that it was hard to be a white woman on an otherwise all-Roma team. I had heard this before, and I pushed her: "What do you mean, the work is hard for them? Is it not too hard for the Romani women?" After all, many of the Romani sweepers were smaller, older, and appeared sicker than the robust-looking white woman who temporarily joined them. Ani explained, "Bulgarians aren't used to it, that's it."

Romani sweepers also described their ability to "get used to it," but with a different implication—namely, what it takes to "collectively manage the conditions of living within a racial capitalist economy."[17] It wasn't a matter of white women needing time to adjust or feeling culturally out of place, my Romani colleagues told me, but of their inability to measure up to Romani power and endurance. Incidentally, there were two white women on the team, apparent exceptions to the rule, but my Romani colleagues told me that they weren't "totally well"; one should have been home on a disability pension due to mental illness, and the other swept to be closer to the stray dogs she liked to feed. But the sweepers broadly categorized the other white Bulgarian women they encountered on the street as *kifli*—sweet, croissant-like rolls typically eaten for breakfast and a term used to imply a spoiled, usually attractive young woman without financial stressors. Romani women, they said, worked too hard and faced too much to stay sweet and airy. Bulgarian women, on the other hand, would never last on the streets: "Bulgarians aren't used to working hard, like animals, like machines." As they explained matter-of-factly, Romani women had learned throughout their lives and across the centuries to endure hardship.

Romani women sweepers were also celebrating their own power and ingenuity when they made such comments. Unsure of when they will be paid and often entrapped in debt, workers still manage to provide for their families' needs, often single-handedly. Still, stress takes a toll on their bodies and minds as they are ensnared in the waste-race nexus and, in the eyes of white Bulgarians who both rely on and mock their labor, cast as disposable, akin to the waste they work with. There is little time for rest, or protest. Romani sweepers collect the dirt today, knowing that no matter how hard and long they work, there will be more waste for them to manage tomorrow.

The Racial Politics of Waste

Ani and Mimi, the two middle-aged white Bulgarians who served as middle management, surveilled the sweepers' labor on foot and determined where and with whom each worker swept on a given day. My experiences with Ani and Mimi made clear how street sweepers are both essential to and categorized as disposable in Bulgaria's aspirations for "European progress."

EU environmental mandates focus on achieving environmental sustainability through "resource efficiency and the circular economy," which includes waste management.[18] The current directive on waste focuses on a foundational goal: that the polluter pays.[19] The "polluter pays" policy mandates that "the costs of disposing of waste must be borne by the holder of waste, by previous holders or by the producers of the product from which the waste came."[20] The principle is founded on the idea that "the waste producer and the waste holder should manage the waste in a way that guarantees a high level of protection of the environment and human health."[21] In practice, however, waste producers and holders in Bulgaria are not the ones working to meet these targets—instead, Romani women are. Without them, Bulgaria would risk sanctions and a high landfill tax.[22] In fact, the 2022 EU environmental policy implementation analyses declared Bulgaria to be behind regarding the polluter pays principle, without any progress since 2017.[23] The polluter doesn't pay; instead, Romani women do, laboring within the waste-race nexus.

The entire sweeping team often gathered before and after the workday to discuss various issues, including who would be assigned to which teams. Boyan had taken on a somewhat aloof but grandfatherly role toward me, and his oversight seemed to influence Ani and Mimi's selection of my assignment. On my first few days, they told me and Boyan that they were picking the "calmest" people for me to work with: Lora, one of the two white Bulgarians on the team, and Veronika. They were among the few women who never spoke back to the bosses' authority. Desi, one of the two white Bulgarian women on the team, suffered from mental illness for which, she told us, she was waiting to receive a disability pension. She was often the butt of jokes among the other workers, who laughed both with and about her—not because of her illness, but because she spoke openly about wearing diapers to work so she would not have to pee outdoors. The other sweepers thought that this was absurd and a bit elitist. The rest of the team used the bathroom at cafés with sympathetic owners whenever possible, or else between enclosed dumpsters that offered some privacy, though some avoided drinking anything all day. When I had my period, my colleagues worked hard to find indoor bathrooms for me to use, worried about the "shame" I would face in having to use a makeshift outdoor toilet.

Sometimes, a few men temporarily joined the sweeping team, husbands of sweepers who were waiting for openings in the coveted higher-paying jobs working the back of garbage trucks. But for the most part, street sweeping in Bulgaria is both women's work and a "G*psy job" with low pay.[24] As noted earlier, archival documents from the socialist era reveal that state security forces focused on employing Roma in sectors like street cleaning to provide them with "permanent work [in order to] overcome their wandering (vagrancy)."[25] At the same time, these archives reveal concern that, because so many Roma worked in sectors with relatively low income and high turnover, like cleaning, this strategy might "[lead] to very slow increase of the level of culture within the G*psy population." In response, the government put Romani employment "at the forefront for increasing [Roma] qualifications and general culture." State documents note the need for "organizational, political, and educational work from the party, Komsomol, and trade unions" to achieve Romani "assimilation."

While policies on who should be doing Bulgaria's waste management and cleaning labor are different in the EU era, using the word *chistota* ("purity" or "cleanliness") as the umbrella term for street cleaning is a socialist holdover. Once the name for the state cleaning company, it is still commonly used to refer to the municipal cleaning sector as a whole despite the fact that it has been privatized and divided up between multiple companies. The everyday work of *chistota* is not that different from the socialist era, except, as noted earlier, the shift to a strict eight-hour workday. Although the state socialist strategy of racializing waste work was perhaps more explicit than it is today, the work was also better regarded and better paid. This was due to two factors: first, its focus on urbanization as critical to large-scale socialist development, with waste work seen as fundamental to that urbanization, and second, its emphasis on labor's potential to transform social structure.[26] There were, however, contradictions between ideology and practice. While socialist policy promoted work as critical to equality, the state also intentionally used labor organization to implement racial assimilationist goals. Labor was intended to discipline Roma into good socialist "Bulgarians," but at the same time, the state degraded that racialized labor.[27] Despite the state-sanctioned value of sweeping labor and the solid remuneration it received, it was still labor that white Bulgarians did not want—or expect—to do.[28] And, as street cleaning's technologies and economies shifted, so too did the processes and particularities of racialization they facilitated.

My colleague Lora was acutely aware of the low status of her sweeping job, and that she was one of the few white Bulgarians doing it. She had been a secretary for a socialist administrative office in the 1980s, becoming a hairdresser after the postsocialist transition of 1989. She told me about her college-educated children who worked in Sofia's courthouse and her ex-husband who lived in the United States. The other sweepers often wondered aloud about why Lora would do "G*psy work" when she clearly had other options. Some suggested that it must be because she loved stray dogs so much. She spent much of her time on the job feeding street dogs, picking ticks from their fur, and scratching them behind the ears. She had even proudly named several of them.

Nobody on the team particularly liked Lora. They complained of her incessant talking, while she bemoaned that her colleagues spoke only Romani to each other and ignored her. At the same time, she distanced herself from her Romani colleagues by emphasizing her whiteness—or as

FIGURE 1.6   Lora working with stray dogs around her. Photo by the author.

she and many other white Bulgarians encoded it, "Bulgarianness"—and her class status, reminding anyone who would listen that she lived in Bankya, a famously rich suburb that was home to Bulgaria's prime minister at the time, Boyko Borisov. In the mornings, she would sit on the curb and take a mirror from her uniform pocket to put on bright red lipstick. She told me that she hoped it made her seem less "G*psy," but acknowledged that it might have the opposite effect. She repeatedly told me that she felt safe sharing the workplace, and all the talking, food, and time it entailed, with me since I was like her: a white woman.

One day when Lora and I were working together, some teenage boys yelled at us: "Look at those white *m*ngalki*!" They laughed as they threw plastic bottles and potato chip bags at our feet. *M*ngal* is the most derogatory racist slur for a Roma person, used only—and used commonly—by white Bulgarians.[29] More than one Bulgarian-language teacher taught me this term as they chuckled while I explained my research to them. The slur was ubiquitous; the president's website even used it in the filename of an English-language PDF on their EU Roma integration strategy. The document was saved as *13.NationalStrategyIntegrateM*ngali.pdf*.[30]

The boys' actions were far from unusual. Sofia residents often threw garbage at uniformed street sweepers. Some passersby would aim garbage directly into the *farazh*, what sweepers called their long-handled metal dustpans. Others, however, threw their waste directly at sweepers' bodies, at times including lit cigarettes. This struck me as another way workers were dehumanized as yet another object in the waste landscape. But both sweepers and other Sofia residents told me that these actions also reflected residents' frustration with the urban waste system at large. Municipal funding, which regulated the number and placement of waste bins based on population size and budget, was insufficient. Instead of appealing to the municipality for more bins or more regular collection and cleaning of existing dumpsters—actions that would involve navigating a bureaucracy so complicated and inefficient it was basically futile—residents targeted the frontline, uniformed Romani workers.

Many of my colleagues ignored verbal insults and dodged the objects thrown at them from apartment windows. But Lora interrupted the young men: "We aren't *m*ngalki*," she declared boldly. She pointed to me, "She's an American and speaks better English than you, and I am Bulgarian, from Bankya." The boys stood silently. I asked them, "So why do you say such a thing to us?" One looked down at his sneakers and replied, "He didn't say it. Didn't mean it."

"That's just racist," I told him. "You're young, don't talk like that." One of the boys looked at me directly. "Have you finished twelfth grade?" he asked. "Yes," I replied, "and university."

He thought for a minute. "So why do you work on the street like that?" His friend echoed, "So why are you working here?" I explained my research—I was accustomed to such questions by then. They asked me how much I got paid. "Not enough," I told them. "She's doing *research*," one explained to the other, sounding incredulous and sarcastic.

"You know, people work on the street because they have to," I told the boys.

"Well, the other sweepers haven't finished high school," they announced, as though that made it okay to shout slurs at them.

"You can't use the word *m*ngalki*," I insisted.

One boy replied, "We didn't mean it for you." The other nodded. "We didn't mean it for you, he just talks like that." We had been conversing for a while when a police officer came over to investigate the commotion. On learning I was American, he asked me a bit about the United States, including what I thought of the president at the time, Barack Obama, and whether I liked life in Bulgaria. Then he sent the boys back to school and

WASTE AND RACE

left us alone. I imagine that if he had found two Romani sweepers trying to convince Bulgarian boys to be less racist, the story would have ended quite differently.

Lora and I spent the rest of the day discussing what had happened. She told me that the young men should be thanking us, the laborers who clean their streets, not calling us names and dropping trash at our feet for us to pick up. But she also kept repeating, "And I'm a Bulgarian!" It was hard not to hear her protest as insistence that her relation to the work was different from her Romani colleagues—a lament for her own lot in working a job that made people see her as part of a group she herself looked down upon.

I had only been sweeping for a few weeks when I realized that, although my whiteness was obvious to my colleagues, many passersby assumed that I was Romani. This almost never happened in other contexts, but while I was sweeping, Romani pedestrians would address me as though I was a Romani woman who was new to the area, perhaps newly married or living with relatives. They would ask whose "daughter-in-law" (*bori,* in Romani) I was and in what Romani neighborhood (*mahala*) I was living. Non-Romani residents also recognized that I was new on the job and alternated between asking where I came from and throwing their waste at me like they did with my colleagues, assuming our brooms to be an extension of uniformed bodies. My body became raced through the work I was doing, the uniform I was wearing, and the instruments I was holding—not the color of my skin.[31] To be a sweeper in Bulgaria is to be apprehended as Roma.

Race has long been a colonial technology designed to advance material and ideological claims to whiteness and power, and it continues to operate this way on Sofia's streets.[32] White Bulgarians, hungering for Europeanization and its racialized modernity, carry on the long-normalized devaluation of both Roma and their work. Sweeping city streets in a city aspiring toward Europeanness places Romani workers at the heart of the waste-race nexus.

Europeanization as a Racial Project

Under socialism, the responsibilities of Chistota were essentially the same as today: ensuring streets were clean, tidy, and meeting mandated aesthetic criteria. The socialist aesthetic also required workers to clean before, during, and after the many festivals and parades intended to boost morale and political compliance. During these events, workers themselves had to adhere to an aesthetic standard in the form of clean uniforms and overall look. This was particularly important because when most workers were Roma, they were assumed to be dirty unless they were being forced by the state to comply with its cleanliness regulations. Chistota managers worried about the errors and messiness of human labor and looked to mechanization as a solution.[33] For the socialist state, cleaning was important to state presentation; this is still the case today in the name of Europeanization, although workers are no longer conceived of as an essential part of the state apparatus.

The Europeanization of Bulgaria has been an asymptotic process, a goal that is always out of reach and mired in white supremacy. This was true well before the promise of EU accession was on the table. In fact, in the 1920s and '30s, "eugenic scientists, politicians, and laymen in these countries insisted on the racial and cultural homogeneity of their nations and asserted their nations' place in a European civilization attached to racial Whiteness."[34] However, much like colonial constitutions of "the human," Europeanness is, by definition, unobtainable for those who do not already conform to its preestablished and continually policed contours. For Bulgaria, Europe has remained a neocolonial power and an almost-but-not-quite-obtainable ideal.[35] Bulgaria continues to strive for Europeanness, knowing that its position in pan-European frameworks is that of an Eastern bloc country still entrenched in its socialist past, and a fundamentally Balkan space with a deep Ottoman legacy. Although Bulgaria has instituted changes to conform or "harmonize" with European Union policy, it has never fully achieved Europeanness in the eyes of most Bulgarians. Political, social, and aesthetic Europeanness, for almost all my interlocutors, is categorically unobtainable. Throughout my research, waste company CEOs, government officials, and Romani residents alike repeated variations of the same sentiment: "The promise of Europe was always on its way but never arrived."

The idea of an asymptotic Europe, an ideal that can be approached but never reached, materialized through my attention to environmental policy on waste management. As I finished my street-sweeping gig while interning part-time at the Bulgarian Ministry of the Environment and Water during the summer of 2013, a delegation from Kosovo came to meet with the ministry's waste directorate. We sat with strong coffees and plastic bottles of water in the meeting room of the ministry's headquarters. The Kosovo delegation wanted to learn how Bulgaria "transposed" EU waste law and policy into the local context. Kristina, one of the delegation leaders, explained, "As we are located so close to Bulgaria, this was one of the main reasons to choose to visit your country, and we also have the same way of thinking." She spoke with simultaneous translation into Bulgarian, which was typical at this kind of international meeting. Kristina went on to clarify that Kosovo and Bulgaria have "the same mentality." After the slight translation delay, the Bulgarians in the room laughed. They knew what she meant. They explained that "the same mentality" was a "Balkan" one, and that it was quite difficult to smoothly impose waste laws from Germany and France into these countries.

These expressions of concern and frustration about the imposition of Western European models into the Eastern European context were typical in the international waste meetings and conferences I attended. It was not just that the countries had different histories. As more than one official explained to me, the economic makeup of the countries differed. During a formal interview I conducted in her office, Irena, a ministry official, waved her arm westward toward Germany or France as she told me: "Over there, they don't have the informal sector that we do." "Informal sector" was coded language for Romani labor. During after-work drinks at a bustling café, she made the same point more openly: "They don't have the G*psies over there that we have here. How can we become France?" She pointed to the people going through nearby dumpsters, "Just look outside." Another ministry official who had joined us asked me, perhaps rhetorically, "Tell me, how can we be Germany when we don't have cleaning machines but just have G*psies to rely on?" This line of thought expressed a deep-rooted frustration that Western European countries imposed impossible measures but did not have to conform to EU regulations as strictly as Bulgaria did, since they were not subject to the same post-accession environmental sanctions imposed in new EU countries. They did not have to prove their Europeanness.

People also expressed anxiety about the daily circulation and social significance of waste. I wrote in my field notes one day during my internship at the ministry, "Waste is really just a kind of temporary loan." It had struck me that, like the loans my sweeping colleagues managed, waste itself was a similar type of temporary accrual, appearing and disappearing only to materialize again. For white Bulgarians and for those not involved with street cleaning, waste moved in and out of urban space almost magically. The waste-race nexus did not pervade their lives except in that they wanted both waste items and nonwhite bodies removed from view—from the urban landscape they sought to Europeanize. Almost all older white Bulgarians I spoke to waxed nostalgic for the invisibility of waste labor during socialism. In the past, they told me, the street sparkled and you had no idea how: "You would just wake up that way and never see a sweeper out in daylight." Some older women on the sweeping team confirmed this. "Yes, I worked early in the morning," Nadka told me. She would sweep while it was still dark and be home in time to take her children to school. Then the next day, the waste would be there again. Waste moves and is removed, and it requires constant management. It is most visible to those who do the labor of removing it. Successful labor, in essence, renders invisible the struggle of the laborers themselves.

To hear white Bulgarians tell it, Romani waste workers today are entirely too visible. Their labor is integral to Sofia's ability to appear aesthetically European, since Europe, according to residents and urban planners I spoke with, should be "orderly and tidy."[36] But more than one interlocutor also told me that, in Europe, "there aren't these G*psies everywhere, going through trash" like there are in Bulgaria. Europe, they suggested, is a place in which Roma do not exist—or at least are not visible. For them, Romani bodies should remain out of view, much like trash on the streets.

In contrast to their memory of socialist times when their labor was better remunerated and they "were people," street sweepers know all too well that the European aesthetic to which Bulgaria now aspires is one in which they don't exist. High-interest loans enable workers to take part in the Europeanization project, to maintain their always-precarious employment, and to continue to pay for electricity and household needs. They are trapped in cycles of late pay and debt, but know that sweeping work is one of the most stable jobs they can find. They recognize that the Bulgarian government and Sofia municipality have deemed it more economical to continue to employ them (while not paying them on time) than to invest in new machinery. They are effectively made to be less than human through their labor, even as that labor, through the waste-race nexus, enables Bulgaria to adhere to an aesthetically idealized Europe.

Europeanness and Bulgarianness are at times proximal but at other times seemingly distant.[37] In this space between Europeanness and Bulgarianness, Romani Bulgarians—including sweepers—navigate conditions of impossible resolution.[38] When Bulgarianness and Europeanness seem proximal, they do so at the expense of Roma, who are seen as outside of both the nation and white Europeanness. On the other hand, when they appear distant, Roma are still stuck in the absurd navigation of asserting themselves within and between preexisting categories of the human, nonhuman, and object.

And, as street sweepers are racialized as disposable, the material waste objects that are part of urban sustainability regimes accrue more value than the people who work with them. Although it is never acknowledged, Romani women compensate for the failures of EU waste policy, especially Bulgaria's failure to meet the EU-mandated polluter pays principle. Romani women, not polluters or manufacturers, pay for the waste that accumulates on city streets in the form of financial limbo, emotional duress, and physical hardship—all of which reinforce the marginalization that drives Romani workers into the waste sector to begin with.

TWO

Recycling

Colored bins began appearing regularly on Sofia streets in 2006. They were placed there in preparation for Bulgaria's 2007 accession into the European Union. Each bin had a small hole in the front where passersby could insert waste by category, with labels and pictures showing what was supposed to go inside. Blue was for cardboard and paper, green for glass, and yellow for plastic and metal. Most residents found these bins difficult to use: How could cardboard packaging fit into such a small hole? So, instead, the bins—intended for residents but also illegally used by neighborhood businesses—typically served as a structure around which to discard all kinds of recyclable and nonrecyclable waste. The bins also served as charity sites where people hung old clothing or piled unwanted items for anyone who passed by.

When I first encountered these bins in 2008, two years before I began street sweeping, I wondered if their small openings were designed to protect against animals, like the stray dogs for which Sofia was infamous.[1] Yet this seemed unlikely, because the metal mixed-waste bins remained completely open and were much more likely to contain food. Perhaps, I thought, the holes were intended to protect the items inside from inclement weather that would destroy their integrity and make recycling more difficult. Yet that struck me as unlikely too. When I

FIGURE 2.1 Plastic bins for EU-mandated separate collection recycling in Sofia. Photo by the author.

asked, nearly everyone—urban residents, waste workers, recycling firm CEOs—told me the same thing: They were meant to "keep garbage in and G*psies out."

The bins had been installed to help Bulgaria meet the recycling quotas required by the European Union, an uphill battle, given how publicly unpopular recycling was, and the firms wanted to keep recyclable waste for their own profits. They made the holes small to prevent people, understood in Bulgaria as inevitably Romani collectors, or *kloshari*, from "stealing" "their" waste. To the extent that Bulgaria manages to meet EU quotas, however, it does so because of these same criminalized laborers who collect recyclables, transport them to local collection points called *punktove* (pl.), and sell them to official producer responsibility organizations (PROs). PROs then report these items in their accounting of recovered packaging materials, as mandated by the European Union. Even PRO officials told me that they probably wouldn't meet EU targets without the work of *kloshari* and *punktove*. The institution of the *punkt* dates back to Bulgaria's socialist period.[2] While some of the *punktove* have changed their technologies and appearance, many others look the same as they did decades ago.

Liberal European sustainability is framed in terms of "stewardship," "protection," and "responsibility." Article 3 of the Treaty on European Union, one of the two treaties upon which the EU is based, states that "sustainable development is an overarching objective for the EU, which is committed to a 'high level of protection and improvement of the quality of the environment.'"[3] Within the waste-race nexus in Bulgaria, these objectives are enacted by Romani laborers, including street sweepers, waste collectors, recyclers, and those working at conveyor-belt waste sorting sites. Their work props up the very waste regimes that, insofar as they help Bulgaria become European, also cast Roma as racialized others who are excluded from full European personhood. EU environmental sustainability is thus ensnared within long histories of racist urban "cleansing" projects, and contemporary recycling programs solidify these existing racial hierarchies.

FIGURE 2.2   Women working at a waste sorting facility in Sofia, Bulgaria. Photo by the author.

Transformations of Waste Work

Bulgaria's shift from socialism to democratic capitalism, which began in late 1989, was initially calm. Unlike other countries, such as neighboring Romania, it did not undergo a violent transition or face immediate political-economic upheaval. In fact, most Bulgarians I knew understood the collapse of the socialist regime, or "the changes" (*promenite*), in Bulgaria as an antirevolutionary revolution. Those who had been in power under state socialism stayed in power under "democratic" capitalism. Their labels and formal political associations were restructured, but this was often explained as a sleight of hand designed to legitimate Bulgaria's shift from Eastern European socialism to the democracy associated with Western Europe and, over time, the EU.[4]

Nevertheless, both Romani and non-Romani Bulgarians often recalled state socialism as a time of relative comfort and abundance, one that stood in contrast to the severe economic crisis the county fell into not long after signing the European Agreement in 1995 to seek EU membership. The crisis lasted for years.[5] Those in Western Europe and the United States often picture communism as an era of bread lines and overwhelming lack, but in Bulgaria, such images are associated instead with memories of the 1990s.[6] Throughout the 1990s, Bulgaria's official standard-of-living markers were as much as 40% below what they had been during late socialism.[7] By 1997, Bulgaria was experiencing one of postsocialism's worst cases of hyperinflation, defined as rapidly rising inflation rates of over 50% per month.[8] During this period, the exchange rate fell from about 70 leva to the US dollar in 1995 to almost 500 leva at the end of 1996 and peaked at about 3,000 leva per dollar in early 1997.[9]

It was not until mid-2004 that the country again reached pre-1989 standards of living.[10] The first time I traveled to Bulgaria, in 2003, a friend of mine followed my every step. He walked me to the bus stop, picked me up each morning outside the educational desegregation NGO office where I worked with him, and accompanied me on my lunch break. After a few weeks of this, I asked him why he did not leave me alone. He told me that, not long before, thieves had tied his cousin up in the entryway to his downtown apartment building, took his keys, and stole his car in broad daylight. He knew of enough similar stories, he said, that it would take hours to tell them to me. Most were from the 1990s, he explained, but he wasn't certain that the crisis was actually over.[11]

By official metrics, though, Bulgaria's economy had recovered. Hyperinflation had been remedied by pegging the leva to the German deutsche mark in 1997 through a currency board implemented at the insistence of the International Monetary Fund.[12] And, by 2003, the country was on its way to EU accession, which meant mandates that Bulgaria continue to work on privatization and democracy building. These efforts specifically included sustainable environmental development, corporate de-monopolization (especially pertinent for the waste sector), and the integration of minorities like the Roma.[13]

As this political-economic transition took place, so did waste management reform. Under state socialism, waste labor had been more highly valued than it has been since socialism's collapse, in terms of both remuneration and public esteem. In fact, state archives show that, in as early as the 1940s and 1950s, the state socialist Sofia city cleaning entity, Chistota, was desperate for laborers and increased worker salaries as an incentive.[14] This resulted in some experienced sweepers and waste collectors making as much as, or more than, indoor office workers. Other documents show the cleaning enterprise's strategies to accomplish its state-mandated goals, which included offering incentives such as prizes and acclaim to the best and longest-term workers.[15] Early on, most of the city's Chistota workers were men from villages. But as it became harder to bring them to Sofia, separating them from their families and homes, the workforce modulated until most waste laborers were Romani women from Sofia, as is still the case today. One major shift in the political economy of waste work is that in the postsocialist period, cleaning labor has been increasingly devalued. Financial incentives have become unnecessary as the cleaning firms have realized that there is a seemingly interminable workforce of otherwise unemployed Roma who will work for minimum wage. In addition to being devalued in city development plans, the labor has become increasingly racialized and gendered.

The transition to democracy also brought an increase in consumer waste. As an example, under socialism, most food purchases were made in bulk and without excess packaging, and there was a highly institutionalized culture of reuse. My friend Vera told me that she remembered going to the local store with her mother and grandmother in the 1980s to buy yogurt. They would take a glass bowl or casserole dish to the clerk, who would weigh it, zero the scale, and then fill it with as much yogurt as requested. Vera contrasted this practice with how yogurt was sold currently, in small plastic containers that are infamously difficult to recycle.

Though recycling in Bulgaria now is motivated by the "green" capitalist ideology common to Europe, the practice itself is not new.[16] According to Zsuzsa Gille, although "industrial ecology and the project of ecological modernization may be seen as revolutionary approaches in the West, a strikingly similar social experiment was initiated in state socialist countries half a century ago."[17] Like other socialist countries, Bulgaria had baked recycling into its production programs in ways that, while not framed in terms of environmental protection, prevented what would have otherwise resulted in massive amounts of landfilled waste. During socialism, these initiatives involved both local and state-sponsored attempts to reclaim materials needed for industrial production. At times, citizens would be asked to collect items that were needed for a specific industrial project; in Sofia, for example, this included domestic metal food containers to be melted down for the renowned state-owned Kremikovtsi metallurgy factory, the largest metallurgy factory in Bulgaria from 1963 through 2009. These arrangements were not sustainable after the transition to capitalism, in which it is often cheaper to purchase new materials and harder to compel collective recycling efforts.

Where consumer waste was concerned, the socialist state relied primarily on low-paid Romani workers for urban cleaning as well as independent door-to-door scrap collectors (mostly Romani men) to meet its recycling goals.[18] But it also promoted community-based recycling efforts to materially support the nation's ideological goals. Communist leaders throughout the region focused on linking consumer-waste recycling with state pride in industrialization. In Bulgaria and throughout the region, the metal waste that was materially necessary for industrial production was treated as though it represented all waste, becoming emblematic of socialist and Soviet development.[19]

Many of my interlocutors remember participating in recycling programs as part of socialist public schooling, with teachers and school officials framing their efforts through the lens of socialist modernization. Schools would ask students in a particular class or grade to collect one category of waste—in contemporary waste management terminology, a "waste stream." (In spite of metal's symbolic power and its role in heavy industry, nearly all my interviewees told me they collected paper.) When they had gathered enough, someone at the school would take it to be sold at the local *punkt*. Whatever money they made would either go to a sick child in the class or be shared between classmates as extra pocket money for things like ice cream and the sugary carbonated yellow drink of socialism, *limonada*.

Many elderly Sofia residents remembered spending the summers collecting recyclables, selling them for extra cash to buy trinkets at the seaside.

While some people spoke about such memories with nostalgia, others recalled state socialist recycling as yet another authoritarian order to comply with, under the propagandist guise of helping Bulgaria achieve its industrial goals. Indeed, recycling was enforced so strictly throughout the socialist period that many people have come to relish the freedom to discard things as they wish since the 1990s. Today, many Bulgarians reject the idea of voluntary recycling. Numerous Sofia residents, including those working in waste-related sectors, explained to me that there is no point in discarding items in color-coded recycling containers; they do not trust the state and assert that all waste "goes to the same place."[20]

Statistics from one of Bulgaria's prominent state-run recycling entities reveal how quickly the decline of industrially driven recycling took place. The aptly named Phoenix Elite (*Feniks Elit*) (which was renamed Phoenix Resource [*Feniks Resurs*] in 1989) remained state owned through the late 1990s and primarily recycled scrap metal. Even after socialism's end in 1989, Phoenix Resource conducted campaigns during which they hosted designated weeks "for gathering and buying of recyclable waste all over the country." These continued the legacy of Leninist *subbotnik*, or "voluntary" (the socialist euphemism for mandatory) Saturdays spent cleaning public space.[21] According to the 1991 bulletin of Phoenix Resource, "during the week held in 1989, 20,248 tons of scrap were sold/bought, including 7,839 tons of paper; whereas in 1990 the same period saw a 50% increase in the supply of exchange goods—caps, sanitary paper, fiction books, and others—with only 8,790 tons of scrap being sold/bought, including 3,240 tons of paper."[22] The recycling landscape had changed: Despite the presence of more goods on the so-called free market, state mandates had relaxed and lower quantities of recyclables were being collected. The 1990 Phoenix Resource report explains that the "situation in the country and its economic partners" as well as "the influence of the economic crisis, the political struggle and the strong political polarization of the population" had significant impacts on the materials collected.

While Bulgaria had long framed recycling as a communal endeavor, capitalist-era recycling became a matter of individual post-consumption decisions: Should waste be dumped, incinerated, or reused? EU programs promoting "Zero Waste" encourage post-consumption recycling, but their aims are quite different from the original meaning of this phrase, which was closer to socialist Bulgaria's approach to material recovery. In the 1970s, Paul Palmer, a chemist living near California's Silicon Valley, coined the term "Zero Waste" to describe a way to recover tech-business chemical waste that was still valuable but was being discarded by producers.[23] But contemporary Zero Waste programs in newly accessed EU countries like Bulgaria do not focus on waste prevention at sites of production. Nor do they support what Samantha MacBride, writing about the original Zero Waste approach, characterizes as "priorities of social justice" by addressing the "injustice inscribed in waste-related infrastructure upon urban landscapes."[24] Instead of regulating how much waste is produced, these programs endeavor to find a "sink" where it can go, after consumption, so that the national programs can meet international standards.[25] Zero Waste implementation in Bulgaria has meant moving, transferring, and transforming waste so that it no longer counts toward EU-imposed landfill reduction targets, and so that it remains outside of the white Bulgarian purview.[26] This includes burning nonrecyclable, combustible waste like plastic bags as refuse-derived fuel (RDF).

FIGURE 2.3 Baled waste being stored at a recycling installation site in Sofia, which will be incinerated as refuse-derived fuel (RDF). Photo by the author.

EU-era neoliberal reforms establish quantifiable markers like landfill targets to measure how much waste is accumulated from consumer goods; these markers were decided upon by wealthier European countries decades ago. Western European "green dot" recycling programs, implemented in the name of Zero Waste and codified into EU regulations, also shape waste disposal internationally.[27] The green dot is a proprietary trademark used primarily in Europe as a symbol on packaging. It indicates that the company that made the packaging has financially contributed to a registered national packaging recovery organization "set up in accordance with the principles defined in European Packaging and Packaging Waste Directive 94/62/EC and the respective national law."[28] In other words, it shows that a fee has been paid to fund the recycling of that packaging when it becomes post-consumer waste. Thus, the green dot is a financial trademark in that it indicates a country's ability to conform with EU environmental standards for package recycling.

During the summer of 2013, when I worked as an intern in the Bulgarian Ministry of the Environment and Water, I met Ryan, a Swedish waste management consultant who had been hired on an EU contract to help the ministry achieve its EU-mandated goals. Ryan was well versed in EU-wide waste programs and explained the significance of waste accumulation to EU accession processes to me. We met one late afternoon at one of Sofia's vegetarian restaurants, with American jazz music playing and my recorder on, so that he could tell me in English about his take on things. During the meeting, he told me that many European indexes have used waste as a marker for capitalistic—and, by proxy, democratic—development. This was especially true for Bulgaria in the 1990s, when the country was focused on economic privatization.

In the early postsocialist period, Bulgaria had to adhere to a set of mandates known as the Copenhagen criteria in order to join the EU. These mandates were vast. They required not only economic privatization but also political reforms regarding "the stability of institutions guaranteeing democracy, the rule of law, human rights and respect for and protection of minorities."[29] Environmental issues were not explicit in this first set of criteria. In fact, early postsocialist economic reforms worked in direct opposition to the environmental sustainability criteria that later became crucial to EU accession. In the 1990s, waste production was valorized because it served as a material index of Bulgaria's free-market economic growth.

This valorization continued for decades. In 2012, a former government official gave me an unpublished draft of a previous version of the National Waste Strategy for Bulgaria, which summarized statistical data on municipal, construction, industrial, and hazardous waste generation and linked waste with economic growth: "The quantity of the municipal waste generated will grow as a result of the expected economic growth, the increase of incomes and of consumption by the private households." Employees from the Ministry of the Environment and Water told me that waste generation was important in the early postsocialist period because everyone knew that more waste indicated rapid economic growth—the capitalist bottom line for Bulgaria's EU accession.[30] Bulgaria needed to expand its economy at all costs. By the late 1990s, however, this valorization of waste coexisted with another model that relied on waste reduction, putting economic markers of progress at odds with indicators of EU-mandated environmental sustainability. Officially, Bulgaria shifted from the "freedom to discard" model to mandates rooted in an EU-legitimated Zero Waste model. And yet waste policy documents (many unpublished) show that greater quantities of waste were still esteemed in terms of economic development. The paradox remains: less (or zero) waste as an environmental goal alongside more waste as a sign of higher income generation that would pave the path toward economic Europeanization.

"Freedom to discard" undergirds racial capitalism, including the particularly postsocialist form found in Bulgaria. More waste requires more laborers to clean it up in order to meet European aesthetic ideals. This is crucial for Bulgaria's aspiring Europeanness and also marks a particular mode of waste management under capitalism that relies on racial hierarchies. And so, this so-called freedom is wholly contingent on the exploitation of Romani workers. Waste thus becomes an indicator of progress as it constitutes a new political economy, one that is simultaneously attached to ideals of Europeanness and fundamentally outside the official European project.[31]

Western European recycling campaigns espousing "green" sustainability ideologies have not been effective in Bulgaria, primarily because most people believe that separated collection infrastructures are futile. As noted earlier, they claim that all the waste gets picked up in one truck and "goes to the same place." Bulgarians also associate recycling with compulsory socialist programs and thus see this freedom to discard as inherently linked to democracy. The EU continues to promote recycling as something novel despite Bulgaria's long socialist history of waste reuse and recovery, and despite the fact that EU programs are only successful because of the predominately Romani unofficial workers who collect waste and bring it to socialist-era *punktove* for resale. Without their labor, Bulgaria would not meet its packaging waste recovery targets.

Underlying EU environmental and urban recycling policies, then, are ideologies of who and what can be discarded, saved, reused, and transformed—and who and what are left over. This reveals the discordances between environmental sustainability politics and minority integration projects. In turn, these contradictions highlight how environmental sustainability becomes racial practice, showing how once again the European project is premised upon racial hierarchization, this time through racial sustainability.

Criminalizing Recycling

As Bulgaria moved toward EU accession, Romani communities found themselves poorer and in more precarious positions than during socialism. By most Romani accounts, "everyone" had a job during socialism, but many quickly became unemployed after the collapse of the socialist state. They faced new and explicit forms of white supremacist anti-Roma racism, as well as minimum-wage pay for waste labor (and other manual labor) that could not keep up with rapidly rising costs for housing, food, and medicine. With the demise of local heavy industry, including Sofia's Kremikovtsi metallurgy plant and the famous Balkancar factory that manufactured forklifts, along with the offshoring of manual labor jobs that Roma formerly occupied, they lacked access to steady employment.[32] The Romani men who had previously worked in these sectors were subject to mass unemployment, and thousands of Romani women lost their jobs in the textile industries in which they had been well employed as seamstresses, cleaners, and technicians. As jobs in Bulgaria became harder to find, everyone had to seek new kinds of work. This was especially the case for Roma, who faced explicit workplace discrimination, naturalized prejudice, and insufficient opportunities to gain the education needed for emerging job sectors like information technology.

One strategy was to take previous expertise gained in the primary markets for heavy industrial and textile production and apply it to contemporary secondary markets for discarded materials. Romani men and women would stop at dumpsters to collect what had been discarded both inside and adjacent to the bins. Their labor tended to be divided along gendered lines. Romani women, like Baka, worked on foot with bags, gathering items for reuse and resale, while Romani men often bought or rented horse carts to collect raw materials for recycling, such as cans and paper to be sold at local *punktove*. Horse carts were especially useful for collecting metal waste, which was impossible to collect and transport on foot. When white Bulgarians wanted to get rid of a car or construction waste without paying to do so via official procedures, they often summoned Romani men with horse carts to make it "disappear."[33]

One of these unofficial waste laborers was a distant cousin of my friend Sylvia. While much of my ethnographic work focused on women's spaces, Sylvia suggested I accompany Petko because he was a trustworthy person and "too old" for our proximity to look inappropriate. He didn't want to take me with him at first (explaining that I would slow him down), but Sylvia told him that he had to do it for my research, and he relented. He asked me to call him Uncle Petko, a sign of respect and an acknowledgment of our wide age gap. During the socialist era, Uncle Petko had worked first as a bus mechanic and later as a bus driver, but in the wake of socialism's demise, he found himself unemployed. He explained that nobody in charge of municipal transportation services would hire him, "a G*psy." But by working for so long in the automotive repair sector, he had acquired a strong knowledge base about discarded materials, mostly from how he used them as part of both state-sanctioned repairs and socialism's thriving secondary reuse market.

I had met men who worked like Petko before. When I first began this component of research in 2009, I would naively ask people I saw collecting waste on city streets about what they were doing. Only men, typically older ones, tended to answer. Many told me they had previously worked in Sofia's factories, like Kremikovtsi. Since the collapse of socialism and the subsequent decline of heavy industry sectors like metallurgy, many former employees turned to collecting and selling items discarded in Sofia's dumpsters. They had extensive knowledge about metals and could easily detect what was worth collecting, which items would be worth more or less on the market, and which plastic-coated wires would lead to the most cash flow (i.e., copper). Many of these workers reminded me that they were experts in these materials, with knowledge that was once valued and well compensated but that they could now apply only by collecting waste.

FIGURE 2.4 Looking for reclaimable metal in a downtown dumpster. Photo by the author.

Petko, whose income was supplemented with a disability pension from years of hard labor that had taken a toll on his body, traveled with a pushcart to collect recyclables each morning while his wife tended to their one-room home and cooked lunch. Once he collected enough to fill the cart, he would approach one of Sofia's many *punktove*, where he could weigh items at a weigh station after waiting in a typically long line. These socialist-era sites are located on side streets and often sit between apartment buildings, and despite being somewhat hidden, they are well known by recyclers who have long sold collected items there. The amount Petko would earn depended on the prices for goods that day, which were established by international market. On our work rounds in 2011, aluminum cans were paid at thirty-five stotinki (twenty cents) per kilogram and paper was eight stotinki (five cents) per kilogram.

Petko used a handmade cart divided into two parts, one for paper and one for aluminum cans, and he insisted on removing the idea of "trash" or "garbage" from the equation. When I asked when he started collecting trash, for example, he joked, "Trash?!... Where is the trash? Here it's just pure money." But as Petko uncoupled trash from his labor, he also solid-

FIGURE 2.5 Weighing collected paper at the local collection point (*punkt*) in downtown Sofia. Photo by the author.

ified it with his sarcasm. It is not pure money at all. Instead, his labor is deeply stigmatized and enmeshed in the waste-race nexus on multiple levels, in terms of both its racialization and its reliance on the materiality of other people's trash. He acknowledges the social realities of the

FIGURE 2.6 Payment for recyclable materials at a local collection point in Sofia. Photo by the author.

waste-race nexus in terms of how white Bulgarians see him as he works, contrasting this with a socialist past in which, despite being Roma, he had steady contracted work and the respect that went along with it.

Petko narrated his life to me as we traversed his regular route. We stopped outside an apartment building where he had once lived with his family, near the high school from which his two sons graduated. We also stopped at places newer to his routine, such as the bench where he took a daily cigarette break and the park where he fed pigeons, and finally at the *punkt* where he sold his collected objects to a middle-aged white Bulgarian woman. After five hours, Uncle Petko had collected nine kilograms of paper, three kilograms of aluminum, and a broken copper-plated kitchen pot. He sold all of this at the *punkt* for 2.80 leva (about $1.50). I asked Petko what he was going to do with the money, unsure if it was a good or bad day for him. "I'm going to buy us some coffees, maybe a beer for later, take a lev home. That's a day." Compared to the collectors who used horse carts or the women like Baka who sold items secondhand, Petko's routine did not seem lucrative. But he explained that money accumulated little by little, and that collecting was a great way to get out of the house

FIGURE 2.7 Uncle Petko's cart, divided into sections for aluminum and paper. Photo by the author.

and work, something he missed due to his chronic disability and lengthy unemployment.

What Petko describes as a way to stay active and earn some money, others treat as criminal activity. As more and more Roma found themselves unemployed and took to the secondary recovery economy, they became targets of anti-Roma violence at the hands of white Bulgarians and were criminalized by waste officials for "stealing" trash. Readers will recall Irena, the official at the Bulgarian Ministry of the Environment and Water. Irena told me about a recent case that had occurred a few months prior to our 2013 interview in which a kilometer of railroad tracks went missing. She said that this was very common in Bulgaria and should be categorized as terrorism. She explained, "The problem is that the rails bounce sometimes from the way they are bolted together and it is easy to remove them. And, if a train passes on them, it can cause a crash." She then shared what she considered the root of the problem: "These people are mostly from Romani origin, but there are some Bulgarians too. . . . Most of these people are in perfect condition for working, but

CHAPTER TWO

most of them don't want to. They want to do things easily and they have no education. . . . It is very hard to integrate such people."

When I looked into this case on my own, I learned that a kilometer of rails had indeed been stolen outside of Sofia over the May St. George's Day holiday, and that, as Irena observed, the old rails were bolted in ways that made them very easy to take apart. I watched a recording of a televised interview with the local transportation police chief, given two days after the crime was registered. He presented the rail theft as one of many similar problems: "There are different companies. Their complaints are that the electricity stops, cables are stolen. It's the same things as everywhere there is G*psy population close to the railroads." Here too, Roma were interpellated, called into being, as criminals. The fact that they were assumed to have dismantled the tracks has a particular local resonance because of the railroads' role in connecting Bulgaria with the rest of Europe. In this imagining, Roma were breaking, or blocking, the material and symbolic lifelines to both Europe and Europeanness. Yet local NGO leaders and politicians disclosed something that was excluded from media accounts: The tracks had not been in use for years. The state-owned railway had run out of funds to operate them, so they existed in an interstitial category between waste and non-waste. But within the racializing and criminalizing discourse, this did not matter.[34] Instead of blaming the state, in the majority-public consciousness, Roma were scapegoated for preventing Bulgaria from becoming a "normal," well-connected, European state.[35]

In Bulgaria, casting Roma as criminals, often in ways that distract from the state's shortcomings, has a long history. It stretches from Ottoman accounts in the 1500s that describe them as thieves who cannot be trusted, to socialist-era stories of Roma stealing communist housing materials for firewood, to the pre-EU-accession introduction of recycling bins with small holes designed to keep "thieving" Romani hands out.[36] Indeed, the criminalization of waste collection, particularly scrap metal, hinges upon its associations with "G*psy labor."[37] The language people use to refer to waste laborers makes that clear. When white Bulgarians told me about the non-Romani pensioners who, abandoned by the government, turn to dumpsters for income and food, they described this as "pitiful" (zhalko) labor they have to do to survive. But when the same people spoke about the crime of waste theft, they coded it as Roma work. Criminality, their language suggested, was tightly tied to Romaniness, while victimhood at the hands of an incompetent state was a plight reserved for white Bulgarians.

During a question and answer session at Sofia's 2011 Waste Expo, for example, I heard Ivan, the CEO of one of Bulgaria's largest recycling firms, lament that Western European waste programs implemented in Bulgaria don't acknowledge the country's "scavenger problem," which makes it hard for recycling companies to recover enough recyclable waste from their colored bins. A debate ensued in the conference room over why colored-bin separate collection does not work. When speaking to the panelists via simultaneous English-Bulgarian interpretation, Ivan used the term *kloshari* (scavengers). But when addressing Bulgarian-speaking audience members, he spoke about "G*psies." After the panel, I asked him for his business card and said I wanted to know more about his frustration with Sofia's *kloshari*.

Perhaps my question put him on guard. I initially texted him without reply, but after calling repeatedly, he finally agreed to meet me in his office. We set the day and time, and he told me to call the morning of the meeting to confirm. When I did, he answered gruffly, telling me to make sure I was on time.

I arrived at his office's brightly lit reception area, where an administrative assistant greeted me. She offered me a coffee and handed me a stack of promotional materials, which I happily took and put in my bag. I then waited until Ivan invited me into his large, windowed office. I sat on one side of the desk, small pink notebook in hand, and asked him some general questions about recycling and his own career, hoping he might become more comfortable talking with me. Finally, I circled back to what interested me most: "So why do some of the bins have those holes in them?" He sat up and leaned forward, visibly excited to explain that it was an effort to prevent his firm from "going under."

I asked what the largest hindrance was to meeting their EU packaging recovery quotas. At first, he seemed pleased to explain that the most difficult part of separate collection was to convince the Bulgarian population to throw the correct kind of packaging into the appropriately colored bin. The second major hindrance, he said, was difficulty in "stopping the scavengers from doing what they do." He continued, "I mean, we have no way to stop them for now from stealing waste from the sorting containers and selling it for money...at *punktove* where they buy up the waste. I consider this the most difficult. Everything else can be done according to plan, but not this." I started to follow up. "So, I want to ask you about these scavengers, who actually collect waste on their own, . . ." but he interrupted me: "They are not collecting it. They are stealing it."

When I shadowed Hristo, the CEO of a producer responsibility organization (PRO) much smaller than Ivan's, he had similar complaints. Hristo would often receive phone calls from the municipal inspector in Sofia concerning the firm's legal responsibility to maintain the cleanliness of the area around collection bins. When their trucks emptied the plastic bins to bring the waste to a recycling site, workers on the back of the truck would need to check the area around the containers and, if it was messy, sweep it. When Hristo received a call about a bin that had been turned upside down with items thrown around it, he rolled his eyes and—knowing about my work in the Romani NGO sector—looked pointedly at me in the passenger seat. "*Your* friends created an issue *we* now need to clean. You'll soon see the whole society from this perspective." Hristo was suggesting that the mess his company needs to clean comes from "theft" from recycling bins, a process that involves dumping the bins on their sides to bypass the small holes and get items out.

When Ivan and Hristo talk about recycling in Bulgaria, they highlight their own roles in fulfilling EU sustainability requirements while

FIGURE 2.8 Hristo setting an overturned bin upright. Photo by the author.

naming other people as preventing them, and Bulgaria, from ever becoming European: "the G*psies." In fact, however, they would never be able to meet European regulations without these bemoaned scavengers. Ivan noted that recycling campaigns for the general public failed to produce the necessary results, and he even told me—and insisted I specify in my book—that waste collected by *kloshari* accounts for over 70% of all recyclables recovered in Bulgaria. (There are no official statistics to support this due to restrictions on public accounting of packaging recovery and recycling, but many people repeated this number during my research.) He explained that, since his firm had started in 2004, they had only successfully met their packaging recovery benchmarks because they regularly bought from the *punktove*. He saw this as evidence that the *kloshari* "steal waste" from recycling bins, with the result that his firm was "paying double." He explained, "It is how things work now, but it is not the way the system should be. The waste that is in our containers becomes our property." Still, he said, companies like his would buy from *punktove* "because, whether we like it or not, we have to meet certain EU goals."

Everything I had learned suggested that the people selling waste at the *punktove* were those upon whom the entire system depended, including the income and sustainability of recycling companies like Ivan's. When I pointed out to Ivan that these collection points, according to my research, were legally registered with local municipalities and the national business registry, he responded angrily: "They have registration for their activities, and that is good. But tell me, how can they buy from scavengers without any invoices or without the machine that gives you a receipt for buying something?" He wanted more surveillance and more punishment. "The municipalities are responsible for this in the first place because there are no punishments for the scavengers, and no one is stopping them. And, secondly, those who buy it [collected waste] at the collection points are also to be blamed because they are buying waste illegally and paying the people that bring it to them."

I felt angry watching him both benefit from and deride *kloshari* labor, but I tried to focus on asking questions: "In your view, what's the best avenue for handling this?" Ivan replied as follows:

> Of course there must be a clear law. And there must be those who respect the law. . . . We have already spoken with the Ministry [of the Environment and Water], of course, so they can make some laws for

those people, so they won't be able to sell waste anymore. The law should be organized so that all waste can be turned in for free...and yet, in between all the laws, there are still illegal collection points where you get paid when you turn in plastics, paper, and such. And the ministry is not doing anything.

Most official accounts and documents about recycling that I saw ignored the work of Romani waste collectors. One exception is a 2006 report entitled "Zero Waste as Best Environmental Practice for Waste Management in CEE [Central and Eastern European] Countries."[38] As far as I have been able to determine, this is the only official state document that addresses the intersection of Romani labor and Zero Waste initiatives.[39] Section 5.1.1 of the report, "Waste Crisis in Sofia and Roma Community Recycling Activities," was written by Iskra Stoyanova, a longtime acquaintance of mine who had worked for years at the Romani Star NGO in Fakulteta. For the report, she had interviewed many of the neighborhood's *kloshari*, focusing on Bulgaria's changing waste policy from the perspective of what she saw in the neighborhood. In the document, she explains that the Bulgarian Ministry of the Environment and Water "estimates that roughly 10,000 people are scavenging rubbish bins and landfills to collect and sell recyclable materials in the territory of Bulgaria."[40] On Romani involvement, she notes that "carters usually have two horses each but some of them have 4–5 horses, two of which they rent out to other Roma. Some of the carters have apprentices who are young boys between the age[s] of 10–15 years old who do not receive any wage or money for the materials they have collected during the day but only food and cigarettes."[41] The document concludes that involving local residents, like Romani carters from Fakulteta, can help waste management systems fulfill Zero Waste goals, including those imposed by European Union mandates.[42]

Over the course of my research, collector demographics remained the same, but the recycling landscape changed drastically in alignment with EU law. State socialism focused on metal recycling as the foundation for industrialization and nation-building, equipping people like Petko with strategic knowledge about the production, processing, and repurposing of metal. For waste collectors, metal recycling was critical, and metal again became front and center during my fieldwork. From 2010 to 2014, recycling companies focused not on the importance of metal recovery but instead on how to prevent scrap metal theft. First, in

2012, the government mandated that to sell collected metal to a *punkt*, one needed to present an ID with a personal identification number (the equivalent of an American Social Security number) and be willing to be recorded on video. The law, many people told me, was designed to target Roma in particular. People need an officially registered address to get an ID, but in many Romani neighborhoods registering an address is more or less impossible. If a household does have an address, ten other households might be attached to the same one. This makes getting an ID incredibly difficult since the national office that processes ID cards cannot register so many people at one address.[43] The 2012 ID requirement law thus effectively rendered many scrap collectors unable to work.

I witnessed this kind of racial exclusion, targeting, and surveillance in action one sunny Sunday morning in 2012. I was riding on the back of a horse cart with an artist friend visiting me from New York, my good friend's brother, Emil, and his neighbor from Fakulteta, when a pair of police officers stopped us. They claimed that the cart was illegal because it was within city limits without a valid horse cart license plate. Emil was a taxi driver, well versed in dealing with authorities, and he prided himself on his social skills and ability to talk to anyone and everyone with ease. He climbed out, approached the officer, and tried to laugh it off, eventually pulling out his license and his taxi medallion to legitimate himself. I watched from the cart with Emil's neighbor, who fidgeted nervously with the horse's reins. He was younger, driving his father's

FIGURE 2.9 Reflection of a horse cart before being pulled over by the police. Still image from video by Christina Freeman.

horse cart, and less accustomed to being stopped by the police. Soon Emil walked back to us, smiling. He told us he had resolved the issue by explaining that the driver had the necessary information, just kept in the wrong place because he was not the cart's owner—he was only a teenager. Emil said police stops like this were common.[44]

Beyond city streets, scavengers also look for recyclables at city and regional landfills, a practice that recycling companies also frame as criminal, even though they depend upon it. During visits to nearly a dozen landfills around the country, I found families working on almost half of them, even though such work was illegal, and seemingly nonexistent in EU reports, which do not acknowledge it.[45] But landfill "scavengers" were omnipresent, including in the background of at least one piece of waste company–produced promotional material. In March 2012, I attended an elementary school recycling campaign with Hristo's small PRO where they taught children how to separate their trash and played recycling-themed games, like sorting balloons that stood in for different waste streams. Company representatives told me that they loved this kind of event because the younger generation is the future of sustainability.

After the games were done, the students took their seats and watched a film about what happens to waste after it is discarded. In the video, a well-manicured young white woman in jeans and a sweater narrates the life cycle of things. She visits a Bulgarian landfill, where the camera pans across an expanse of waste, then moves in for close-ups of familiar

FIGURE 2.10   Recycling game. Photo by the author.

FIGURE 2.11 Children in school watching a video about recycling. Photo by the author.

items that could have been recycled: yogurt containers, water bottles, aluminum cans. In the background, there are people sorting through the landfill's waste by hand. It was an image that echoed what I had seen in my own experiences traveling around to Bulgarian landfills. These collectors were not directly acknowledged in the film or in the classroom, but waste industry employees working at the landfills I visited explained that Roma worked, unofficially, at most landfills in Bulgaria. They recovered waste that they could sell to *punktove*, which would, in turn, sell the waste to recycling companies to meet their quotas. In other words, waste was not only "taken" from recycling containers on the street, but also retrieved from landfills where it would otherwise languish.

When I returned to Bulgaria in 2017, recycling companies had taken over most of Sofia's *punktove* in order to cut out the middleman. Now, they were buying "stolen" trash directly. In effect, socialist-era waste infrastructures, once formalized and mandatory, began to function in a space of legal ambiguity. Through the *punktove*, the companies implicitly admit to needing Romani labor yet refuse to make this dependency explicit or offer adequate financial compensation. Through the

FIGURE 2.12 People going through waste at the site of a landfill in central Bulgaria, 2012. Photo by the author.

government's strategic lack of regulation, the *punktove* and those who sell to them together help Bulgaria meet its EU targets while manifesting the racialized criminalization of certain waste workers (manual laborers) and denying the criminality of others (recycling companies).

Cleaning Up and Out in the Name of Europe

Bulgaria is faced with making more than just its own waste disappear. Before and during the initial years of EU accession, finding sinks for Western Europe's waste meant sending this waste eastward, to Eastern Europe and China. Bulgaria became a key recipient of Western Europe's waste, including for countries like Italy, Germany, and Spain.[46] From 2010 to 2017, Bulgaria's waste imports increased almost fivefold.[47] When I asked environmentalists, government workers, and waste firm executives where imported waste went once it entered Bulgaria's borders, they told me that they did not really know, variously speculating that it was landfilled, hidden in bales or under tarps, or illegally incinerated in cement plants as low-quality refuse-derived fuel. Others told me that the waste accumulated haphazardly throughout the countryside, like scenes from the 2008 Disney Pixar movie *WALL-E*. In fact, the movie's art director, Anthony Hristov, is Bulgarian, and many people asserted that he had taken inspiration from Bulgaria's 2007–2008 waste crisis. (When I asked Hristov about this via a Facebook messenger exchange, he told me that the similarity was merely coincidental.) Environmentalists confirmed that the country was sequestering waste in places that served as unregulated sinks, including Romani neighborhoods, rural riverbanks and ravines, and landfills where numbers are regularly "reformed" (i.e., manipulated) to comply with EU standards.[48] EU Zero Waste policy in Bulgaria has effectively meant zero waste where it can be monitored.

Even as the EU sends its garbage to Bulgaria, a common perception remains throughout Western Europe that Bulgaria's pollution comes from its hyperindustrial socialist past. Never mind that recycling was a major part of that past; now, as the EU sees it, Bulgaria is a landscape that needs remediation. It serves as an example of the possibility to transform a degraded space into a laudable site of Europeanization—an opportunity for the EU to model how to steward and repair a "historically" polluted space. The EU focuses on how Bulgaria, particularly as a postsocialist and newly accessed EU country, is caught between two sets of environmental principles according to Bulgaria's postsocialist Environmental Protection Law (EPL): "In Bulgaria, the ecological legislation is based on the polluter pays principle (the owner is liable for current contamination)—from one side, and from the other, that at times of restitution and privatization of property, the new owners 'shall not be liable for ecological damage caused by past actions or lack of actions.'"[49] But, whomever is blamed, EU policies are understood as a means to Europeanize Bulgaria's waste sector and its streets. Somewhat counterintuitively, EU waste targets end up being achieved only through the reuse of socialist-era waste infrastructures like the *punktove*.[50]

In sum, international Zero Waste efforts focus on reducing waste at all stages of production and consumption, but in Bulgaria, the term has become synonymous with post-consumption recycling and reduced landfilling. To the extent that EU quotas are met, it is only because of the work of *kloshari* who traverse streets and landfills, salvaging recyclable goods and taking them to *punktove*. Yet this primarily Romani waste work is framed as a criminal activity, undertaken by a group racialized as nonwhite who are stereotyped as holding the country back from attaining the presumed aesthetic of cleanliness—which is to say, the whiteness—of Europe. Progressive policy designed to "green" the system thus entrenches local hierarchies, and racial sustainability rolls along. White Bulgarians depend on Roma to recycle their trash, but they also see the Roma as disposable. Zero Waste thus sustains both an imagined white European future in which there is no trash, and the ongoing erasure of the racialized laborers propping up the system.[51]

As the far right has become mainstream in Bulgaria over the past twenty years, the desire to discard the Roma from Bulgaria has become much more explicit. Political parties like Ataka, Revival, and VMRO—Bulgarian National Movement run on platforms that call for ethnic cleansing in the name of Europeanizing Bulgaria, blaming Romani neighborhoods for polluting nearby white areas to justify destroying entire communities.[52] With the perceived threat of the demographic rise of Roma, a concern used to incite anti-Roma sentiment since at least the socialist period, politicians call for "cleaning up" Sofia's urban space in the name of creating a "Bulgaria for the Bulgarians."[53] In fact, populist right-wing parties across Europe construct campaigns around the presumed disposability of Roma.[54] In Bulgaria, the trope of Roma expendability was commonly called up in conversations where Roma were also categorized as trash (*boklutsi*), while public campaigns incited WWII-era Nazi rhetoric of Roma as vermin needing to be exterminated.

And yet, as European waste-cleaning regimes attempt to transform Sofia, many of those people actually doing the cleaning refuse to sustain the racist and racializing project of Europeanization. Petko, like the uniformed and contracted waste workers with whom I swept, labors each day to make and remake life on his own terms, to the best of his ability. People like Ivan see him as a criminal, but Petko understands his work, at least insofar as it hinges upon his expertise in metals, as directly connected to the more socially acceptable and lucrative jobs he used to have. It connects him to a world outside his home and gives him a sense of purpose. It serves as an ongoing project of figuring out how to live amid structural forces of racial sustainability and how to turn one's daily labors into the work of creation and income generation. Yet he knows that this work is not his alone but is integral to the functioning of EU waste regimes within a Europeanizing Bulgaria.

THREE

Surveillance

Amid white marble columns and a grand piano, just past the registration table, a large cardboard sign reminded everyone who was paying for the conference: "European Social Fund: INVESTMENTS IN YOUR FUTURE." Below the text was a picture of a pregnant Romani woman holding a toddler, wearing gold hoop earrings and slippers, and standing in a small puddle. It was June 2011, and I was meeting my friends Simon and Maria, veteran Romani activists, at the Sheraton Sofia Hotel Balkan (the Sheraton) for a conference, "The Contribution of European Union Funds to Roma Integration." As I made my way through the revolving glass doors to find them, I looked at the poster in horror: Even as it promoted so-called integration, it invoked a strand of the popular fearmongering of political campaigns that focused on Roma "overpopulation."[1] Simon and Maria just smirked. "Of course, she's pregnant," they noted, telling me that they expected nothing less.

Simon had been my close friend for nearly a decade, and he and Maria were planning an action to take place at the conference later that day, in front of European Union and Bulgarian political officials. They were frustrated with the fact that EU funds earmarked for minority integration in Bulgaria were not actually being used to improve Romani lives. What's more, the ostensible availability of that money triggered anti-Roma sentiment and unprecedented surveillance from governmental entities, which seemed to believe that Roma organizations were neither worthy of nor to be trusted with such funds. When Simon asked me to join them, I readily agreed.

Having attended similar meetings for years, he and Maria knew that conference organizers would record their attendance to claim that Roma had participated, even though their voices would not be welcomed or, most likely, even heard—especially if they voiced anything that challenged EU rhetoric. Instead, they wore their message on T-shirts for all to see: *Europe, Stop Funding Roma Exclusion*. "Take a photo of us with this G*psy," they instructed me. I obliged. They half-smiled.

As we took our seats with other conference participants in the hotel ballroom, Simon and Maria opened their vinyl swag bags. Inside were but-

FIGURE 3.1 Poster at Sheraton conference with Simon and Maria on either side. Illustration by Izabela Ivanova.

FIGURE 3.2 Photo of poster at conference. Photo by the author.

tons, notebooks, brochures, and a bright yellow vest with an English-language promotional slogan on the back: "Making a DIFFERENCE IN LIFE." Below was the URL of the European Social Fund website.[2] Snickering, Simon explained with sarcasm, "Of course they give this [vest] to us—they want to make sure they can always find the G*psies, even in the dark." He then joked, "We also have reflective bracelets! I think they do this so it is clear who are the Roma and who are the Bulgarians."

FIGURE 3.3 Left to right: protester at conference holding up vest, conference participant wearing vest, street sweepers in uniform. Illustration by Izabela Ivanova.

I had become accustomed to the jaded humor of Romani attendees at similar conferences, which they referred to as "absurd" (*absurdni*) or "bullshit" (*gluposti*). Simon shook his head. "European Union, come on, European Union," he muttered under his breath. "We want them to stop making fun of us. They mock us for twenty years. We want them to stop. We want to stop being excuses for somebody else to profit." He was fed up.

Dragomir, a Romani radio journalist and fellow conference participant, looked over at us and scoffed. Eying the yellow reflector vests, which seemed purposefully similar to those that street sweepers had to wear when working, he leaned over to joke, "So, are you here visiting from the sweeping company?" Yellow reflective vests in Bulgaria indexed street sweeping and its labor-based racialization; when someone sees such a vest in Bulgaria, they typically assume its wearer is Roma.

As another NGO activist, someone who was not planning to join the protest, walked by, Dragomir called out, "Are you one of us?" "Of course I am," he replied dismissively, rushing to his seat. "Well then, put on a vest!" Dragomir reached into the vinyl gift bag exaggeratedly. "Here it is. The vests are in the bags. Put it on and be one of us. There are cameras and media. You put it on, so they can film you as a *real* G*psy." The fellow attendee smiled in what struck me as both a knowing acknowledgment of what the vest signified and a way to politely get out of putting it on. The Romani conference attendees that day, including the protest organizers, were part of what they characterized among themselves as a kind of Romani intelligentsia. They tended to have more formal education than many Bulgarian Roma of their generation, along with more social mobility, and many (although not all) lived in or near urban centers, rather than segregated Romani neighborhoods. Some had studied English, both in Bulgaria and abroad, sometimes as beneficiaries of George Soros–funded programs for equal access to education and general promotion of post-socialist democracy-building initiatives. Many had become NGO workers in the 1990s, when funding flowed in from international foundations and foreign governments. Simon, for example, had taken part in a variety of Soros and Open Society Institute (OSI) initiatives and had worked in the NGO sector while earning an advanced degree at Sofia University. He is fluent in Bulgarian, English, and multiple other languages. We met in 2003 while he was working at a Romani education organization. Simon, along with the organization's other members, often attended international conferences, hung posters of Martin Luther King Jr. on the walls of their office, listened to Tupac, and readily hosted foreigners.[3] They hoped to improve the schooling conditions of Roma, believing fiercely in closing segregated schools in Romani neighborhoods in order to force the majority society to integrate Roma into mainstream Bulgarian public schools.

By the time of the conference, however, the Roma NGO sector had been so thoroughly defunded that many had lost their jobs. It struck them as cruelly funny that they were now being given the uniform of one of the only jobs Roma could find in EU-era Bulgaria: waste work. The phrase on the back, "Making a difference in life," seemed patently absurd.

Later, during a coffee break, I asked one of the conference organizers, an EU representative from Brussels, about the decision to provide yellow reflector vests in the swag bags. "In Europe," he told me, "everyone needs to have such vests in their cars because of EU automobile safety laws." This was also technically the case in Bulgaria as an EU member state, and some people did keep reflector vests in a packet in the trunk of their car in case of a police check or an accident. However, in a room full of Romani activists, the vest had a very different charge. In Bulgaria, it had become emblematic of racialized waste work, a realm in which Roma were both hypervisible and undervalued. Activists made it clear that they were caught in a similar double bind.

———

During the lead-up to Bulgaria's EU accession in 2007, there may have been reason to hope that the country would follow the EU's goal of Roma integration, which included programs focused on education and access to health care. But as Simon and Maria both told me, and as race studies scholars have argued for decades, the integration framework can be woefully inadequate. It implies that minorities need to be brought into the larger society by transforming them into that which can be recognized and accepted by the ruling class rather than demanding that the larger society change the systems into which they are to be integrated.[4] In Bulgaria, integration programs have focused on promoting Romani education, not on changing the other aspects of systemic institutional racism that have resulted in shockingly high child mortality rates, housing insecurity, and mass unemployment. EU healthcare programs placed a conspicuous emphasis on birth control, reinforcing politicized fears of an increasing Roma demographic.[5] And, to conform to liberal EU-approved ideas of human rights, what was understood as "forced," "early," or "child" marriage in Romani communities has been heavily stigmatized.[6]

As Simon and Maria explained to me, the "integration problem" is like the "vulnerable population problem" (referring to rhetoric describing Roma as a disempowered group, vulnerable to the whims of others). Both invoke European Union terminology like "progress" and "tolerance" to further exploit Romani populations for ruling-class gains. Furthermore, the ambiguity of terms like "vulnerable groups" allows the ruling class to distribute earmarked money to any groups they deem vulnerable, thereby diverting it away from specifically Roma causes.

Integration initiatives were critical to Bulgaria's acceptance into the EU. After EU accession, however, external pressure subsided.[7] When Bulgaria became an official European Union member state in 2007, the EU turned monitoring over to the ever-changing but increasingly right-wing national government. As part of this shift, funding streams for many Roma NGOs dried up because Bulgaria, as a new EU country, was no longer a priority for international donors like George Soros, the World Bank, or the United Nations Development Programme (UNDP) that focused on building democracy in developing countries. In the EU era, many organizations were taken over by white Bulgarian "experts" drawing support from right-wing politicians. For example, Valeri Simeonov, the founding leader of the far-right party National Front for the Salvation of Bulgaria, was egregiously appointed Chair of the Council on Ethnic Minority Integration in 2017.[8] At the same time, racist smear campaigns were run by the Bulgarian government itself, which also set about gutting the Roma NGO sector. Today, Romani communities are used opportunistically by the Bulgarian government, targeted by violent white supremacists, and forced by their economic conditions to clean up Sofia neighborhoods in which they will never have a chance to live. Romani activists have long sought to change these conditions, but in the wake of EU accession, their task has seemed nearly impossible.

Despite, because of, and in rejection of such structural conditions, my Romani interlocutors in the NGO sector, as well as those working in the waste sector, refuse to be denied full personhood.[9] This refusal has not typically involved overt protest. Bulgarians have a well-practiced history of furtive action, solidified under communist rule, that subverts the state in quiet, routine ways that generate and maintain sociality while avoiding government crackdown.[10] Bulgarian Romani communities especially have had to hone such modes of protest. They have experienced widespread violent ramifications for their protests in the past and have been subject to hypersurveillance during state socialism and racial profiling by police in its aftermath.[11] The Sheraton action I describe in this chapter has thus lived on in participants' memory as being one of the first of its kind. Yet the wit and dark absurdist humor that Simon and Maria brought to the occasion are consistent with other Bulgarian Romani efforts to create life on their own terms. Available political pathways may seem slim to nonexistent, but when confronted with the demeaning image of the pregnant woman at the conference, empowered Romani activists stood tall beside it, highlighting how they are anything but that stereotype. Their juxtaposition of real and imagined bodies was simultaneously comical, pointed, and filled with pathos.

Affiliation and Integration

Authoritarian state socialism had a sweeping disciplinary regime that honed everyday surveillance of individuals and communities with the aim of quelling political dissent. Socialist leaders and the state's police force feared that Roma might become a "nationalistic" group unto themselves or, worse still, might affiliate with Turkish power structures for a unified opposition.[12] The Turks in Bulgaria had a history of political organizing, and with Turkey just across Bulgaria's southeastern border, solidarity posed a serious threat to state power. In attempts to prevent this, the state recruited Romani agents to report on any potential uprisings.[13] A 1950 Bulgarian Communist Party document entitled "Strictly Confidential Plan for Intelligence and Operational Work with the

CHAPTER THREE

G*psy Minority" reveals the state's agenda.[14] Entire Romani neighborhoods, as well as specific cultural producers like publishers, poets, and artists, were highly surveilled, typically by local informants and embedded academic researchers (including ethnographers) who would write long reports to the state with their findings. Of special concern were links between Romani political organizers and leaders of other minority groups.

The government responded to these perceived threats with efforts to "affiliate" (the socialist term for "integrate") Roma into Bulgarian society, including forcing all working-age Roma to be employed in state enterprises and rehousing Romani families into apartment buildings inhabited by white Bulgarians. Nearly all the Bulgarians I asked about these efforts remembered that each apartment building had one or two Romani families living on the ground floor during socialism. State archives confirm that this was part of the "re-education" program for culturally "lagging" Romani communities.[15] In a concerted effort to "bring them up to the level of Bulgarians," Roma were moved into apartments where they were "placed under constant surveillance, even in individual cases for years, by a dedicated police officer who checked them in the morning and evening to see if they are in the home."[16] Across decades and political-economic systems, the state has used surveillance in ways that racialize Roma and quell the possibility of Romani uprisings.[17]

I often struggled with my relationship to this history of surveillance, in part because it has gone hand in hand with the history of cultural anthropology (or ethnology, as it is often called in Europe). For hundreds of years, non-Romani researchers, writers, and artists have lived among or visited Romani settlements, engaging in poverty tourism and exoticization in the name of cultural preservation, and subjecting Roma to the surveilling—and exploitative—gaze of outsiders.[18] Many of my interlocutors specifically recalled the ethnologists who worked as state agents, learning Romani dialects and living in Romani neighborhoods to provide information to socialist authorities. No wonder, then, that I often found myself fighting the presumption that I was a spy—perhaps working for the Americans, but more likely, people suggested, for Bulgarians seeking to infiltrate Romani communities to prevent political organizing. The history of anthropologists' complicity with state control is profound in Bulgaria but also significant throughout Europe and includes figures like the Nazi-trained anthropologist Eva Justin, who specialized

SURVEILLANCE 101

in scientific racism and used her anthropological research tools for the annihilation of Romani communities in Nazi Germany.[19] I always felt the presence of the ethnographers who came before me but tried to differentiate myself by acknowledging this history and focusing on action I believed in: making my research agenda public, joining in protests, and being as candid as I could about my discomfort with the legacy that I was, and am, a part of.

As the end of socialism approached in 1989, surveillance measures heightened the more that party leaders realized they were losing power.[20] The postsocialist period of the early 1990s was the peak of "democratic" NGO activity in Bulgaria, and external funders helped ensure that Romani-rights NGOs were well resourced.[21] Romani civil society developed through a direct-donor, project-based model that required Romani activists to quickly produce proposals and concrete, preferably photographable, results.[22] These outcomes were desirable for external funders but also critical for Bulgaria's pending European Union accession, which was contingent upon Roma integration (and evidentiary markers of it).

In the lead-up to European Union accession in 2007, Bulgaria had to meet specific standards, called Copenhagen criteria, to be eligible to enter the European Union. These criteria included minority integration via educational desegregation and healthcare but also environmental sustainability, justice reform, a well-functioning market economy, and what was framed as democratic governance and human rights.[23] In order to fulfill these criteria, there were also efforts to clean up—and clean out— any vestiges of socialist power and spending from the public sphere, including eliminating what were considered excess funds spent on public services and 1990s-era NGOs. When Bulgaria joined the European Union in 2007, EU guidelines suggested that Roma integration should take place with EU funds under Bulgarian supervision. As a result, direct-donor aid for Roma integration initiatives, once considered essential for both the geopolitical securement of Eastern Europe and EU accession, quickly dried up.

Throughout these changes, Bulgaria's increasingly right-wing governments continued to cast Roma as perpetual outsiders requiring integration.[24] For example, in 2019, in the name of increasing the efficiency of Bulgaria's EU-sponsored integration programs, Deputy Prime Minister Krasimir Karakachanov proposed a new Roma Integration Strategy focused on the "inclusion of asocial people from the G*psy ethnic group to the traditional values for the Bulgarian society."[25] This strategy entailed, first and foremost, reducing the Romani birth rate and "preventing criminality."[26] Couched in the language of equality, the integration strategy also involved video surveillance "with a special focus in the settlements with a predominant G*psy (Roma) population, in order to prevent crime and protect public order."[27] Karakachanov was proposing another form of cleanup, evoking long histories of genocide and coerced sterilization of Roma in the region, as well as their criminalization and surveillance.[28]

For grassroots Roma organizations interested in supporting rather than denying or policing Romani life, funding became much more difficult to acquire in the wake of EU accession. Obtaining European Union Structural Funds requires knowledge of the neoliberal language of quantifiable results and short-term, project-based approaches, or what some of my interlocutors call the ability to speak *bryukselski*.[29] *Bryukselski* is an EU-era Bulgarianism that can be translated as "Brussels-speak," a term that implicitly critiques bureaucratic language as absurdly opaque. Many Romani NGO activists in the post-EU-accession period were not fluent in *bryukselski*. This contributed to the replacement of Roma-run NGOs with professionalized organizations led by white, non-Romani professed experts who had more formal education, connections with both the national government and EU headquarters, as well as fluency in *bryukselski*.

Despite major political transformations after EU accession, it soon became clear that Roma integration initiatives had not been successful in the way Romani NGO leaders had hoped for. White Bulgarians often complained that the EU privileged Roma by funding them so much—a trope that became popular across Europe—but as Simon documented, EU funding rarely reached Romani communities.[30] Instead, as many Romani activists explained to me, high-up Bulgarian officials would siphon "European money" to their own friendly experts (or their own pockets).

The results are telling. According to the EU Agency for Fundamental Rights (FRA), in 2011, four years after accession, the general unemployment rate in Bulgaria was 12.3%, but the Romani unemployment rate was 49.8%.[31] In 2020, nearly a decade later and thirteen years since EU accession, the estimated Romani unemployment rate remained at about 50%, although the white Bulgarian unemployment rate dropped to less than 6%.[32] Studies have also shown that Roma are less likely to be hired for jobs than non-Roma across Central and Eastern Europe, even at the same educational level.[33] Besides this, having employment does not mean having health insurance or receiving adequate wages for that employment. Even among the fully employed, a non-Romani person in Bulgaria is almost twice as likely to have health insurance as a Romani person.[34] No wonder, then, that in 2011, the Romani life expectancy in Bulgaria was ten years lower than the national average—the same average life span difference between Romani and non-Romani populations across Europe.[35] In 2021, Roma in Bulgaria had the highest percentages of both employed and unemployed individuals living under the poverty line.[36] In a country where nearly half of all Roma are unemployed, uninsured, and dying young, it is clear that top-down integration efforts are not working to sustain Romani life.

Many Romani activists and NGO leaders told me that while Roma NGOs had to focus on short-term quantifiable goals to stay afloat after EU accession, the activities that would meet these targets did not provide the support their communities needed for long-term institutional development. Others explained that "the sector" had become a self-propagating force, driven by available funding sources and project opportunities rather than local needs.

Though the sector originally provided highly educated Romani activists with employment outside of the racist hiring protocols they faced elsewhere in the workforce, it was also a source of precarity. One of my good friends, who held multiple master's degrees and had worked for over a decade as an upper-level NGO program officer, had a fortune-telling costume at home that she explained she kept "just in case she needed to go abroad and make money." "Now, fortune telling, that's reliable work for a G*psy like me," she noted, only half joking. Since the sector was project-based and relied on external donor funds, most employees knew they could lose funding and their jobs at any time. Moreover, NGO employees were acutely aware of the rampant workplace discrimination in other sectors, where even candidates with advanced postgraduate degrees were asked in interviews about their ethnic background and mother tongue.

Most of the activists I knew—former and current NGO sector workers—had become disillusioned, deciding that protest was largely futile. This accords with a broader Bulgarian understanding of politics, widely thought to be hopeless. Harkening back to the 1989 postsocialist transition, when most would argue not enough had actually changed, there was a sensibility among progressives in Bulgaria that formal politics were doomed to fail because, as I was told over and over again, "power, no matter what the regime, just stays in the same hands." Despite this deep sense of futility, Bulgarians across the country, including Romani activists at the Sheraton in downtown Sofia, still sometimes protest.[37] While they claim that all hope is lost, their actions show something different.

Simon once told me outright that "protest is not our culture," yet he, Maria, and many of my other activist friends also often discussed what they called a "politics of passivity." Drawing on their collective readings of Gandhian resistance, they explained that this meant that there were possibilities for alternative futures and claiming some measure of power, but these would not be achieved by direct action; more lasting change would come through rejecting or refusing the formal institutions that they saw as fundamentally exploitative. Their approach overlaps with what Cedric Robinson calls "retreat": a frame for action rooted in disengagement with those in official positions of power that makes space for reconstituting community outside of that power.[38] Romani activists' community-building took shape through at-home gatherings, reading groups, debate sessions, and long meetings in local cafés to brainstorm ways to intervene in a landscape where white supremacy and a conservative right wing were becoming the powerful new normal.

When Roma do protest or otherwise take a public stance, Simon explained, journalists have not known how to represent it. "You know, [they assume] 'these G*psies can play music. They can entertain the people. They can say stupid things.'" He took a moment to emphasize, "But no one expects G*psies to raise red cards, to make banners, to wear such T-shirts. [They think] something is not normal, that something is wrong." He laughed as he continued, "Something does not comply with the established perception of Roma people in Bulgaria. They don't want to recognize the existence of Roma intelligence; they don't want to see the truth. They don't want to see the real things." I nodded in agreement. "They don't want to know that there already are such Roma people who have this way of thinking, who disagree with the status quo, who want change, who think, who have a position and an opinion—they don't want to see this." So, they "find another, more elaborate explanation," or they invent one, asserting that "these Roma must be paid off or that they work for someone else."[39]

FIGURE 3.4 Conference attendees wearing protest T-shirts. Illustration by Izabela Ivanova.

Simon and other Romani activists I knew often asserted that it was futile to try to change this point of view, but by the time of the Sheraton conference, they had decided they had nothing left to lose. Roma weren't receiving funding anyway, and Romani NGO workers had been replaced by "experts." A system-wide financial investigation into the Roma-run NGO sector had started to terrorize the community, and they were feeling jaded and fearless. So, my friends decided that it was time to try a new tactic. Local approaches had not worked, but perhaps with an international audience at the EU-sponsored conference, the outcome would be different.

They would be not passive, but hypervisible about their refusal to court institutions or seek funds. In planning meetings before the event, they agreed to call for an end to EU funding for Romani "integration." They wanted to stop white Bulgarians from exploiting the Roma cause for their own financial gain and, I suspect, to trigger anxiety in those same white officials with their own righteous visibility. They wanted to show that EU funding, which measured in the millions of euros, was not helping Romani communities at all. And they wanted to make clear that, given how relentlessly the status quo continued, cutting this funding wouldn't hurt Romani communities either. They may not have been quite sure what should come to stand in its place, but it was clear that something needed to change—or at least be stopped.

"We Are Not Criminals!"

As the conference proceeded, participants and protesters sat in their seats, some wearing the yellow vests. László Andor, European commissioner for employment, social affairs, and inclusion at the time, came onto the stage. By way of introduction, he addressed the audience: "This event is inspired by the understanding of the European Commission that the question of the integration of Romani people is a lot more than a question of human rights, of respectable living, of European values, of justice, but it is also a question of a huge economic meaning." Immediately, I thought back to 2010, when thousands of Roma were forcibly deported from France to Bulgaria. That year, French President Nicolas Sarkozy publicly declared he was starting a fight "against drug traffickers and delinquents" and that "the illegal immigrants must be sent back to their countries."[40] Sarkozy focused explicitly on Roma: "I am therefore asking you to put an end to the out-of-control mushrooming of Roma camps. These are lawless zones that cannot be tolerated in France."[41] This anti-Roma deportation regime continued in France and across Europe.[42] As Bulgarian Roma knew well, when the EU channeled funds into Bulgaria to promote Romani inclusion, they did so with the additional aim of preventing Romani migration to Western Europe, even though they were legally allowed to move per European Union Law.[43]

Andor continued:

> It is a question of a better future together, which we, as citizens of Europe, deserve. I hope that this is not just a singular event, but that it is a part of an initiative, which takes on the ambitious task

to inform everyone included in the process...representatives of the institutions, of the international institutions, of the public administration, of the multiple [Romani] organizations I see represented here, so that they can use better the existing mechanisms and instruments for integration.

Some of the T-shirt-wearing protesters sat throughout the audience, but the group I was with, the main organizers, stood together because they had planned an action for this very moment.

As Andor paused briefly, Maria and I walked to the front of the room and blocked the stage with a banner that read "Europe, Stop Funding Roma Exclusion." In the back of the room, Simon and another protester held the banner they had worked on the night before: "Don't Fuck with 12,000,000 Roma" (*Ne se ebavayte s 12 000 000 Romi*). The slogan referenced the estimated Romani population across all of Europe; the organizers had determined it was more appropriate for men to hold this sign at the back of the hall, since it was more controversial. Andor did not acknowledge any of these actions; he simply continued his speech throughout the demonstration.

Following Andor's speech, Tsvetan Tsvetanov, the Bulgarian minister of the interior, took the stage. About a year prior, Tsvetanov had told the daily Bulgarian newspaper *24 Chasa* that he had to conduct a "very serious analysis of the problems with Roma because their environments are an incubator for generating crime."[44] In the interview, he discussed an upcoming conference in Brussels where he planned to "have a conversation with the European commissioner for social affairs, László Andor, to demand money for Roma integration to be given to the state, not the foundations." He went on to explain, "In the last twenty years various nongovernmental organizations have received a lot of money, but nothing has been done. Now we see that there are Roma bosses who live in some splendid palaces and the slums for the majority of Roma get bigger."[45] When confronted by an international audience about his comments in Brussels, Tsvetanov announced, "It's just a statement of a fact, it's not a stigmatization." Romani activists came to the Sheraton conference incensed, if not altogether surprised, by his public suggestion that their work in their communities was in fact an elaborate cover for criminal activity.

As Tsvetanov took the stage, my friends started to blow the red plastic whistles that hung from lanyards around their necks. Tsvetanov began

FIGURE 3.5 Protesters holding banner in the back of the Sheraton conference hall: "Don't Fuck with 12,000,000 Roma" (*Ne se ebavayte s 12 000 000 Romi*). Photo by the author.

his remarks with a focus on the previous twenty years: "Bulgaria started a change, which everyone wanted. The Bulgarian economy went through a lot of difficulties and...suspended a lot of the industries in which many Bulgarian citizens and Bulgarians of Romani origin were employed." It was impossible not to hear the subtext in his juxtaposition, the unmarked whiteness of "Bulgarian citizens" and the implication that the nonwhite "Bulgarians of Romani origin" might not count as real citizens. He continued, "Joining the European Union gave us the most priceless thing: the free traveling of the citizens of the European Union. Of course, that led to serious migration issues..."

At this point, Maria stood up and exclaimed loudly, "We are the only ones left!" In this she invoked a common refrain that only G*psies and "losers"—society's trash—remain in Bulgaria, while those who can afford to leave, do. This links to the widely publicized "brain drain" that has been a topic of national concern since 1989, when Bulgarians began to migrate en masse. In the midst of this emigration, many Roma have come to see Bulgaria as a place devoid of hope for reliably livable Romani life. The sweepers, along with Baka, her daughter-in-law Tanya, and nearly everyone I encountered, reiterated the same thing. Baka often rhetorically asked me when we were working our trash rounds, "Who would be stupid enough to stay if they *could* leave this place?"

Tsvetanov continued, ignoring Maria's interjection. "The key to the improvement and well-being of the nation is to have a healthy well-developed citizenry living in normal conditions for a democratic country. Regrettably, these conditions are lacking for a great number of Roma." He explained that the "failures of the past have resulted in grave consequences not only for Bulgaria but other EU countries...[due to] the repercussions of Bulgarians leaving Bulgaria and going to other European cities. More and more talking has been devoted to the topic of Roma integration Europe-wide." The entire EU conference, it seemed, was a direct response to the deportations of 2010. "The low social status and the lack of opportunities for personal and professional realization," Tsvetanov went on, "leads to high levels of dependency on Romani leaders in various communities, including criminal schemes related to money laundering."

Simon yelled out: "Mr. Tsvetanov, you here are giving an example of how to speak about Roma: 'the Romani criminality'..." Someone else from the crowd interjected, "And who controls the money lenders?" implying that it was the Bulgarian mafia-cum-government, in which Tsvetanov was deeply implicated, that controlled EU money while Romani communities were criminalized as the face of such schemes. The protesters in the crowd broke into a chant: "We are not criminals! We are not criminals!" They blew their whistles and held up red cards, as in a soccer match when a player has committed a particularly egregious foul.

Tsvetanov asked, visibly angry but trying to maintain a professional manner, if he could continue. Simon shouted back: "Do you see the vests they gave us? Look, if you want, *you* can wear it. This is a vest that the organizers of this conference put in each bag, and their message to us is clear where [they think] Roma belong. If this is the inclusion of the Roma, then so be it." In other words, Simon was suggesting that European "inclusion" was absurd; it meant sustaining a status quo in which Roma should remain working on the streets, hypervisible and underpaid, cleaning up other people's waste. Tsvetanov replied from the podium, "I am not responsible for the conference organization or promotional material which have been made for the conference today. I am just invited." Linking Tsvetanov and the EU organizers within the same systemic frame, Maria interjected: "This is all of your attitudes toward us."

"Thank you," Tsvetanov said as he tried to regain composure. "I think that such an attitude is not the best.... Because when we speak about the problems that we have today, we have to name the problems and the truth with the real names." He began to list the liberal, EU-approved catchphrases for Romani inclusion, the first being the education of Roma. He continued, "In second place is health care. In third place is the way of life.... I want to apologize if somebody has been affected by what I said, but fellow ladies and gentlemen, we have to say the problems with the real names." This strategy of apparent frankness—"real talk" and "naming names"—was of a piece with the global politicking of those on the right who dodge accusations of white supremacy by claiming that they refuse to conform to the standards of "political correctness."[46]

Tsvetanov finished quickly, and then Tomislav Donchev, then-minister of EU funds management in Prime Minister Boyko Borisov's government, took the stage. He spoke first about the vest, disputing that it had anything to do with the racialized waste work shouldered primarily by Roma: "The important message when putting on the vest is that the bright color should draw your attention...and the nice writing on the back. Personally, I have no problem putting it on." Maria rolled her eyes. "Before I get to the main point," Donchev continued, "concerning what just happened, I believe this is the democratic way. Since we have the right to make presentations here, the public also has the right to represent themselves." His efforts at pacification struck me as an attempt to quiet the protesters, roping them into the "democratic" framework they were actually up against—all while using the *bryukselski* that would also please the European Union commissioners in the room. The public discourse proceeded in this way, and the protesters soon left the room to field questions from journalists in the hallway until the session ended.

———

After the conference, officials continued working to take back whatever power the protesters had tried to claim. A front-row attendee, a long-term employee of the United States Embassy, came up to me after the speeches ended and told me that the protest was inappropriate. A few weeks after the conference, another representative of the United States

SURVEILLANCE

111

Embassy emailed me to schedule a meeting in a downtown Starbucks. At the meeting, she told me that, because of the protest and some other remarks I had made at an embassy-sponsored party that were deemed anti-American, I had become what they call "water-cooler talk." Because of this, she commented, I would likely never be hired by the State Department. She explained that I might have had my funding revoked if I had done this while I was a beneficiary of a government-funded Fulbright grant (at the time, I was thankfully receiving private Wenner-Gren funding and awaiting the start of my Fulbright-Hays grant, which ultimately was not a problem).[47]

When I called Simon a few days later to tell him what happened, he paused briefly then told me we should only discuss this in person and immediately hung up the phone. He and Maria later told me in person that they had expected that such a public display would result in their own surveillance or worse by the Bulgarian government. After all, Bulgarian politics at the time focused on preemptively quelling dissent. And in the following months, the crackdown intensified.

"Europe: You're Too Late!"

Sitting outside a pizzeria near the entrance to Fakulteta in the early summer of 2011, Martin, the leader of the Romani Star NGO where I was volunteering, pointed to the flowers in a nearby flowerbox. His eyebrows raised and his eyes glimmered as he leaned in to say something, so I expected one of his jokes. "So, Elanka, do you know what we call these?" "Impatiens?" I asked, remembering the name my mother used when we grew the plants in window boxes at home. They were a flower that liked shade, something I knew from my childhood. "Little g*psies" (*ts*gancheta*), he told me and cackled in his signature way, waiting for my reaction. "Why?" I asked naively, performing my part in our regular dynamic. He smiled, "Because they will grow anywhere." I took his joke as a satirical acknowledgment and reclaiming of the stereotype about Romani "overpopulation" but also a more somber acknowledgment of the need for Romani strategies of survival.

I worked with Martin at Romani Star for nine months in 2011 before he died. Romani Star was a grassroots organization based in Fakulteta, founded in 1995 to focus on educational desegregation and social justice issues more broadly. The NGO was supported by the Open Society

CHAPTER THREE

Foundation for a time but had many other funding sources over the years of its existence (1995–2011). Throughout this period, it also became a community-wide clearinghouse for all sorts of issues, providing legal services and housing assistance and serving as a home base for international visitors from organizations like the World Bank and the United Nations. I had visited their offices in 2003 and 2009, and from January to September 2011 I worked with them as a daily volunteer. Officially, my hours were 9 a.m. to 5 p.m., but they often ran from 9 a.m. to 9 p.m.

Romani Star had previously had a large staff, but by the time I joined, substantial funding cuts linked to the changes after EU accession had made it impossible to pay anyone a full salary. Often there were only three of us at the office: Martin, the founder and executive director, his colleague Anton, who was in charge of the daily running of the organization, and me. They were stretched so thin that I tried to share the labor as much as I could. We would also just pass the time together as Martin tried to push back against the sense of doom that had come over the office as funding became scarcer. I filmed Martin in front of his computer doing dances to the timeless pop songs of Lili Ivanova with my cheap digital camera, and he told me about his life, showing me old military photos of himself and reciting his own poetry. We talked at length about the organization's history, and, alongside my intermittent note-taking, I wrote letters in English appealing to funders for support.

I was at the office with Martin in 2011 when a delegation from the United Nations Office of the High Commissioner for Human Rights came by for a day-long visit. They wanted to hear about Romani Star's work and asked Martin to show them around Fakulteta. Martin explained:

> Whenever you go to a neighborhood like ours, all over Bulgaria, you won't see and you won't hear the presence of the government or local authorities. We are part of a partially finished master plan, which makes our neighborhoods an illegal addendum to the official city plan. So, worst case scenario, when Volen Siderov, the leader of [the far-right, neo-Nazi party] Ataka, is elected mayor of Sofia, he can simply decide to demolish the entire neighborhood. He would have the right to do that.

He changed the subject to tell the visitors about the recent Sheraton protest. He did not organize it, he explained, but he had been there. "They

SURVEILLANCE

113

put up this banner saying, 'Don't fuck with twelve million G*psies.'" He laughed and continued, "Whenever a donor organization allocates money for solving a Roma issue, usually this money will go to solving numerous 'minority' issues but never goes to Romani people." He reiterated Simon's analysis that, because EU funds were couched in *bryukselski* terms like "vulnerable populations" and "underrepresented groups," Bulgarian national bodies funneled them into non-Roma organizations that technically fit these labels.[48]

Martin continued to describe the situation to the visiting foreigners: "When a donor organization comes on a follow-up visit several years later asking us to show what we did with this money, what infrastructure problems we solved, etc., we have no answer...because Roma were never the beneficiaries of the project in the first place." He continued, "The technical excuse would be, 'on behalf of EU services we allocate this money to Bulgaria, and it is the Bulgarian government that decides how to best use the funds.' But if you walked around this neighborhood, do you think these people down here know that they are even part of the European Union?"

Martin had proven this point to me many times, asking Fakulteta residents who came to his office what they thought of the European Union. Most just laughed. One woman waved her arm toward the barred office window that overlooked the neighborhood's deteriorating public school and shrugged. "If you say so, that this is Europe?" She went on to tell Martin that she was just waiting for socialism to come back so she would have the opportunity to work again. Martin explained to me then that this waiting for socialism to return was a common refrain in the neighborhood, as though it was a viable alternative to the democratic capitalist system within which Roma found themselves systemically unemployed. He concluded, "But, there is no external monitoring of the funds. As a result, money is getting transferred from the European Union to the Bulgarian government, and the government self-monitors the spending of these funds."

Martin cited the visit of another American who had recently come to Bulgaria: Robert Zoellick, the 2007–2012 World Bank president. When Zoellick visited Fakulteta, Martin recalled, "We showed him our version of segregated schools…. The idea was to convince the World Bank to give a loan to Bulgaria so that there could be interventions to help to solve Roma problems. That gentleman [Zoellick] was very moved by all the meetings that he had, and he did agree to extend some loans to Bulgaria."

Martin chuckled. "So he gave the Sofia Municipality half a million dollars to make a project here. But the mayor of Sofia decided that he would use the money to build two kindergartens" where, Martin explained, Roma categorically do not attend. Simon, Maria, and the other Sheraton protesters had been trying to make the same point. I wondered if Martin was hoping that now, in a different context, with a different audience, the message might land.

After the UN representatives left, I asked Martin about his thoughts on the protest. He told me that he liked what the protesters did at the Sheraton. He appreciated the text on the posters and their boldness. Then I asked what his banner would say if he made a slogan to show at an EU conference. He answered quickly: "Europe, you're too late!" "Why?" I asked. He did not think long before answering, "No one wants to deal with the problems of the Roma. There is a lot of prejudice in Bulgaria; they think that we're lazy, that we don't want to be educated, that we don't want to work." I nodded. "At the same time, this is a big issue, and only now the EU realizes that, yes, there are a lot of Roma. They only realized this when countries like Bulgaria, Romania, Czech Republic, and Poland tried to join the EU. It was like there were no Roma before, like they suddenly dropped from the sky, just in time for EU accession." He went on: "The EU has no idea what to do with Roma, with poverty, with any of this. They aren't used to it.... Just look at the poster of the woman at the entrance to the conference." He thought for a moment. "It was very ugly. But this is just Europe's view of G*psies."

———

"So, how do you feel about the situation now?" I asked. "I'm depressed," Martin answered matter-of-factly. "My organization is falling apart. It's vanishing before our eyes." He became quiet for a moment. I asked him what he planned to do next, and he responded, "I don't have very many options." After a pause, he continued, "Maybe I'll just surrender to the [white Bulgarian] experts and we'll close down the foundation."

As we were talking, Martin's only remaining coworker, Anton, called. He hadn't been paid in months, and he had a family with small children to take care of. Martin handed me the phone, saying, "You talk to him. Tell him that he must not worry, that everything's going to be okay, that we will continue working and things will turn out great.

He needs you to say that." I took the phone: "Hey, I'm at the office, come by." But Anton told me that his daughter was sick, so he needed to stay home. When I relayed this to Martin before putting the phone down, he looked like he was about to cry. "Just talk to him. Please persuade him that what he does is very important, because he thinks, now, that this job is pointless."

Anton did not return to work over the coming weeks, and Martin also stopped coming in as often. By mid-July, he was only there a few days each week. We met mostly to write letters to potential donors, try to make each other laugh, and continue our ongoing discussions for this book. Martin had a wonderfully sarcastic sense of humor and a long, loud laugh. "Elanka, can I tell you a joke?" Martin asked one afternoon. "Of course," I answered. He launched in:

An Englishman, an Italian, an American, and a Bulgarian get on a plane. Everyone has to throw something out of the window of the plane—something they have an excess of in their country. So, the Englishman thinks for a minute and throws out his history book, the Italian guy throws out a pizza, the American gets rid of money, and then it comes to the Bulgarian. He doesn't need to think: He throws out the G*psies.

I guffawed, used to these jokes that he told me over sweet and milky Nescafé in the smoke-filled office. I rarely pushed him to tell me in earnest what he thought, because it was already so clear.

However, as the months passed and the situation at Romani Star became bleaker, Martin started to talk more directly. One day in early August, as we sorted the mail and looked at the accumulating stack of bills, Martin explained that Europe was too slow to enact real change. "The Roma voice" had not actually been heard at the official conference, he told me. "It just wasn't there. Romani voices haven't been in any reports; there is no real Romani participation at all. It's just some people from Western Europe who have gathered, talking about the Roma people, and the Roma people are staying in the room as witnesses, listening to what non-Roma people think about them." His sentiment echoed everything I had heard from my friends who organized the protest. "There's no life here for Roma," he told me. Sofka had told me something nearly identical soon after I had begun sweeping: "We can't make it in life. There's no life here." Years later, in 2016, when I met with Bobi, a Romani pastor of a church and preschool in Fakulteta, he too asserted: "There's no life, there isn't anything left. Not for the young people and not for us." It was a telling refrain.

I asked Martin what he imagined things would be like in ten years, in 2021. "In ten years," he said, looking out the window and taking a drag of his Marlboro Gold cigarette, "there won't be any significant change to the situation. Instead, the problem will get heavier and heavier. It's like a snowball..." The sector was in a "depression, a crisis," he explained. "The crisis comes from the fact that...the government here is very, shall we say, 'political.' And from the rest, there is fear. A lot of fear in people. That's why what you all did at the conference was very brave." By "political," Martin explained that he meant the government was opportunistic and uncontrollable; it would do anything for the political success it equated with financial gains. "It's brave for those Roma who held up red cards," he continued, "because Tsvetan Tsvetanov might decide to chase these people down with police." I nodded. "He is, after all, the minister of the interior! He isn't just a random person. He has power, he has police, he has people...he has an opportunity to do whatever he wants to them."

Soon thereafter, I spent three weeks on a research trip with an evangelical church group that was missionizing in Romani neighborhoods halfway across the country. I spoke with Martin by phone a few times while I was away, and he expressed deep anxiety about Romani Star's funding; soon, he said, the electricity would be shut off in the office. "We are falling apart; I'm afraid we will disappear." I repeated back what he'd asked me to tell Anton: Not to worry. Change takes time, I reminded him. "I hope you're right, Elanka," he responded hesitantly. I had not heard from him in a few days when I received a phone call from a friend on August 30. Martin had a sudden stroke, presumably stress-related, and died at home.

A few days later, I went to the cemetery in Sofia where Martin was about to be buried. His brother, Todor, invited me inside a small building where his body was being prepared for the funeral. His closest friends and family took turns speaking to him and laying down flowers, stem by stem. I tried to speak, but the words wouldn't come. I cried and Todor handed me a single rose to add to the pile.

Death of the Sector?

Martin's words about the Ministry of the Interior proved scarily prescient. In 2011, the Bulgarian government began investigating what was happening to EU funds coming into Bulgaria for Roma integration initiatives—a process that appealed to a general public focused on transparency and anti-corruption but that in practice was a deeply divisive and racialized "witch hunt," as those close to it called it. The government placed blame on Romani NGO leaders, whom they claimed stole funds for personal gains. Romani activists understood this as a tactic to distract from the government's own embezzlement of European Union money, and it seemed to work.

In what one of my interlocutors called the government's "reign of terror," the police questioned entire Romani families, putting their finances, education, expertise, and reputations on the line. The government publicly ridiculed Romani leaders in interviews and press conferences. News articles claimed that Romani NGO leaders had stolen EU funds to build palaces. Covers of popular magazines displayed Roma stereotypes: faceless, thick-fingered men holding cigars, adorned in gold rings and with big gold teeth. According to both my own interviews and international media coverage, the police investigated, threatened, and imprisoned over a dozen Romani NGO leaders.[49] Local leaders had their phones tapped, their bank accounts combed through, and were threatened by officials not to talk to the media. At the end, nothing of significance was found.

In 2019, when I met with Stefan, a middle-aged Romani NGO leader and political scholar who had tracked the surveillance campaign over eighteen months in 2011–2012, he characterized it as "pure torture...a combination of institutional torture plus media torture" designed to discredit Romani leaders. Ultimately, Stefan explained, none of the Roma NGOs were found to have been corrupt, but the campaigns still succeeded in discrediting and demoralizing Romani leaders. The government, he explained, "cut the wings of the Roma movement."

Martin and I had watched the sweep unfold together, and soon he and Romani Star were targeted as well. His death happened in the middle of this reign of terror. Martin was not the only one. A well-respected leader of a Romani organization in the northwestern Bulgarian town of

Montana died shortly after an invasive investigation.[50] Another respected Romani community leader in the town of Vidin who had been under intensive police investigation suffered a stroke. And nearly ten other Romani leaders lost their jobs.

In Stefan's eyes, even though EU accession had changed the funding landscape in 2007, the Romani movement had been slowly gaining independence up until the 2011–2012 investigations. EU monitoring of Romani "inclusion" had ceased when Bulgaria joined the European Union, but at first, the movement managed to survive on the dregs of dwindling Open Society Institute funding and support from private funders. Soon, however, the government realized there was nothing stopping them from taking down the whole Romani movement.[51] "Since there was no longer international support, no more international allies," Stefan explained, the government saw a "green light" to "smash them [activists] all back." He continued, "They wanted to show to others who are still not beaten what is going to happen to them. It was a very totalitarian move...and unfortunately, there was no reaction from anybody."

I looked at him. "Wasn't there anything that could have been done?" He shook his head. "We, as Romani NGOs, as organizations, were accustomed to functioning in a peaceful way. I would say in a normal democratic way. We were not in the position to react to this. We don't have the power. We didn't have people in the parliament, in the ministries, whatever. And nobody raised a voice about us, unfortunately." He thought for a moment. "It is a very sad story, I would say, especially in the end."

Still, Stefan noted, there was a time in the pre-accession period of the late 1990s and early 2000s when hope was strong and strides were being made toward change. I thought back to my first summer in Bulgaria in 2003 and the optimism I felt as I watched Simon and his colleagues work toward Romani educational desegregation in preparation for EU accession.[52] Stefan explained, "I would say that we achieved certain things. We supported thousands of kids, which changed the lives of thousands of families with the school desegregation initiatives and with a stipend program that supported more than three thousand university students. We created the current young Roma elite in many ways." He knew that they had given voice to many activists and inspired hope for change, but he lamented, "What you see today, that Roma are targets of the government, of racists, and of anti-Roma academic circles—and nobody does anything to [counter] this."

I asked how he imagined the future. "I don't know what is going to happen tomorrow," he said, "but I see a bad tendency. . . . During the last ten years, every year is worse than the previous year in terms of public attitudes towards Roma, and in terms of governmental policy towards Roma. The sector is dying." This was about more than the collapse of NGOs, he made clear. Anti-Roma sentiment and practices had always been present, but, compared to how mainstream they are today, they were "marginal in the beginning of the '90s." He thought for a moment, trying to bring it all together. "I see a severe deterioration." I agreed, seeing this too. He explained that Romani activists are "trying to survive, in one way or another, but we see that there's very little that we can do. There is no room for us." He did believe that somehow they would survive and "someday" it would be better. But, given the targeted violence, criminalization, and growing rhetoric framing Roma as fundamentally expendable, he had no clear prediction about how that might happen.

Endings and Returns

I woke up on the morning of July 19, 2012, to a series of Facebook posts and text messages from friends telling me to go immediately to the website of the president of the Republic of Bulgaria and take a screenshot. Before I was fully awake, I Googled, clicked, and found my way to the website of the office of President Rosen Plevneliev. A document had been uploaded that morning, titled "The National Strategy for the Integration of Roma." However, the document was saved with the filename *13.NationalStrategyIntegrateM*ngali.pdf*, using the term *m*ngali*, one of the most derogatory terms for Roma in Bulgarian.

Soon after this document was uploaded, it was announced that a particular employee had saved it with that name. According to news sources, he was reprimanded but permitted to remain in his position.[53] The filename, once released to the media, was quickly changed to "NationalStrategyIntegrateRoms." From the highest levels of white Bulgarian institutional power to the everyday people taunting waste workers as they do their jobs, Roma are seen as *m*ngali*, as trash on the very streets that they help Europeanize.

FIGURE 3.6 Screenshot from the website of the president of Bulgaria, July 19, 2012. Screenshot by the author.

No wonder so many Roma told me there was no life left for them in Bulgaria. Many of the protesters at the Sheraton ultimately decided to find work abroad, hoping they could make a life elsewhere. Simon, for example, still advances Romani causes, but now does so through virtual political campaigns while working in the hospitality sector in Western Europe. Maria still lives in Bulgaria but no longer participates in the sector, finding other ways to make a living. Many people seemed to have given up hope that the NGO sector would do anything of substance, yet they retained personal connections within the sector on the chance that their collective will might, eventually, make something happen.

Integration efforts, they told me, had failed. International funding dried up or was routed through a racist state apparatus, and the government had capitalized on stereotypes of criminality to take down the Romani NGO sector. The push toward Europeanization was sustaining the racial regime of white "expertise" and control. Martin's joke has repeatedly proven true: Americans might not be throwing money out of airplanes, but Bulgaria continues to enthusiastically discard its Roma.

In 2016, five years after the Sheraton protests, I met with László Andor, the European commissioner in front of whom Maria and I had held our protest banner. This time, we were in a very different setting: a café at Yale University. I did not think he would remember me. I was living in New Haven, Connecticut, writing my dissertation, and had seen that he was giving a talk at Yale's MacMillan Center. I emailed to see if he would meet me with me after his talk, and he agreed.

I told him about the topic of my research and asked his thoughts about being an EU commissioner, a role that he had left about eighteen months prior to our meeting. He discussed the difficulties of getting funding to marginalized communities in newly accessed countries like Bulgaria (and Romania) that were dealing with large amounts of corruption. I asked him what the biggest hindrance was to Roma integration. Sipping slowly from a paper coffee cup, he told me:

> I think the biggest obstacle is the underdevelopment of...and the lack of will in the lower levels of politics. The closer you are to the Roma population, the more difficult it is to create a political organization from local leaders. And that's why it must be created from above. Because maybe it's not a guarantee itself that change will happen, but at least it gives some kind of support for those who want to change things locally.

This top-down approach was exactly what Martin and Simon and Maria had been critiquing.

Several years later, when I returned to Bulgaria for a month in 2019, I met with Todor, Martin's brother who was also formerly part of "the sector," inside of the McDonald's in the subway underpass beneath Sofia University. We sat drinking espressos on a cold October morning as he recounted what he had witnessed during the 2011–2012 "reign of terror" that had immediately followed the conference. Romani leaders "were accused of taking money, stealing, you know, appropriating funding... [it became commonplace] that all G*psies are indeed thieves. No matter what they do. This whole thing reached a point of not only erasing the contributions of Roma people in leadership; it also got to physical destruction of people, of leaders." He explained that Bulgaria neither was nor ever would be a real democracy. "So, you know, I'm done...I used to have a future, but they are not letting me have it. So that's it." He became teary, visibly frustrated by the state of things. "We didn't participate in this, we didn't want to kill ourselves, but they are killing us." I looked away to let him collect himself for a moment, then asked who "they" were. "All of it," he told me. Anti-Roma racism was systemic, institutional, and all-pervasive. It was, as he explained, "inescapably everywhere."[54]

Todor stared past me for a moment, deep in thought. He had come with a small package of oily homemade *banitsa* (Bulgarian cheese pie) for me. It was tradition to give food to honor someone's death, and we met near the anniversary of Martin's death. It had been eight years since he died. He looked at me and changed the subject to the Black Lives Matter movement in the United States. "Roma are a minority," he said, "but now they don't protest. How are we supposed to understand that?" I was quiet. I thought back to Simon and Maria's discussions of Gandhi and the politics of passivity in Romani life, and of Cedric Robinson's analysis of retreat. Todor answered his own question: "Because they have a certain sensitivity...Roma are this sort of island in Europe. They are an island that sustains the humanity that would otherwise be lost."

FOUR

Voting

On a warm Sunday morning in October 2011, thousands of people stood on the main street of Fakulteta outside Elementary School 75, waiting to vote. Families gathered in the schoolyard, discussing the voting process as they prepared to enter the polls. Two police officers stood guard at the entrance, creating a funnel to allow people to enter one by one. Though it was early, crowds of men drinking coffee in plastic cups stood to the side, anxiously watching the pedestrians. The neighborhood's lively buzz seemed to proceed in slow motion, eerily hushed but pulsing with energy, as if everyone was moving in shared anticipation of something yet to take shape.

I soon learned that the men standing streetside were waiting to see what local campaign representatives, acting as middlemen who would organize potential voters—that is, pay them for their votes—would do. Vote buying and selling, I was told, has become de rigueur, especially in Romani neighborhoods. A 2012 Council of Europe report confirmed that it was a widespread practice.[1] However, in the 2011 electoral landscape political parties had developed new tactics to gain votes. Political parties were often threatened by the power of Romani voting blocs and had previously sought to secure Romani votes through cash payments or community "gifts" like long-awaited neighborhood speed bumps. From my experience working as an election monitor during that campaign period,

123

FIGURE 4.1 Voting morning in Fakulteta. Illustration by Izabela Ivanova.

I learned that newer practices of securing votes extended to other, more menacing means, including imprisoning Romani candidates, voter suppression, and physical violence against Romani voters.[2]

Before election day, I had attended meetings of a Romani activist group who quickly mobilized to do something unprecedented: to work as monitors of this unusually sensitive election. The idea behind the meeting was that Roma themselves, not only foreign visitors, should be monitoring elections inside Romani neighborhoods in order to understand what was really happening there on election day. At the meeting I asked how vote buyers could know that vote sellers voted as promised. Some voters, I learned, took cell phone photos of filled-in ballots as proof. Others, I was told, received a filled-in paper ballot—obtained I'm not sure how—that they would submit to the voting site, bringing back the empty ballot they received there as proof that they voted as promised. However, most of the time such surveillance was not necessary. Vote buyers were well connected to local "bosses," and the majority of voters were so dependent upon and fearful of them that nobody would dare to vote in any other way than what they agreed to. Besides, Romani voters seemed to have more or less relinquished hope that "the democratic process" would represent them. Politics had done nothing to help them combat structural racism and entrenched poverty, so why not take whatever small payout politicians offered?

I spent most of election day at the school, from monitoring the voting process in the morning to vote counting in the evening, as a volunteer interpreter for a Danish delegation of monitors collaborating with the Bulgarian Helsinki Committee, a nongovernmental organization for the protection and promotion of human rights in Bulgaria. The delegation had assigned me to Elementary School 75 because I had spent time in Fakulteta and knew the area well. The school had one of the highest proportions of Romani students, nearly 100%, among Sofia's elementary schools. And it had one of the lowest teacher retention rates in the city. Fakulteta parents who could manage it would drive far outside the neighborhood so their kids could attend other schools and were proud when they did. While the school was an everyday reminder of how structural racism and public funding allocations worked in Bulgaria, its role as a voting site was seen as an ironic absurdity for many Fakulteta parents. They had, for the most part, given up on the school as an educational site but saw how politicians relied on it to secure and maintain power.

During breaks and the lunch hour, I walked up the street to my friend Rosa's café to hear the neighbors' and other customers' perspectives on what was going on. A regular, Angela, entered and quietly complained that nobody was being paid the twenty leva they had been promised for their votes. When I asked Angela what she meant, she laughed with embarrassment and quickly created distance between herself and those she was speaking about: "Those G*psies were selling their votes." But upon entering the café, many of my close friends also sheepishly complained about nonpayment, even as they also derided the act of vote selling.

Problematic elections were the shame of Bulgaria on the larger European stage. Bulgaria is one of the few EU countries to receive full election observation missions from international bodies like the Organization for

Security and Co-operation in Europe (OSCE), and it is subject to some of the most intensive election monitoring in the EU. During elections, all campaign materials, including television advertisements, are required to include reminders that vote buying and selling are illegal.[3] However, politicians and the mainstream press focus on vote selling, framing it as both synonymous with the undoing of European democracy and a distinctly "G*psy issue."[4] This effectively renders Roma as democratic refuse that needs to be cleaned up; they are portrayed as polluters of the promised EU-era democracy. Roma, rather than well-documented systemic political corruption, become the culprit.

While I sat with Rosa and her customers, the TV aired scenes of Romani communities allegedly selling their votes throughout the country. There was no mention of the far more powerful forces that purchased votes or, for that matter, kept Romani communities in impoverished conditions that made vote selling appealing. The going rate for a vote, I was told, was twenty leva: the equivalent of one day's wages for many Romani day laborers, and much less than a living wage. Rosa whispered to me under her breath that dire economic circumstances forced some neighbors to vote for whichever candidate paid the most.

The TV coverage also failed to mention what Rosa, other neighborhood residents, and my sweeping coworkers had shared with me: Many Roma simply refuse to vote altogether. The money wasn't worth it, people told me, and, at least in Fakulteta that morning, it wasn't coming anyway. Leading up to the 2011 elections, many Roma were being threatened and so decided not to vote at all in order to preserve their safety. Knowing that their votes would do nothing to change the status quo and having learned that institutional avenues for change do not, in fact, produce change, they simply sit elections out. The same politicians always seemed to end up in charge. Besides, some people said, voting in Fakulteta was shameful because it had become so intrinsically tied to selling oneself.

It struck me that voting for no one—or even claiming to vote for no one—might function as a political statement unto itself. It points out the absurdity of the supposedly democratic process, and, playing out in conversations in cafés or on the street, could rise to something like collective action, what Erica Weiss, writing about refusal to serve in the military in Israel, calls "a politics of abstention" that serves as "a more radical alternative to resistance."[5] Maybe, I considered, it was in line with Cedric Robinson's formulation of what it is to "retreat" from the political, or the "determination to disengage."[6] But when I presented this idea to my friends in Fakulteta, they just waved their hands in my face, explaining that "this is just how it is" (*taka e*). They did not perceive their abstention as refusal or critique; they saw it as an efficient and practical way to save time and preserve something like dignity. What I saw as a politics of abstention or retreat, they took for granted as a commonsense way to avoid expending energy on what would inevitably be futile.

According to most of my Romani interlocutors, the 2011 election was a pivotal moment in the development of Romani political disengagement and the normalization of white supremacy. By this time, it was clear that the liberal democratic systems that EU officials had promoted would not produce meaningful change in Bulgaria, and each election served as another reminder of how little the institutional fabric of Bulgarian life had transformed, despite new individuals coming into power.

Moreover, elections serve as critical turning points in which different parties instrumentalize Roma; for some, that means outright buying of Roma votes, but for others, it entails capitalizing on anti-Roma sentiment as a quick way to gain votes from a white Bulgarian public. Winning elections with anti-Roma propaganda has been the case since the 1990s, but, most claim, it has worsened significantly since EU accession in 2007. The problem is not isolated to Bulgaria. The election-period campaign against Roma in Bulgaria coincided with Nicolas Sarkozy's high-profile deportation of Roma from France as well as Italy's far-right anti-immigration and anti-crime campaigns. As far-right nationalism spreads across Europe, similar dynamics play out with Roma and immigrants from the Middle East, including in France, Italy, Sweden, Hungary, and the United Kingdom.[7]

Given these challenges, many Romani activists believe in reconstituting "the political" on new terms. This means that they sometimes refuse funding, knowing that fiscal reform is impossible given how European Union funding works in an increasingly far-right and nationalistic Bulgarian government. Other times, the political might *look* like a passive acceptance of whatever comes, although the reality is quite the opposite. Activists in Bulgaria know that their idealism consistently results in disappointment, so they remain quietly analytical of the status quo, and they time public action carefully for when it might matter— such as before European Union officials. However, most Fakulteta residents, as well as my sweeping colleagues, equated formal politics with opportunism.

Politics, for them, could never be recuperated. There is a common refrain reiterated by Romani and non-Romani Bulgarians alike: "Every country has its mafia, but in Bulgaria, the mafia have their country."[8] In acknowledging these absurdities and acting upon them, Romani neighborhood residents seek paths out of the present—outside traditional methods of democratic politics like voting—toward a still-to-be-defined "something else" (*neshto drugo*).[9]

Anti-Roma Politics and Protest

After sitting for a while in her café, Rosa asked me to turn on my recorder so I could interview her. We had had many conversations about democratic politics and capitalism in Bulgaria, but I had never recorded them before. Her house was my safe space, my family away from home, and I had made a point to try not to use my time there for research. But now, in the more public space of her café on election day, Rosa wanted to ensure that I got her thoughts down. As I sat with a cup of sugary espresso, she explained that democracy was a failure in Bulgaria. All that came about from "the changes" (*promenite*) from socialism to so-called democracy, she explained, was capitalist exploitation. "All those people who are able, they leave this country...but everyone else, we are scavenging through trash cans and recycling bins. They [Roma] work in Chistota and they don't get paid for five to six months at a time, and they're afraid to say something because 'they're just G*psies' and they might get fired, and they are basically silent members of society." She continued emphatically, "But, when election time gets near, then they think of us." It was true: While some parties target Romani votes, others advance their cause by whipping up a frenzy of anti-Roma sentiment.

While anti-Roma violence is mundane and omnipresent in Bulgaria, it only tends to draw media attention when exceptional acts occur. This includes the 2015 racist attack on a Romani community in the southwestern Bulgarian village of Garmen that sent residents fleeing and resulted in the systematic razing of homes.[10] It also includes the 2019 wave of demolitions in the village of Voyvodinovo, during which white Bulgarians demanded the mass demolishing of Romani homes, and the municipality complied by tearing down so-called illegal housing.[11] However, other more quotidian acts of violence and neighborhood destructions take place without publicity, particularly in pre-election periods.[12]

Couched in terms of urban improvement or safety, these demolitions ostensibly aim to clean up the landscape by cleaning out Roma.[13] They embolden a racist voting base that responds positively to anything resembling anti-crime propaganda.

Such campaigns dovetail with the rhetoric of anti-Roma demonstrations that describe cleaning up Bulgaria by ridding it of its nonwhite population (using the Nazi reference of "turning G*psies to soap") and which have occurred during elections for decades.[14] At the same time, many seemingly mainstream parties, often affiliated with Western European and EU institutions, seek the support of those farther right as a way to increase votes across the country.[15]

Anti-Roma campaigns occur throughout the year, not only during election periods. Simon invited me to attend one such event in late June 2011: a nationalist right-wing protest held across from Parliament in front of the Monument to the Tsar Liberator, built to honor Russian Emperor Alexander II for having liberated Bulgaria from Ottoman rule during the Russo-Turkish War of 1877–78. Simon and I had protested at the Sheraton not long before, and he seemed interested in creatively exploring what could be done in the space of a public demonstration.

Simon had a plan. We would dress as tourists—he would wear a blue and yellow European Union hat and a fanny pack, I would bring my camcorder, and he would speak only in English. We knew from experience eating out together that, if we spoke English, most white Bulgarians would assume I was an English-speaking white Bulgarian and he a darker-skinned foreigner. At restaurants I'd usually get the Bulgarian menu and he'd be given an English one. Evidently, it was incomprehensible to people that someone who had dark skin could both be Bulgarian and speak fluent English. This happened with other darker-skinned Romani friends of mine too. As one friend explained, "They just assume: I'm well-dressed, I speak English—I can't be Roma. I must be Indian, so they give me the English menu." Similarly, these same restaurant employees assume that my whiteness equals Bulgarianness, so if I speak English with someone with dark skin, I must be Bulgarian accommodating a non-Bulgarian-speaking foreigner. Simon wanted us to play on these expectations at the right-wing event, an ironic gotcha joke that only he and I would be in on as we joined the hostile crowd.

As we approached Parliament, Simon grabbed my camcorder and told me that he would do the filming in English; I could translate from

CHAPTER FOUR

Bulgarian to English and back again for him as part of the ruse. About ten reporters looked on as a group of thirty protesters, mostly teenagers, stood awkwardly at the base of the monument, holding shoddily made signs and looking unsure of what to do. Simon, correctly assuming that they would never guess he was Roma if he spoke English, asked why they were there. One young-looking teenage boy answered:

> We want the freedom of the G*psies to be regulated. Now, they don't have rights—they just have freedom. We want them to pay their bills, to be more responsible when looking after their children. Instead, they are just begging on the streets. And there are many villages in Bulgaria where the G*psies [are] causing trouble for the Bulgarians, robbing people in broad daylight. Every day something happens about this in the news. For example, [we hear] "G*psies beat up a policeman, or they are stealing old people's pensions"... The governments are closing their eyes to these things because of the pressures for human rights, but our rights as Bulgarians are actually being destroyed and we are protesting against that.

The protester echoed the most common and stereotypical depictions one could see on the TV news each evening. Simon asked another protester why he was there. He explained, "The G*psies." He continued, "The problem is that our friends, the young people here, are leaving Bulgaria to live a normal life because it is not fair here. They [G*psies] are violent, they steal things, they make problems."

Simon interrupted, "But can I ask you something? I think you have a problem with your government...because the G*psies are the minority in your country, right?" He relished his ability to roleplay, to highlight the absurdity of their claims and of the protest itself. The young protester contradicted Simon: "Actually the Bulgarians are the minority." Simon, incredulous, asked, "Really, the Bulgarians are the minority?" The protester shook his head. "Well, they will be soon." Again, the protester blindly reiterated the fearmongering of the media: That because of the increasing Romani birth rate and the ever-declining white Bulgarian birth rate, Roma will soon become the majority population in Bulgaria—an utterly false claim.

Simon smirked and pointed toward Parliament. "Are there G*psies in this building?" The protester nodded: "Yes, there are one or two political parties for G*psies." "Okay," Simon continued in English, "so they have G*psies in the parliament. But is the president a G*psy?" "No," the protester conceded, "he will never be." In this, the protester was correct; Romani political representation has been virtually nonexistent in Bulgaria and across the European Union.[16]

Simon continued, "But is the prime minister a G*psy?" The protester shook his head, "No." Simon kept pushing: "So these people here who make the policies, they are Bulgarians?" The protester began to speak but Simon interjected, "So why don't you protest against the people making the policies in this country?" The protester tried to explain that the government had its failings, but that "the G*psies were a bigger threat."[17]

As Bulgaria got closer to the 2011 election, anti-Roma rhetoric gave way to anti-Roma violence, some of it local, some of it state-sanctioned, and some of it international. This violence came to a head in the aftermath of the September 23, 2011, killing of a nineteen-year-old white Bulgarian, Angel Petrov, in the small village of Katunitsa. It was initially alleged (and later proven in a criminal court) that Petrov was killed by Simeon Yosifov, a relative of infamous mafia boss Kiril Rashkov, who had been convicted of financial crimes in the 1990s and had established a Romani political party in 1998. News coverage converged on the fact that Rashkov was Roma. The media was already gearing up for the 2011 elections, and right-wing parties capitalized on the story for campaign platforms based on "ending G*psy crime." The case dominated public conversation.[18]

In response to the killing, residents of Katunitsa began burning houses and cars belonging to Rashkov's family, and then demanded that the family leave the village. Within days, large-scale anti-Roma demonstrations spread to over twenty cities and towns throughout Bulgaria. Police were stationed outside Romani neighborhoods to prevent potential conflict. Inside the neighborhoods, residents, scared for their lives, kept close whatever tools they had (mostly baseball bats and firewood axes) for protection. My friends in Fakulteta explained that the families whose children attended schools outside the neighborhood kept them home. Almost nobody left the neighborhood for days. In the weeks between what people called simply Katunitsa and election day, anyone who could not pass as white was frightened to go outside at night. Protesters walked the streets throughout the country chanting neo-Nazi rhetoric like "Death to G*psies," "G*psies into soap," and "Turks under the knife."[19]

FIGURE 4.2 Anti-Roma, white supremacist protest in downtown Sofia, October 2011. Photo by the author.

The case against Rashkov quickly transformed into an indictment of all Roma. Many of my activist friends and political interlocutors explained that the protests were strategically timed to take place right before the presidential elections on October 23. While political parties did not publicly lead the protests, people I spoke to told me that they were "pulling the strings" in ways that would benefit their campaigns. It was no accident, they said, that among the many crimes taking place in Bulgaria each year, this one had become a national story, cited in political speeches and used to motivate protesters by politicians hoping for gains in the polls.

When Rosa reflected on this dynamic on election day, she kept checking to make sure the recorder was on. She wanted this documented. "Katunitsa was a distraction during the elections in which Roma were turned into scapegoats for the ills of Bulgarian politics." She continued, pointing to the TV that was switched on for customers to watch:

> The news always tells us, "G*psies don't pay their electric bills, the G*psies steal. The G*psies have put this country in bankruptcy!" But why don't they turn their eyes towards how Bulgarians live, the ones

VOTING 133

in parliament? They're all criminals. Much bigger than Kiril Rashkov. What kind of criminals are the G*psies? And what kind of a criminal is Kiril Rashkov? Well, they [government officials] turned him into a criminal. Who has been hiding behind him all these years? Why did they close their eyes while he was helping their schemes? And now Kiril Rashkov doesn't pay taxes, but is he the only one that doesn't pay taxes? The most famous and the biggest don't pay taxes, all over the world. Oh, look at Kiril Rashkov—*the G*psy*! So, when a G*psy decides to do something, it's all out in the open, but when a Bulgarian decides to do something, it stays in the dark.

Rosa pointed out that Rashkov got called out not as a member of the mafia for which Bulgaria is infamous, but as a G*psy. While he was part of the network of mafia bosses who are known to run Bulgarian politics, he was lower in the hierarchy than his white bosses—a likely scapegoat. He was made the public face of what white Bulgarian politicians did behind closed doors. Much like how EU environmental standards and the related European aesthetic rely on unrecognized Romani labor, European and democratic ideals are upheld through criminalized Romani labor.

In Rosa's understanding, the whole system was designed to work against Roma while also depending on their votes for critical political leverage. She explained that, as a Romani person, "you live without a sewer system, without water." She continued, "Our rights are trampled on and the Bulgarians always say that the Roma live off the country's back. But that's not the case!" She continued, "Okay, so some get 125 leva [68 dollars per month] to support five children, and how can you manage to raise five children with 125 leva and integrate them, as they say? Where are the funds for the integration? That money is not only in the [pockets of] Roma bosses, but in Bulgarians' [pockets] too because they [white Bulgarians] are the first who come up with the idea for how to use these funds, not the G*psies."

I was reminded of Simon and Maria's calls at the Sheraton to stop EU funding altogether. Rosa made a similar objection but wanted the funding to continue—just with better allocation to help with the actual issues that Romani communities like hers were facing. It was common knowledge that funding for Roma integration more often supported ultranationalist and racist Bulgarian politicians than community-based Romani initiatives. In practice, integration was just another

CHAPTER FOUR

mafia-controlled political money-making scheme reliant on abundant European Union funds. Rosa concluded that these so-called integration initiatives institutionalized Romani disposability.

Under socialism, she told me, Roma were laborers who constituted an important part of the societal fabric in Bulgaria.[20] They may have been low on the labor hierarchy, but they were paid a decent wage for their work in state enterprises—at least compared to what they made today. And they had hoped that their diligent work might reduce the degree of state surveillance they faced. Although the Romani language was outlawed and Romani leaders were repressed, Rosa recalled a better life during what she and others commonly referred to as "before." "Before," she could even buy enough inexpensive clothing to resell for a good profit at flea markets in Sofia.

In postsocialist, EU-era Bulgaria, however, waste labor lost its position as instrumental to urban modernization and nation-building, and Romani citizens lost status as well. Now, Romani laborers have become locked into a category of those in need of integration, in contrast to those who are seen as quintessentially Bulgarian contributing to the country's development. Moreover, economic precarity among Roma has increased. Rosa told me, "Everyone has a loan from the bank to pay back and a mortgage. Everyone is sick and everyone is in need...but this is our country. We were born here. So, what do they plan to do to us now—what Hitler did and put us in a gas chamber? Let them, but this, this is not a nation."

I asked Rosa what she thought could be done. She got up to make a coffee for a waiting customer and continued talking as she expertly packed the espresso machine with a plastic tamper. "Leave this country, don't vote, there's nothing left here for us except to work with trash, to be treated as trash." Rosa's sentiment is characteristic of widespread critiques of liberal democracy in the region, such as those prevalent in local think tanks, academic lectures, and casual conversations that express cynicism about what Europeanization has done to Bulgaria. However, her critique was also rooted in the particularly racialized conditions of EU-era postsocialist capitalism.

Most people in Bulgaria share the understanding that Bulgaria has become valuable for the European Union as a site for consumption of low-quality goods (e.g., where Western Europe can sell its waste) and a source of cheap labor for Western European profits, serving as a site of pan-European exploitation to grow the wealth of already-wealthier countries.[21] At the same time, I saw evidence of large-scale efforts to push against the status quo throughout my fieldwork. This included abundant calls for ending political corruption. Widespread internet memes, like the ones used in online organizing for Bulgaria's 2013–2014 year of protest, played on Bulgaria's EU-era insistence on keeping the streets and landscape clean.[22] The best cleanup, such memes suggested, would be both material and political: In one, a figure discards all of Bulgaria's political parties into a waste bin. Beneath the image is the hashtag #DANSWITHME, which had spread on Facebook as a play on the abbreviation for the Bulgarian State Agency for National Security, DANS (*Darzhavna Agentsiya "Natsionalna Sigurnost"*). Protesters coalesced against the election of infamous oligarch Delyan Peevski as head of DANS.[23]

In other forums, protesters chanted the phrase "red trash" (*cherveni boklutsi*), an imperfect rhyme in Bulgarian that signifies that the "red" former communists still in power have out-of-date political frameworks and should be discarded.[24] The phrase "red trash" became so ubiquitous that it even entered official parliamentary discussion. In 2019, members of parliament used this chant to call out policies and members of the Bulgarian Socialist Party during official debates.[25] Many of my interlocutors told me that, while Roma are often cast as trash, the real problem is the "recycling" of politicians, who continually change political affiliation in order to stay in power. Many people told me that "politicians are the most recycled thing in this country." Unlike in neighboring Romania, where the president of the Socialist Republic, Nicolae Ceaușescu, along with his wife Elena, were executed on national television in 1989 during the overhaul of power, "nothing actually changed in Bulgaria," many of my interlocutors commonly reiterated.

In Bulgaria, political metaphors of recycling and waste also have material resonance because actual waste has been critical to multiple elections.[26] For example, waste piled up on Sofia's streets in 2007 and again in 2009 when waste companies went on strike. At the time, the waste firm managing Sofia's trash was affiliated with the Bulgarian Socialist Party—a leader of which was running in Sofia's mayoral election. To gain popularity in the election, they instigated a strike, which was then blamed on the mayor at the time, Boyko Borisov. They wanted it to appear as though Borisov could not keep his city clean and therefore should not be reelected. The manipulation of material waste may have helped: Borisov still won the election, but only by a very small percentage.

FIGURE 4.3 Meme of a person throwing political parties into the garbage. Party names include the Bulgarian Socialist Party (BSP), Movement for Rights and Freedoms (DPS), Attack (Ataka), and Citizens for European Development of Bulgaria (GERB). Below the image is a protest hashtag: #DANSWITHME. Screenshot by the author.

FIGURE 4.4 Waste on the street from a strike in Sofia, Bulgaria, 2009. Photo by the author.

It is true that many recent political leaders in Bulgaria have been recycled. In other words, they have strong ties to previous power regimes, socialist and otherwise.[27] Boyko Borisov, who became prime minister in 2009 and held that position until 2021 (except for a hiatus when he resigned in 2013 and was reelected the following year), was the bodyguard for former Communist Party leader Todor Zhivkov in the 1990s. Bulgaria's prime minister from 2001 to 2005 had a political past that predated socialism: Simeon Borisov Saxe-Coburg-Gotha reigned as Simeon II, the child tsar (king) of Bulgaria, from 1943 to 1946 before he was forced into exile in Spain, not returning until 1996. Representing Bulgaria's hope for the most "untainted" politician they could find (as he had spent so much time outside the country), he became prime minister in 2001. Many other politicians have followed the ideological winds and shifted from being staunch communists to devoted democrats to contemporary socialists. As Simon used to tell me, "The best communists are now the most outspoken democrats." Power has changed hands in name only.

For some politicians, gaining or retaining power involves exploiting fears of Romani criminality. For others, it means courting or outright purchasing Romani votes. For others still, it involves anti-Roma violence and voter suppression. All three strategies lead to a political stasis, wherein white Bulgarian leaders and their constituents benefit from reinscribing racialized inequities even as they call for integration. Instead of advancing the standing of minority groups, Bulgarian democracy props up racial sustainability, and many Roma see little to no means of escape.

Sausages and Beer

Entering many Romani neighborhoods in Bulgaria means encountering a variety of phenomena, stemming from both a lack of public infrastructure and local attempts to remedy those gaps. The roads are deeply potholed, although, as I was told, this was sometimes remedied right before elections. In fact, before elections, it was common to see construction crews quickly repaving neighborhood roads. Once, weeks before a national election, I witnessed uniformed crews reinforcing the speed bumps on Fakulteta's main road, a constant safety concern for neighborhood parents. They finally arrived to perform the overdue work at what everyone assumed was a strategically timed date. I later learned that the various satellite dishes adorning houses in Romani neighborhoods were, like the speed bumps, "gifts" from politicians to residents during campaigns. The same was true, I was told, of other Romani neighborhoods throughout Sofia. Pastors who worked with neighborhood residents joked that "you could name each satellite dish after whose election it came from."

Bulgarian politicians typically only provide municipal services to Romani neighborhoods in the period leading up to elections. They rely on the premise that Romani communities are so underserved that they will take whatever is offered, because it's the only time they can expect to see city-sponsored development in their neighborhoods.[28] In fact, people from many backgrounds, including white Bulgarians, Roma, even politicians themselves, would say that only in Bulgaria could politicians buy votes with "a few sausages and a beer." People take what they can get, and where Bulgarian Roma are concerned, people know that they and their landscapes will be essentially forgotten soon after the elections conclude.

VOTING 139

Nothing about this dynamic was particularly hidden. Consider a sketch from the popular late-night comedy show *Komicite* (The Comedians), in which "Lyuba-the-G*psy" confronts a census-taker at her door. At first, she thinks he is asking for something, so she tells him she has no money. He explains that what he is there for will not cost her anything. She looks at him suspiciously. "Okay," she asks, "so will we have to vote after that?" He looks comically shocked, and she goes on: "Because usually when someone gives something for free in the neighborhood, then they take us to make us vote." Although lacking an actual bribing politician, the sketch casts Lyuba as a cynical opportunist, entrenching the stereotypes of Romani criminality that even avowed white progressives in Bulgaria often hold.

———

This became clear to me during the campaign of one well-meaning progressive candidate, Petar.[29] Petar, a longtime research consultant and friend, was a centrist, democratic candidate in the 2013 parliamentary elections who listened intently when I told him about my research and my thoughts on Romani political participation. After I insisted, over the course of many months of friendly rapport, that politicians should approach Romani communities as constituents rather than voting blocs to buy off or suppress, he decided to organize a Romani outreach initiative and invited me along. I accompanied him on his first campaign trip to a large Romani neighborhood in Vabrava, the Northeastern Bulgaria town for which he was the designated party representative.[30]

Petar did not want to deliver "business as usual" and was staunchly opposed to anti-Roma violence. But as I accompanied him on the campaign trial, I began to see the problems in his form of progressivism, which involved trumpeting the importance of democracy and condemning vote buying and selling with a range of EU-beloved buzzwords like "education," "dignity," and "transparency." Although his ideas pointed to hope for systemic change, it soon became clear that, to borrow a phrase from Savannah Shange, his reliance on "the universalizing rhetoric of the liberal state [was] itself the problem.[31] It made for a rather hopeless sense of what the future might bring. It was hard to imagine how following the same frameworks that had created systemic oppression could lead to meaningful change.

———

CHAPTER FOUR

My time with Petar's campaign started before dawn on a chilly Wednesday morning. Petar picked me up at home in Sofia in his SUV, which had plush leather seats and a young hired driver who remained mostly silent. Petar sat in the passenger seat. I climbed into the back alongside his childhood friend and campaign manager. We drove across the country toward Vabrava, stopping at rest stops, cafés, and businesses to meet with local party members along the way. In central Bulgaria, we stopped to eat at a hilltop restaurant that was part of a Vegas-like castle complex, complete with a plastic-stone moat. Then we drove to the parking lot of a nearby bread factory, where Petar stepped out of the car to take a meeting. I stayed in the back seat and could only make out parts of the hushed conversation. When I asked him what the meeting was about, he just shook his head: "Bulgarian politics are nuts sometimes."

In the late afternoon, we finally arrived at the Vabrava headquarters of Petar's party, Democratic Citizens of Bulgaria.[32] In the office, we planned what we would do over the weekend. Petar made sure we would travel to one of the local Romani neighborhoods. They organized the logistics of the trip, which included ensuring we drove there in the old sedan of one of the local party leaders, not his shiny SUV with Sofia plates. "We need to look more modest," he explained to me. "You know what I mean." Along with the local team, he discussed what to take on the visit, deciding to leave their jackets in the car and the laptop safely at the office. Niki, a local collaborator and music producer, would supply amplified music to get everyone out of their apartments to gather in the communal yard between their socialist-built buildings. In a hushed voice, Petar told me, "I just don't want to see any belly dancing when the journalists come," expressing both a common stereotype of Romani "belly dancing" to a locally popular music genre (*kyuchek*) and his worry that it could have negative effects on the campaign's publicity. Niki, who worked with musicians from the neighborhood regularly, warned the team: "At least they let people into this part of the neighborhood—Bulgarians I mean. In the typical ghetto parts of these neighborhoods, it is very hard for outsiders to enter." He echoed the common refrain that Romani neighborhoods were closed communities, something I'd heard again and again but which had not been my experience at all.

The next day, Petar talked to Niki as we drove over. "The point is not to manipulate them," he emphasized. "They will just vote for whoever they are told.... This is the future of Bulgaria. They are still hungry, they have to eat." Admitting defeat before we even arrived, Petar acknowledged that democratic voting structures relied on Romani poverty. In this view, Roma were not disposable but rather the opposite: essential to the political victories of those parties with the power and money to pay for votes and, when necessary, suppress Romani voter turnout.

We parked outside the neighborhood's center, next to a plot of open space surrounded by communist-built housing complexes in various stages of disrepair. Music played loudly on outdoor speakers close to a table with posters of the party's local candidate taped around its sides. Children ran back and forth across the yard while their mothers stood watching nearby. Others, mostly women, sat on a building's stoop, cracking open salty shells and eating the roasted sunflower seeds inside. Marina, the party's local administrator, took the microphone that had been set up and called the neighbors together. As she assembled the group, I stood on the sidelines, filming with a small Nikon digital camera beside a radio journalist who seemed more interested in recording me than the campaign visit.

Petar stepped forward, looking purposefully casual in jeans and a baggy white T-shirt. "There's something wrong with this microphone," he complained. He cradled a handful of sunflower seeds, handed to him by a woman sitting on the stoop. Eating sunflower seeds is a widespread Bulgarian pastime but has also long been part of the representation of Roma in Bulgaria, often used to exemplify the aimlessness of people who don't do anything but sit around killing time. Petar took a handful of seeds and expertly chewed them in what struck me as an invocation of an "everyman" folksiness. "These seeds that Slavka brought are very good, so I can't speak at the moment," Petar mumbled as he munched. He finished eating, then began speaking to the small but growing crowd:

> This here is not an agitation, my friends. I came here to tell you only one thing: Just think before you go out on election day. Go and vote for the one you want. Be proud and honest people. I came here today not to give you a speech and promises, no, nothing like that. I came here today to take a walk among you and to have a discussion with you. I came here to tell you that even though I am a candidate for representative in the next parliament, I am not here to bribe you to vote for me. I am not here to treat you to beer and sausages, and I will not mock you like all the others do.

Petar continued, "The others will bribe you and then you will remain living in these miserable conditions and this big social mess. If you want better roads and streets in the neighborhood, you will have them when you stop selling your votes for small amounts of money. It's easier for other politicians to bribe you and, after that, to leave you to live in this misery."

Rather than sharing his particular campaign platform—the type of material that might, say, chart a way out of "this misery"—Petar continued to bemoan vote selling: "When you don't allow them to bribe you, then you will be rightful citizens who are able to demand all kinds of things." Petar suggested a political framework in which short-term financial gains could be replaced by a righteous citizenship, as though the state would accept them and their demands if they just refused bribery. But he did not account for the fact that their demands might never be met and that, thus far, most people had no reason to believe they ever would be. Petar reiterated that he was not there as a typical politician: "You can vote for whoever you want to, just don't forget you should be dignified people. I want you to prove the people wrong who think that you do not know what is going on.... I will take a walk now with you, and please feel free to share all kinds of problems you have with me. If there is a coffee shop nearby, we can go all together and take a coffee while discussing it all."

There was no coffee shop of the sort Petar imagined nearby. This neighborhood was on the outskirts of town and far from anything resembling a pharmacy or supermarket, let alone a sit-down café large enough to accommodate such a group. But the audience did have some questions. A woman in the crowd took the microphone immediately: "Hello, sir. First, I want to thank you for making time for us in your busy schedule, but why do you do that now, when the elections are almost knocking on our door? Is this when you only decide to solve some social problems that the G*psies have in order to gain more votes?" Petar nodded professionally, mouth slightly open and appearing to fight off an urge to interrupt her. I knew he expected this, but he was sweating as he responded:

Yes, of course you are right. I have been in [other neighborhoods] and Sofia until now, and all those G*psy neighborhoods, or you may call them ghettos, look just like this and have the same problems. As I repeated multiple times, I did not come here to ask you to vote for me or agitate you. I just want one thing from you: Be proud and don't let others make fun of you and bribe you. Because this all is also making fun of your human rights.

Another woman, a resident of the apartment building we were standing outside, interrupted: "It seems like we G*psies have been socially abandoned. We have no place to live, no money to pay our bills, no jobs, and we are always given only empty promises." Petar responded, "This is exactly why we are not making any promises; we are just coming to get to know each other." Nobody in the crowd seemed to take his claims at face value. They were well versed in people who opportunistically exploited them in the guise of democratic reform.

A man in the audience started speaking aloud to whoever was in earshot: "But this is why people don't want to vote in elections at all, because they were bribing us way too much before, as though a couple of meatballs and sausages can do the trick." He explained that the politicians just wanted votes but would never do anything for them. A woman nearby overheard the conversation and joined in: "This is mission impossible. We are fed up, no more.... We have children to feed, rents to pay, bills. With 130 leva [about 72 dollars per month] pension, tell me what I can do. I can't even go to work anymore because of my problems with my legs..."

Another woman jumped in: "I don't even have a place to live. [The current mayor] promised to give us places to live in and now we are supposed to vote, really? They all promise and do nothing in the end. They just make promises until we vote for them, and after that, they forget about us." At this point, a woman standing next to me, whom I later learned was named Sara, interjected: "I just don't trust even a single politician anymore. I want to vote but there is nobody.... Everyone is part of one big mafia. And you want me to vote? I will not vote for anyone. I just want all the politicians out of my life."

At that point, Petar stopped the official part of the campaign event, which was clearly not going the way he had hoped it would. He walked over to where Sara and I stood, and Sara invited us upstairs to show us "the misery" she lived in, guiding him by the hand. Petar, Niki, and some of the other campaign organizers followed her up the dark collapsing stairwell to a broken door that, when pried open, revealed a tidy, lavender-wallpapered apartment that smelled of citrusy cleaning fluid and baked goods. The linoleum flooring was brown and coming up at the edges, but the floral wallpaper was shining in the sunlight and the furniture was arranged, in typical Bulgarian fashion, with all usable flat surfaces displaying matching decorative glassware atop multicolor crochet doilies, with ornate picture frames of the family's children throughout. Sara and her husband offered us Bulgarian Easter cake and juice, explaining that they are Muslim and don't drink. We sat down on wooden stools and an overstuffed couch, eating cake and drinking juice from small, decorated glasses.

Sara shared her concerns about her daughter Kristina's safety in school, where a boy had ripped her dress the week prior. "I might be a G*psy, but I don't want to raise my daughter in such an environment, I want to raise her in a normal environment. It is not really normal when things like that start to happen." She continued, "We want to stop this practice where they bribe us during every election for votes with fifty, maybe one hundred leva, and with sausages and music as well..." As she spoke, the music that Niki had organized was still blaring outside.

Niki hurriedly came to the door and told us that it was time to go. But before leaving, Petar looked at Sara and explained to her the importance of education, echoing standard EU Roma integration rhetoric: "If you give your children the right kind of education.... You need to send them to school, to learn and learn more, because this is the most important." Kristina's father looked at Petar in jaded disbelief. He explained that their son had finished high school with excellent marks and high hopes, but then he had to work as a day laborer because he couldn't find any steady work. "He wakes up at 6:00 in the morning and comes back home at 10:00 p.m., making ten leva each day."[33]

Petar nodded. "Because there is no industry now. What sector does he work in?" Sara explained, "He is good in everything, but mostly in computers.... When they see he is black (*cheren*)...when they see him, they just turn him down." Her husband added, "He needs to have money for breakfast. But what is he supposed to do by lunch, stay hungry? Why are they even learning in the first place if they can't get hired after finishing their education?"

Petar tried to interject with a personal story from his childhood. "I learned from my grandfather..." Sara interrupted him quickly: "So, tell me, what is this education for? There is no work. And they are racists when they hire someone. If they continue doing this, it will always just be the same." She took a breath, looked Petar in the eye, and repeated: "When they see he is black, they just turn him down."

Sara and her husband were explaining that efforts to integrate educational institutions do not carry over into hiring practices.[34] They took the time to convey their situation to Petar despite Sara's insistence that voting was not the answer and that the premise of democratic electoral politics could do nothing for them. Yet they wanted to host us in their apartment, to show us how they lived, and to recount for a few minutes what their lives were like to one politician who listened. Petar, for his part, was campaigning in a Romani neighborhood not in the expected way (by buying votes), but in what he had earlier described to me as a "European way." He wanted to connect with people, and this situation, on the couch, drinking juice, had seemed promising. But much as he tried, he seemed unable to hear them, talking over and past them instead.

Sara explained yet again the reason for her family's hardship: "There is no work. And sometimes they are racists when they hire someone. If they continue doing this, it will be all the same." Petar responded by waxing nostalgic for a better time: "We never really hated each other before, and it has never been [like] this." He tried to relate anti-Roma discrimination to electoral populism, saying, "I think at the moment this whole fake scenario with the hate is because it is just convenient, an opportunity, for some people."

Sara was not having it. "There is no work, no open positions anywhere. What are we supposed to do without work? I am just getting enraged because I can't raise my children properly because of this." Petar stumbled toward familiar, universalizing liberal rhetoric: "We are going to keep you safe from all that...because we are all Bulgarians down to the last one." But Sara continued, "And where am I supposed to get the money to pay my bills? They want me to pay for the water, for the electricity and the rest of the utilities...and, if other people are not working too, what are they supposed to pay with? If they had normal work, of course they would pay their bills. If there is no work for them, they just cut [the wires to tap into electrical lines]."

Petar was silent for a moment, and then Niki called for us again from outside the door. As he rushed to leave, Petar assured Sara, "Even if we don't win these elections, we will come here again, for sure." We walked down the stairs with Niki escorting us to ensure we did not end up in a neighbor's apartment, since most of Sara's neighbors were now waiting by their open doors to invite us inside. Once inside the car, it was suddenly quiet.

146   CHAPTER FOUR

After a few moments, Petar reflected on the experience and explained to me, in English, "This whole thing is really fucked up. Their apartment is like thirty-eight times cleaner than mine. But their building..." It was a socialist-era apartment building in which people took good care of their individual apartments, but no one was funding the repair, cleaning, or even lighting of the common spaces; it was likely that this had been the case since the early 1990s. It occurred to me that Petar had probably never expected Romani homes to be cleaner inside than they appeared outside. In fact, it might have been his first realization that Romani neighborhoods appear to be in decay mostly because the municipally owned buildings, streets, and other urban infrastructures are simply not kept up to livable standards despite relevant national and EU policies.[35]

Niki switched on the radio and told Petar our next stop on his campaign trail: a senior center in a majority-white area, where we would meet with elderly residents and provide them with actual sausages and beer. It was a rampant stereotype but also a very real part of many election campaigns in Bulgaria. Later that night, over dinner, Petar told me that it was hard to imagine change in the Romani neighborhood. Everyone there, including Petar, had believed that elections would do nothing for the residents. Petar had tried to promote a vision in which race played no role—"we are all Bulgarians down to the last one"—but away from the campaign trail, he told me that Bulgaria would never have a "clean" (chista) democracy. Instead, it would continue to propel itself forward by recycling former politicians and through continued disenfranchisement of potential Romani voters. As neighborhoods fell out of public concern, except to criminalize the people who lived there for populist purposes, residents like Sara focused on what they could: maintaining the insides of their homes and their ability to express their refusal to sustain so-called democratic politics to whoever would listen.

Petar naively insisted that Romani communities could leverage their votes for infrastructural improvements or focus on their education. His response to their own articulation of their positionality reiterated the buzzwords of liberal EU-sponsored notions of change: education, self-determination, pride, dignity, human rights. The most pervasive response to his visit was one in which Romani communities are well versed—a strategic disengagement born from disappointment and cynicism, in which voting makes no difference. Still, community members talked to Petar and invited him inside. I wouldn't call that hope, but it was, at least, an opening.

"Nothing Ever Changes"

As voting day in Fakulteta came to an end, I was tired but looking forward to discussing my experience with Rosa. She had long told me about how democracy had failed Romani communities in Bulgaria, such that election day was nothing new or remarkable. It was just another instance of democratic promises that are taken up as absurd, a "joke of a political system," as she and her neighbors called it. And like Sara, Rosa articulated that the only way to deal with such a system was to opt out, or laugh at its absurdity, or both. Diagnosing the absurd serves as a collective critique of the status quo that reveals part of what constitutes contemporary Romani politics. This diagnosis is in fact political because, in the terms of Audra Simpson, it "[imagines] how action will unfold" in relation to the distribution of power in order "to reach back to that distribution for a re-sort, but also for a push on what should be."[36] And it does so outside of the results-oriented lens with which international structures (like the European Union) validate what does and does not count as change.

International and national analyses of the 2011 elections concluded that election fraud had been widespread, especially considering mass anti-G*psy protests, intimidation, and imprisonment of Romani leaders in the days and weeks prior.[37] While these findings interpreted vote buying alongside intimidation and voter suppression as part of the larger structure of poverty and political manipulation, most white Bulgarians still see individual vote selling as the crime; they interpret the issue within a popular framework of perceived Romani criminality.[38]

As Roma are criminalized for allegedly selling votes, they are also criminalized through their waste labor. Both of these phenomena are needed by Bulgaria to meet its EU goals.[39] Like EU recycling initiatives, democratic elections in Bulgaria rely on Roma and their institutionalized infrastructural neglect and generalized poverty. Politicians pursue "the Roma vote," knowing, as I was told repeatedly, that it could swing an election. Romani votes are critical to sustaining Bulgarian liberal democracy that functionally fails them and that reinscribes the racialized power hierarchy in which they are at the bottom. Therefore, withholding a vote is in fact a move toward a redistribution of power, even if it is only temporary.

In response to the elections, Rosa compared the socialist past to the capitalist present in which Roma go through white Bulgarians' trash and clean the streets without getting paid on time. Sara articulated how hard it is to receive an education in a "free" Bulgaria and how, even with an education, one might never get hired because they are "black." The exact moments when democracy seems most tangible—in elections, campaigns, and the "free" capitalist labor market—make clear how Romani people are positioned as expendable if they refuse the role into which they have been cast. Their disposability comes to the fore, yet again, between elections when they are no longer deemed essential.

Furthermore, during election periods, state-sanctioned violence continues because the threat of Romani death wins votes. This trend is reinforced time and again as the Bulgarian political landscape turns even more nationalistic and the far right is increasingly perceived as centrist. Politicians view Roma, paradoxically, as both necessary and disposable. Moreover, their (necessary) votes are often won by the same politicians whose campaigns focus on their expendability and express disregard for their lives and their homes.

While Roma are portrayed in populist propaganda as "dirty" criminals that need to be cleaned out of Bulgaria, and from Europe, most of my interlocutors identified the true source of corruption as the stasis of Bulgaria's political system and the decades-long recycling of politicians it facilitated. Rosa told me, often: "Nothing ever changes." I heard the same sentiment from Fakulteta residents, activists, and waste workers alike. The system had changed, but they understood their positionality as one of stasis. As sweepers told me, "It's all the same, the work gets harder, but our job stays the same. Only the color of the uniform changes." They were expressing a common sentiment: No matter who is in charge, and no matter which party they might be affiliated with, the system remains.

When Petar visited the Romani neighborhood, he was part of this same failing system. His claims of doing something different, what he thinks is his liberal best, were met with sharp critique. He drew on well-trafficked EU ideals of how change should happen, through voting, education, and political representation, without acknowledging that these strategies had already failed his audience. The ideals and ideologies upon which

Europeanization depends are not the solution to the Roma's problems: These ideals are the problem now.

Romani communities acknowledge that the state and its politics are predicated on their racialization and exclusion; most would say they have never been adequately politically represented in Bulgaria.[40] But the state is not worth engaging, most of the time. People I met with told me they had been so repeatedly disappointed, that now they just expected the worst. However, as much as they insisted that they had given up, it seemed that they still found spaces, perhaps webbed crevices, among the democratic politics of the EU imaginary to create new avenues for incremental or transitory transformation. This is a form of politics that lies among but outside of liberal European normative frames. Some might term this a kind of "infrapolitics," along the lines of how James Scott describes "the active political life of subordinate groups [that] has been ignored because it takes place at a level we rarely recognize as political," or how Robin D. G. Kelley names "politics from below."[41] But their not voting, for example, is not so simply infrapolitical. I think anyone, including Petar, would acknowledge the blatant, out-loud politics of reckoning with the fact that there is no way to fight what Bulgarians call "the octopus" of their political system.[42] Yet people continue to build the social relationships and collectivities that emerge from such knowledge. Emergent Romani politics, then, inhabits thin slivers of possibility, outside of the "overly determined, effective capacity of the state," because the state's capacity isn't effective to begin with.[43]

Simon, along with Rosa, Sara, and many Romani activists and Sofia waste workers and residents I knew, would agree that neither the state nor democratic elections are the answer. When Simon and Maria organized the Sheraton protest, they made sure it was in fact not the state they were appealing to. It was a much more amorphous and all-encompassing European Union to which they addressed their refusal. And Sara, like Rosa, knew that the state and its representatives in elections couldn't solve their problems. After all, they suggested, why make the state the focus of their attention when it is such a joke to begin with?

In dismissing the possibility that Bulgarian politics could result in meaningful social change, my Romani interlocutors both acknowledge and reject the capacity of the Bulgarian state and democratic electoral politics altogether. They refuse to vote and refuse to believe politicians who come to them professing their dignity. Sometimes, like Sara, they invite a conversation, but other times they just walk away shaking their heads, knowing that it is not worth their time.

Many Roma reject Bulgarian politics as they know it while not completely giving up. They temporarily disengage or retreat from normative politics but also look for moments when it might be worth it to intervene, if only for a day. To remove oneself and one's community from institutional EU political machinations also creates the space for something else to take its place. When Rosa, Sara, and so many other Romani Bulgarians refuse democratic politics, they assert a different theory of change. They refuse to succumb to their circumstances; instead, they work, in Cathy Cohen's terms, "to create greater autonomy over one's life, to pursue desire, or to make the best of very limited life options."[44] The remaining chapters in this book turn to the resulting collective solidarities, structured by workplace friendships and material repair, that may not be explicitly political but facilitate a disruption of the status quo that, in the meantime, provides new regimes of value, meaning, and senses of possibility.

FIVE

Friendship

Most of the sweepers I worked with told me that they used to live a "normal life." By this, they meant that they had either stayed home to raise children or worked indoors as cleaners in offices or government buildings. Zlatna, like many of my colleagues on the team, recounted how she had been relatively middle class before. I often heard other people use "before" to mark a time before an immense political change, like the end of socialism in 1989 or EU accession in 2007, and I asked Zlatna what "before" meant for her. She explained that she saw the year delineating before from now as 2001, when Deyanova Mahala—the Romani neighborhood where she and more than half of the other sweepers on the team had lived, reared their children, and mourned their parents—had been razed.[1] That year, some 240 residents suddenly lost their homes.

A decade later, Zlatna and the rest of the sweeping team were responsible for cleaning the shiny new development that stands atop what was once Deyanova Mahala. BILLA, a massive Austrian-owned supermarket chain, is the anchor store, with bright yellow signage on a cherry-red metal roof. Pictures of yellow-and-red plastic shopping bags, floating pineapples and strawberries, and flying salty crackers frame the entrance. A giant yellow and red shopping bag spinning inside of a silver metal halo on a massive pole makes the store's presence visible from miles away.

In the expansive parking lot out front, round directional signs like those found throughout Europe indicate the flow of traffic. To the left of the supermarket stands a KFC, brand-new when I was there, complete with a drive-thru and plastic picnic-bench outdoor seating. To the right is a metro station where sweepers buy single cigarettes, bags of pretzel sticks, and thirty-cent espressos in plastic cups from the socialist-era kiosk in the underpass. In the mornings, we often gathered with the bosses—a sea of bright red uniforms—outside of BILLA to prepare for our day or sat on the curb where we would not be in anyone's way. During sweeping breaks on cold winter days, we sometimes would walk inside the big box store briefly to warm our hands and browse the aisles.

Before demolition, BILLA had offered meager compensation to some of the landowners in Deyanova Mahala on a haphazard basis, but those without valid deeds to their homes or legal personal identification cards were simply ordered to leave.[2] The Bulgarian Regulations for the Enforcement of the Municipal Property Act considers individuals "who have lived in non-inhabitable premises such as shacks, cellars, attics, etc. for not less than one year" to be in need of social housing.[3] But to be eligible for municipal housing under this act, people are required to show address registration documents proving that they had lived in Sofia for at least five years, something many residents of Deyanova Mahala could not do. One needs a permanent legal address to obtain registration (and personal ID) documents, trapping them in a catch-22 situation. As a result of residents' ambiguous status, they were forcibly removed from their homes and relocated to provisional train car housing, which remained as "temporary" accommodation for over a decade, on Europe Boulevard (*Bulevard Evropa*), the main thoroughfare between Bulgaria and the rest of Europe (crossing the Serbian border).[4] I remember some of my activist friends, including Simon, laughing at the irony of the street name, conjuring up an imagined greeting sign while joking, "Welcome to Europe."

Where they were resettled was more of a settlement than a neighborhood. It had no running water, no stable electricity source, and virtually no space between train car homes, which often resulted in deadly and devastating fires. When I visited in 2011, eleven years after this temporary housing was built, over thirty families still lived there. Some were employed by sweeping companies, but many had family-owned horse carts and worked as informal recyclers and waste scavengers. Still others had turned to alcoholism or other addictions, and nearly all residents were the targets of Bulgarian evangelical churches aiming to improve the community's spiritual conditions while they continued to wait for material improvements.[5] Other residents of Deyanova Mahala had moved in with friends and family or relocated to a falling-down communist-era apartment building serving as public housing, where Wonder Clean Sofia cleaned. Sweepers nicknamed this sweeping region, not just staffed by Roma, but where predominantly Roma lived, simply "the G*psies."

I imagined that it must be painful for Zlatna and her colleagues to clean the area around the supermarket on land where they once lived, and I asked for their thoughts on what I considered land dispossession and state-sanctioned violence. However, Zlatna, like most of the sweepers, just nodded and told me that she had become "used to it."[6] Besides, the sweepers said, they had no other choice—and the BILLA was a good place to warm your hands on a cold workday. The transformation of the site from home to supermarket to workplace was part of a larger life history in which landscapes once intimate are destroyed by forces beyond one's control and then become intimate again in new ways.

While BILLA was a reminder of what they had lost, most sweepers did not want to dwell on it. It was better to keep going and find ways to cope with the realities they faced in the present. As Zlatna explained to me many times, "It is our fate, that's all, and we move on." By "our," Zlatna referred to both her fellow street sweepers and also a larger Romani collectivity; there was common understanding among my interlocutors that Roma had been persecuted for centuries and that this persecution was ongoing and relentless.

Despite ongoing subjugation, "moving on" is a critical aspect of how Romani women transform their lives, living beyond what many Romani activists, residents, and waste workers described to me as "no life." For the Romani women sweepers I knew, moving on meant not so much stoically accepting their place in the waste-race nexus, but rather engaging in different kinds of creation, of making "something else" out of the conditions of the here and now. They remade the landscapes where they labored by remaking other things, buoyed by the intimacy of their shared labor: relationships, experiences, and ways of being in public space.[7]

One day, for example, as several sweepers stood in BILLA's fluorescent-lit entryway to warm up and avoid their bosses' surveillance, Donka and Rada pressed me, loudly, on the typical things they asked me when the day got boring: if I smelled "down there," or if the reason I slept so badly was because I desperately needed sex. Donka, a mother of two and grandmother of five, got louder and louder, smiling in response to the looks of horror she got from me, her shyer colleagues, and passersby. Donka and Rada reveled in their ability to take up public space and make people nearby uncomfortable, engaging in something like the "endless play" of confronting expectations of their racialized and gendered positionalities—in this case, the stereotype of Romani women as volatile, dependent, and hypersexual.[8]

They were also embarrassing me in part, as I understood it, to test my allegiances. Like other sweeping colleagues, they liked to loudly refer to me as "their American," showing me off to acquaintances along the work route: newspaper salespeople at sidewalk kiosks, local café owners, sweepers from other regions who passed through. It was clear that I was always an outsider, but they played with what it meant to have an American among them. When a crew from the national TV station came one afternoon to film us sweeping during the first snow of the winter, the reporter evoked racist Romani stereotypes by asking how many children sweepers had and whether they cleaned condoms off the street. Many of my colleagues, not wanting to be publicly shamed, ran beyond the camera's view. But Sofka, who was even more outspoken than Donka, put her broom down and stood in the center of the frame. The reporter asked if she shared food with the American. Sofka paused, looked straight into the camera, and declared, "We drink from the same water bottle." Sofka's assertion took aim at the knowledge that such bodily intimacy between a Romani cleaner and a white foreigner was transgressive in Bulgarian society. Her lightning-fast response both asserted the closeness of our relationship and refused the lens through which public forums tend to view Romani women, of which she was acutely aware. When the video later appeared on the evening news, featuring Sofka's interview, the voiceover focused on how an American girl had left her luxurious life in New York to sweep the streets of Sofia with Romani colleagues.

Romani women sweepers contend with the hypervisibility of "regulated nonnormative heterosexuality" through daily street harassment.[9] But instead of responding by trying to be invisible, Sofka, Donka, and other women sweepers I knew played with the stereotypes of hypersexual Romani women through a parodic excess. They catcalled white men, shouted about sexual desire on public buses, and performed white womanhood to parody it. In this way, they boldly assert their own uniformed presence and, at least momentarily, destabilize the racialized gender dynamics to which Romani women are routinely subjected. This play is part of broader strategies through which Romani women come together and refuse to be limited by the gendered racial logics designed to dehumanize them. They also do this by consoling one another in the wake of loss and, on International Women's Day, they did so by forging their own forms of communal celebration. Rather than accepting no life, street sweepers work to sustain their created lifeworlds and support each other in the process.

The solidarities generated through their friendships diagnose the absurdity of Europe's racializing logics. And their affective intimacy emerges through experiences of shared struggle and joy.[10] These deep-rooted friendships between sweepers are grounded in mutual responsibility, obligation, and love. At the same time, their friendships transgress many things: normative local expectations of family-based sociality and of spending most of one's time with in-laws and children, as well as the inherited narratives of kinship that are deeply embroiled in racist political and anthropological projects of Romani bloodlines, reproductive surveillance, and relational charts. As a result, sweepers' connections—their friendships and solidarities—generate their own kind of power.

As this chapter shows, sweepers' intimacies have the potential to create something new within the waste-race nexus, if not an avenue out of it. Furthermore, intimacy creates the conditions for "something else," an alternative future in which, through collectively disruptive solidarity, a different way of living might be possible.[11] And it does so as part of a broader Romani politics of refusal, alongside the subversions of surveillance and rejections of voting discussed in earlier chapters. This intimacy builds enduring relationships that reconstitute what being a person feels like amid white supremacist conditions naturalized as the European status quo. The friendships that sweepers cultivate while cleaning city streets may not seem conventionally political, but they enable women to outright reject society's suppression of their power by coexisting in and reproducing loving, kind, collaborative "otherwises"—different and better scenarios, over and over again.[12]

FIGURE 5.1 Friends Donka and Rada laughing on a break, with brooms and dustpans, the tools of their labor. Illustration by Izabela Ivanova.

Queens with Men's Hands

Ani and Mimi, the two middle-aged white Bulgarian bosses who surveilled sweepers' labor, constantly reminded them that they were there to work, not "to sit on benches and do whatever you want." Multiple times a day, Ani and Mimi yelled to whoever was in earshot, "You are not here to enjoy the outdoors, you are here to clean it." They would scold workers, telling them that they must not talk out of line or interrupt during roll call in the dark early morning hours before each sweeper was assigned their duties. In after-work walks to the bus stop, when I could catch Ani and Mimi alone, they told me they had to take on multiple jobs because this one did not pay enough, especially considering the challenges of managing "such women...[who] show no respect." But it was hard for me not to see their annoyance as self-serving, given that, as addressed in Chapter 1, Mimi also worked for a high-interest loan company that targeted sweepers, entrapping them into sometimes lifelong and even intergenerational debt. She benefited by exacerbating the servitude relations that sweepers entered when they began sweeping and by exploiting their low wages.

Ani and Mimi goaded me too, but it was different from the way they treated the Romani women on the team. Since I only worked part-time, I moved between established sweeping teams, filling in when someone was absent or a street was particularly dirty and needed an additional person to clean it. This meant that they sometimes made me work with the sweepers' husbands who swept while waiting for higher-paid positions on the backs of trucks to become available—jobs held almost exclusively by Romani men. When EU projects like wheelchair ramps and handicap-accessible elevators materialized, sweepers were tasked with preparing public space for the official ribbon-cutting ceremonies. Ani and Mimi knew that the team's work would be closely examined by the attending city officials, so they would remain nearby to ensure that the team met the municipal cleanliness standards.

One day in March 2012, our sweeping team was cleaning in preparation for the official opening of one of the newly accessible elevators at the BILLA metro station. Typically, cleaning work was done with a broom, but that day Ani and Mimi forced me to pick up cigarette butts on a large swath of grass by hand. After I returned to the barracks at the end of the day, sore and exhausted, the others on the team told me similar stories of pain and humiliation. Lilia, a great-grandmother and one of the oldest workers on the team, shared that she was once instructed to clean her work detail (*naryad*) until it was spotless, even if it got dark outside. She cleaned so thoroughly that she crawled down under a bush to collect the stray garbage that had gathered beneath it. When the boss drove by to let the workers go at the end of the day, releasing them with a quickly shouted "go home with your instruments," she was so deep in the bush that she could not hear him dismiss her.[13] She ended up working into the night, going home well after dark. It wasn't until she arrived at work the next morning to the laughter of her bosses that she realized she had taken their instructions more literally than they intended. I knew Lilia was trying to help me feel better, but such expressions of sympathy always made me feel worse since I knew I would soon leave the job and return to my graduate student life, whereas my colleagues were bound to the workplace.

Sweeping can be humiliating, especially when working under white bosses who can impose their will at any time. The labor also takes its toll on the body. When I began sweeping, I could not help talking about how painful it was. The skin on my face was sunburned and chapped from exposure, my hands blistered and bled, and my back ached so much each night that it was hard to sleep. The women on my team would ask me how sweeping was in New York, where I was from. "There's poor and middle class and rich there too, but the workers who do this job make much more money than you," I told them. Donka nodded and said, "Well, here, the rich just think about themselves. Nobody considers us. And now from day one you're working extremely hard." The others in the group agreed.

Neli, who had been standing quietly nearby, piped up: "Ask Boyan to show you *his* hands." How calloused someone's hands were served as a sign of how hard they worked. Boyan, who, readers will recall, was the manager who secured my employment "in," spent his time in the driver's seat of a Jeep surveilling their labor, so Neli knew that his hands would be softer than the women's. "Your hands, they are soft, you haven't worked in a while," Donka told me as she looked at my open palms. Neli leaned over and touched my not-yet-calloused hands. "I was also like that at the beginning," she recounted. "Your hands are softer, but now our hands are hard, like men's."

When sweepers talked about the difficulty of their work, or my inability to sweep as well as them, they would often allude to both the power and shame of having "man hands." The phrase shows their critical attention to how sweeping transforms the body into a gendered tool for labor. It also highlights how ingrained gender dynamics play out through the bodily transformative potential of sweeping—"man hands" are both more powerful than "woman hands" and an index of the psychic and physical toll of waste work. Mingled with the pride and humor of "man hands" was a profound sense of loss. Efforts to reclaim an idealized and unobtainable femininity ran deep throughout team members' discussions, and many sweepers saw their jobs as a transition from a prework self to a differently gendered personhood. They expressed nostalgia for the time before they swept, when they still had "woman hands."

However, even these imagined woman hands of a former life are somewhat fantastical. Most workers had been cleaning tirelessly at home since before they were married, often since the age of nine or ten. Many sweepers recounted to me, often regretfully, that they never got educated because they were taking care of the house and their siblings while their parents worked. And Romani homes, as I witnessed and they told me, "are spotless—not like how Bulgarians live." Many of my colleagues were in their thirties or early forties when I worked with them in 2012, meaning they were of domestic caretaking age right around the time of Bulgaria's "changes" in 1989. Even before the 1990s, many families relied on their children for caretaking while parents worked in state socialist factories or other professions. This meant that the generation of Romani women with whom I swept typically could read and write but called themselves "illiterate" (*negramotni*) since they did not learn such skills in school. It also meant that they had entered Bulgaria's labor force in the 1990s while their young husbands struggled to find work. During that decade, many construction projects that had promised employment to uneducated men as builders quickly shut down when funding dried up due to Bulgaria's inflation crisis. Many sweepers identified this period as the hardest, when their husbands developed anxiety and chronic stress-related illnesses. The result was that Romani women became heads of households, both working outside of the house to provide financially and doing most of the caretaking labor at home.

After lunch one day, as the bosses called roll and read out our assignments, Zlatna smiled at me. We were assigned together to clean a big boulevard, one of the main arteries of the city, commonly called Tsaritsa Yoanna (Queen Yoanna). The sweepers simply called it *Tsaritsata*, The Queen. The Queen was one of the major thoroughfares in the area we worked and, according to municipal protocols, should be cleaned every day. Zlatna laughed. "Now we are queens, with crowns on the intersections, right, Elanka?" I looked at her, unsure of how to respond. "What?" I did not understand the linguistic play on the name of the boulevard. "We are queens now, so where is your crown?" Zlatna replied, laughing at the confusion on my face. In hindsight, I understood her joke as an acknowledgment that Bulgarian society was built upon the denial of Romani dignity: Roma would never be queens, but they would sweep The Queen's dirt.

Sweepers would often joke that their white bosses might as well be their pimps, for they were basically just "street workers," paid in cash. The cash that each worker was paid, in a white envelope monthly, was both coveted and a source of shame for many sweepers. Wonder Clean Sofia paid less than competing firms and did not offer benefits like food coupons or as many paid holidays, but the tradeoff of being paid in cash prevented sweepers in debt from having their paychecks turned over to the bank. When the paper bills were handed out in personalized envelopes at my first payday, my colleagues fanned themselves with the cash and told me that it was like they were "cheap prostitutes or strippers."

Maya, who was about my age and was sweeping with us on The Queen that day, appreciated the value of a good joke. At one point, she looked in my direction and said, "I mean, we are so beautiful in these uniforms, we might as well make some extra money working these streets." She lifted the baggy pant leg of her bright red uniform to reveal a bare calf. "Come on, sexy ladies, let's go from the boulevards to the highway and make the real money." Zlatna and the older women on the team laughed. It was a common stereotype that Romani women worked as prostitutes

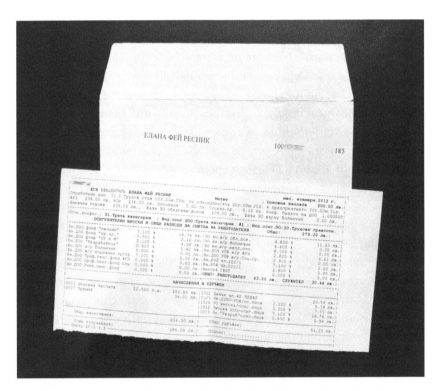

FIGURE 5.2 Payday envelope of cash, with a breakdown of how the salary was calculated. Photo by the author.

along Sofia's ring road, a highway that encircled the whole city and divided urban space from the industrial zone. It also skimmed the edges of Filipovtsi, where many sweepers on the team lived, and we all knew how uncomfortable it could feel standing there, even just waiting for a bus. Bulgarians commonly joked about what they could pick up by driving in slow traffic along the ring road.

Such banter hit upon deep, ambivalent feelings about womanhood and waste labor. Maya's joke substituted one version of gendered social marginality (street sweepers treated as trash) with another (ring road prostitutes) to play upon ideas of desirability and beauty—something that sweepers described themselves as having lost. In other, quieter times, sweepers made it clear that jokes about prostitution also reflected anxiety about their visibility and vulnerability at work, as well as how hard they strove to maintain self-respect amid the job's dirt.[14] Many women, including Zlatna, told me that although they were accustomed to working outside, the job was dehumanizing. Except for Desi, their white Bulgarian colleague who wore an adult diaper to avoid urinating outdoors, the team regularly had to pee on the streets like "stray bitches," as they joked, since the company did not provide restrooms and most stores (except, sometimes, BILLA) prohibited their using public bathrooms. In addition, a wave of anti-Roma attacks occurred in the area around this time. Sometimes, sweepers had to manage people screaming obscenities and threatening violence as they worked.

Joking, however, was not only a refuge from such travails but also a pleasure in its own right. Workers on the team explained that they loved working with Donka because life was long and hard, and they needed to laugh—something she made easy. One warm October day, I was sweeping in a team of five, along with Hristina, Raya, Jesus, and Donka. Our lunch break was over, and we had two hours left in the workday until we would reconvene for roll call before being released to go home. But with only about a block left to sweep, we knew we could, and should, move slowly. We always needed to appear to be working in case one of the bosses or a municipal inspector came to check on us. If they knew we had finished early, we would just be given more work to do to fill the time until the end of the workday.

While we walked along the road, Raya ran ahead to see what was in a large metal municipal waste bin behind BILLA. Donka yelled after her, telling her to grab the apples dangling from a tree branch over the

CHAPTER FIVE

sidewalk. "What am I, your pet squirrel?" Raya retorted. She reached deep into the metal dumpster with one arm, holding the frame with the other so she would not fall in. A moment later, she emerged holding a white leather purse with shiny silver-toned metal clasps and a bundle of blond hair wrapped in tissue paper.

"Raya, what on earth have you brought us?" Donka shouted, pointing to the hair. "You know, people are really buying these," I intervened. Hristina responded slowly, "Yes, yes, I know. But I don't know what kind of hair this is, I'm scared. Can you recognize it? I don't know who it belongs to or where it is from. Throw that away!" Eyeing the white bag slyly, Donka picked it up. "Look what I found ..." Hristina interjected, "And it's a nice one, on top of that.... Do you know how much money you can make from that?"

As we passed the purse around, considering its potential market value, Donka grabbed the silky hair from the ground where Raya had thrown it. Quietly, she attached it to her head with the elastic band that held her own sun-bleached, dyed-red hair. She resumed sweeping with exaggerated movements that made the ponytail sway side to side. Raya threw the handbag to Donka who placed it on the crook of her arm daintily, as though going to a ladies' lunch, then continued to sweep. We laughed as Donka pranced, exaggeratedly impersonating the imagined owner of the found goods: a blond woman who would flitter around the street, calling attention to herself and her white handbag on a Tuesday afternoon. We all recognized the stereotype: Donka was impersonating a *kifla*. This word for a sweet, crescent-shaped baked good, readers will recall, is used colloquially to denote a well-off and materialistic girl who is distinctively Bulgarian, blond, and unmarked as white (not Roma).

That the items with which Donka performed were someone else's trash was part of the joke. The sweepers knew all too well that the trash we cleaned mostly came from white Bulgarians, and they often remarked about the waste as leftovers—what I called in my notes an "index"—of a life that has already been lived. White Bulgarians have the privilege of avoiding the afterlife of consumption, but Romani waste workers do not. Donka's jokes suggested that recovering waste is, in a way, a resurrection. Donka was imagining the past life of trash and animating that trash to resurrect a *kifla*. While Donka would rarely have such close personal contact with a white Bulgarian woman, the "public reproductive labor" of street sweeping connects her with such women's detritus.[15]

If we think about humor as rooted in the element of surprise, Donka surprised via material juxtapositions—her red uniform and Romani womanhood at odds with the *kifla* hair and bag.[16] She both mocked white womanhood and played with claiming it, refusing to unambiguously embody the service work sweepers do. Humor is often defined as a subversion of traditional categories. But in contexts where "nothing is disrupted," jokes can function as "agents of conformity."[17] Donka's performance with trash brings attention to both the enduring strength of hierarchized racial and gender categories and the potential to denaturalize them by underscoring their absurdity. There is a greater subversion at work too. The joke takes the practice of collecting other people's trash and turns it into play, entertainment, joy, and unruliness, all while on the job.

Donka's joke cut in particularly transgressive ways as she diagnosed the absurd.[18] Donka's embodied parodic performance, crossing both racial and class lines, points to how race and class are already gendered; Romani women's racial identity is encoded into their gendered class performance.[19] The significance of Donka's performance may be understood in its contrast with the recurring TV character Lyuba-the-G*psy—a white man parodying a Romani woman (discussed in Chapter 4). While Lyuba naturalizes white Bulgarians' fears of Romani "overpopulation" through comedy, Donka's performance parodies white womanhood. In doing so, it draws attention to the coupling of whiteness and class-based femininity, showing it for what it is: constructed yet powerful, even as it is absurd and laughable.

———

Returning to the barracks later that day, we hoisted our sweeping instruments (broom and dustpan, or *farazh*) onto the bus, as we often did. But the ticket controller, who circulated between buses checking and punching tickets, told us we weren't allowed on without tickets— something the company never provided to its workers. We complained but ultimately got off and waited a long time for another bus without a controller on it to arrive. When we finally climbed on, Hristina seemed actively bored. She looked around, then began to boisterously expound upon what she thought I wanted in a man. Laughing, she asked whether I wanted "some chocolate," and when I did not answer, continued, "The American, our American, likes herself some chocolate, if you know what I mean." The bus got quiet. "Some smooth, dark chocolate is what she wants, isn't that right, Elanke?" she said, using an affectionate diminutive form of my name. "You like it dark, don't you?" I looked at her and smiled, not liking to be the center of attention but wanting to support her public display. "Or maybe some milk chocolate? What is it today, our American?" I began to feel the sensation of shared power bubbling up and remained quiet. I was used to playing the team's comedic foil. Frustrated after the long wait, Hristina was going to say what she wanted, asserting her presence and letting everyone know she had just as much right to occupy public space as anyone else, while also acknowledging the transgression involved.

Hristina's teasing also got at the heart of a core part of racialization in Bulgaria: colorization.[20] Among Romani women, whiteness was esteemed and a constant point of discussion. They would often remark that I could easily pass as Roma because their children were "even whiter" than me. When I complained about my single status, they comforted me by saying that most men desired a "white bride," so it would not be a problem. How Romani racialization as nonwhite intersected with other racial systems (like the American one, for example) was also a constant source of debate. Ideas of who could pass, as what, and in what spaces, were key to how sweepers understood not only race but their place in the world. Most sweepers explained that they worked on the street because they were "black G*psies." "The white ones," they told me, typically worked indoors at the mall or cleaning hotels. They explained that, if I needed money enough, it was fine to clean with them. But I was white enough that I could work inside a café or luxury hotel where I'd receive tips.

The sweepers continued to engage the stereotypes commonly attributed to Romani women that day, with Donka taking the lead. After we got off the bus, we still had some time to kill until roll call, so we sat atop our brooms on the sidewalk, watching people walk by. Emboldened, we commented about everyone we saw. There were old men we ignored, elderly women out shopping, kids dashing past—then Donka saw a man about my age in a tight black Diesel T-shirt and screamed out, "Hey, sexy, we like how you walk in that shirt! I have some American stuff for you right here." He looked around, unsure who was screaming. Donka looked at him directly. "YOU, I'M CALLING YOU." I laughed and, continuing to play it straight against Donka's bravado, ran away. The man turned red in the face as Donka and the other women laughed. Hristina's whole body was shaking, and Raya hid behind her hair and slapped the ground. I waited until the man was out of sight to return. Eventually, we picked up our brooms, figuring it was about time for roll call and release. We fell silent when we saw the bosses waiting, having come by to check that we didn't leave our work detail early—which, of course, we had.

The workspace enabled an intimate solidarity that was powerful; it helped workers garner the confidence to go so far as to yell at white men walking by. When Donka addressed the man in the tight T-shirt, she used the collective "we," stressing "*we* like how you walk." It might just seem like a group of women bored at the end of the workday, which maybe it was. But it also instigated an effervescent group intimacy that allowed Donka to mock the absurdity of their situation, aloud, for passersby to witness and deal with.

Sweepers are aware that these ways of playing with their public misrepresentations and stereotypes of their hypersexuality could trigger popular ideas about Romani women and overpopulation, which have become mainstream as politicians use demographic fears ("Roma will outnumber Bulgarians in the next twenty years") to garner support. Politicians and their propaganda explain that Romani women and their predilection for having children represent the quintessential hindrance to European progress in Bulgaria. Even seemingly progressive Bulgarian professors would tell me that "according to scientific data," "there would soon be more Roma than Bulgarians in their country" and they would become "the minority."

Here we can recall "Lyuba-the-G*psy." When the census taker goes to her house, he asks: "How many people live here?" Lyuba, a white man in "G*psy" drag, responds, twirling her long hair around her finger, "Ohhh, wait, I have to see…. Do you know how long I've tried to count but it just doesn't happen?" The camera pans to the audience, where a white woman is laughing. Lyuba continues, "They hide under the beds, under the fridge. Do you know how rude they are?" The white census taker chuckles and gestures toward Lyuba's protruding belly, "I see you are expecting." Lyuba rubs her stomach and replies, "I am, I am." The census taker asks if it is a boy or a girl. Lyuba tells him that it is a boy and that the doctor announces, "We need to name him Louis." There is a pause for the joke.

The census taker asks why. "Because he is the fourteenth," Lyuba responds, straight-faced.

The census taker remains serious, looking down at his clipboard. "Yes, but here in this column I have to write how many children you have." Lyuba shrugs and waves her hand nonchalantly, saying, "You write whatever you want." She begins to count with her fingers, as though trying to keep track of her children: "I have four from my first marriage, I have four from the second marriage, and three are mine personally." The studio audience, most of whom appear to be white women, laugh at this joke that three are hers "personally," suggesting both that she doesn't understand how procreation works and that there is no father responsible for them. The census taker looks down. "Apparently you give birth to a lot of children…" Lyuba interrupts with a wave of the hand. "A lot, but I have lots more to go…"

FIGURE 5.3 Protest T-shirt on a man sleeping in the Sofia University metro station: "I don't want to live in a g*psy state." Photo by the author.

This broadcast television representation rings funny for its white audience because of widespread fears of Romani overpopulation that structure everyday life in Bulgaria. These are the same tropes that link Roma with waste itself. In front of another television camera, when Sofka highlights sharing her water bottle with me, the white American ethnographer, she preempts the commonplace understanding that Roma, like the waste they collect, are superfluous, excessive, and frustratingly overabundant. Announcing that she shares the same bottle with "the American" while staring directly at the camera, she flips the question and, at least momentarily, rejects the assumption of her disposability.

Transforming Tears into Work

Amid pervasive racism, Donka yelled the loudest and laughed the hardest. However, the Donka who found joy with her colleagues at work was quite different from the Donka I visited after work at her home. The first time she invited me over, Rada met me at the bus stop and walked me through Filipovtsi's muddy streets to Donka's small, tidy, and perfectly arranged home. Embroidered cloths rested under glass figurines, and a freshly scrubbed patterned pastel rug covered the uneven parquet floor. Donka sat me down on a wooden stool at her kitchen table. She laid out a placemat, napkin, soup spoon, and porcelain bowl with flowers on the rim and then served me meatball soup from a big pot on the coal-burning stove. She sat beside me on another stool, cutting me pieces of fresh bread and repeatedly asking if she could fill my bowl. She explained that her daughter could run across the street and get me a soft drink or Nescafé if I wanted. Once she decided I was settled, she moved to the couch where her husband was half asleep, giving me space as she watched me eat. Donka's husband had severe health issues that prevented him from working. He received a hundred or so leva (sixty-two dollars) every month in disability benefits. Her children and grandchildren, who also lived with her, relied on her income for food, clothing, heat, electricity—for every basic need.

After her boisterous daily interrogations about my sex life, it was unnerving to see Donka as a traditional homemaker, occupying in earnest a version of the femininity she satirically performed on the street. But this was her life at home. While home can serve as a respite from the everyday experiences of environmental degradation for many Romani waste workers, it also comes with its own set of gendered expectations.

Only in the workplace did she have the space to demand that I teach her obscenities in English, so she could try out screaming them at her colleagues in the middle of a public park, checking to make sure she was pronouncing them correctly. On another morning, Donka explained that instead of crying about her problems, she sweeps, or, as she put it, she transforms her tears into labor. She did not see this as unique. For many workers, she said, sweeping is a form of emotional catharsis, a way "not to go crazy at home." Tears are not to be avoided but worked through with bodily labor, even when that labor might transform the body in ways that render it unrecognizable. Despite their bosses' surveillance, many of the women described the workplace as relaxing, since the repetitive motion of sweeping, as well as time outdoors, could help to "soothe nerves." What's more, work was a place where the women could distance themselves from family obligations and find new relationships that their neighborhoods did not typically afford. Female solidarity at work helped sweepers regain calm and control, even while facing challenges that could seem insurmountable.

Many of the sweepers were mothers, grandmothers, and, like Donka, the sole income earners for large extended families. But even women with more familial support spoke of their persistent nervousness. Valya, a twenty-year-old who typically talked on the phone with headphones while sweeping, regularly brought her husband and children to payday. She explained that her husband was her best friend, and her face lit up every time she talked about him. Life at home was good, she said, although money was a problem, especially when payday was delayed, as it often was. She worried constantly about keeping her family well fed, her home clean, and her kids in school. She told me that her friends had started taking medicine, both herbal and prescribed, to deal with their nervousness, and she wondered if that could help her.

The women on the team were constantly dealing with bills that they could not pay. Some had lost their electricity long ago, so they made do without, living in darkness and warming their homes with wood or coal-burning stoves. Neda, one of the oldest women on the team, had not had electricity in months. She told me one day while sweeping that she needed to close her eyes for a bit because she was so tired. During the night, she forced herself to wake up every hour to light a match and check a battery-powered watch, to make sure she wouldn't be late to work and lose her much-needed job. Neda's husband was paralyzed and could not work. She was raising her teenage grandson so his mother could work abroad.

When husbands and children fell sick or were involved in tragic accidents, sweepers had fragile safety nets. One morning, our typically good-humored colleague Kali arrived at work shaking. Since there was not enough money at home to pay the electricity bill, her twelve-year-old son had offered to climb a pole and connect a neighbor's electrical line directly to their home. However, he fell from the pole and was electrocuted on his way down. Luckily, he survived both the electrocution and the fall, but his hand was badly burned and he had gone to the hospital for emergency surgery. Now he couldn't move his arm, and though she wasn't sure what to do and was racked with worry, she had to leave him alone at the hospital and come to work. Otherwise, she would be fired.

Another sweeper on the team, Ivanka, went through a long and difficult period after her son was taken into custody by the police and incarcerated for a crime he did not commit, leaving his wife and young children at home. It was obvious to everyone I spoke to that the authorities had presumed him to be criminal because he was a Romani man. This was a common scenario across Bulgaria, as described by the 2011 judgment of the European Court of Human Rights in a case about the police raid of a Romani household (*Lingurar v. Romania*): The authorities "automatically connected ethnicity to criminal behavior."[21] Public officials often pushed Romani citizens' concerns to the bottom of their rosters, and the state-appointed attorney for Ivanka's son seemed to be doing the same. Ivanka kept her phone with her at her all times, waiting and hoping the lawyer would call. She was uncertain about what was happening with her son's case, and no one knew when he would come home. In the meantime, she went to work each day and relied on her colleagues for support and camaraderie. They checked on her continuously, asking her how she was and reminding her to eat, not to just nervously smoke all day. The friendship of the other sweepers, she told me, kept her alive. "We are around each other all day. There's nothing to keep from each other...and tomorrow we are here again, so what could we even hide?"

The intimacy of the workplace, as Ivanka explained it, was both emotional and embodied. If one of them lacked food, other sweepers would share theirs: "If it's only half-loaf bread, we are both going to eat it." After all, "tomorrow is another day" and nobody knows what it will bring. Working with her colleagues, moving beyond her family networks at home, was important for Ivanka's survival. "When I'm having a hard time and I can't keep it in myself anymore, I tell it to my colleagues, and then I feel better." Their friendship transformed her individual pain into something collectively shared. "If it wasn't for these women, I'd die," she told me as we worked. "When we sweep, I go up one side of the street and they go up the other. When we meet on the way, in the middle, they tell me, 'Don't cry, Ivanke, don't be angry. Look at you, you'll get sick.' And I know that this is hard for every mother." I nodded. "This is a mother's child," she continued, "you can't ever stop thinking about your child, even if he is in jail, because he's a part of you." I nodded again, feeling the pain in her voice and realizing that, not yet a mother myself, I could not understand fully. But her colleagues were also mothers. They understood and empathized, sometimes even crying with her, as they met up between work duties throughout the day.

Ivanka told me that she was helped most by Petya, whom she had first met on the job when their bosses assigned them to sweep together one day. "Petya, the blond one...you know her?" I knew her well. Petya's son had been killed when he was seventeen years old, and years later, as Ivanka summed up, "no one knows anything about it still." Petya had spoken with me about her son at length. At her house, she showed me photo books of him, along with photos of her other son's wedding where her husband refused to dance in honor of his deceased son. He still won't dance, Petya's young daughter explained to me. I slept there that night, and before we fell asleep, Petya's daughter told me about the brother she barely remembered but who she knows was killed, wanting to make sure I knew his name. She passed me a square of her chocolate bar and reminded me that a bit of chocolate before bed helps ensure sweet dreams.

———

One day, while sweeping as an assigned team of three, Ivanka and Petya told me about their bond. "We sat down, and we really talked to each other," Ivanka recalled, "and she's looking at me smoking, and she's like, 'Stop smoking. If you were in my place, you would die. And you're so young, Ivanke.'" Ivanka recounted Petya's advice. "'Stop for a moment, remember that your son has two children. So, you must pay attention to those children as well, to take care of them.'" Ivanka took a sip of her strong coffee, her hand shaking, and nodded. "She's right. So, I went home, and that's that. I was looking out the window, alone at home, with my husband. I needed to take the grandkids outside still. Children are children, they can't always stay inside with me.... 'We are going to the [supermarket] Fantastiko,' they told me, so I told them, 'Okay,' and I gave them fifty stotinki to buy Coca-Cola. And then I stayed home, looking out the window and thinking of what she told me. And I knew Petya was right."

Petya talked to Ivanka a lot about life and death as they worked. Ivanka recalled, "'He's alive, Ivanke,' she told me. 'It doesn't matter that he's in jail. It doesn't matter when, a year will pass, two, three, four, five, twenty, then he'll come back.'" Ivanka accepted Petya's words. "I need to be careful so something doesn't happen to me, she told me. Because we work on the road and I really thought about what she said—I thought, she's right." Working on the roads was dangerous. Each sweeper regularly had to sign and renew legal documents absolving the company from responsibility in case they are injured on the job. Though the sweepers were often the sole income providers for entire extended families, they rarely expressed worry about getting hit by a car. They only brought up their need to be vigilant on the road in moments of crisis and death.

Ivanka continued, "[Petya] told me, 'One way or another, he's going to come back. So, you will fight. You will pay if you have to. You'll give as

FIGURE 5.4 Sweeping a major boulevard during rush hour. Still image from film footage by Bojina Panayotova.

much as you can give, and he'll come back to you.'" She looked at me. "So now, it's been three days since she told me those words and honestly, I feel so much better." I looked into Ivanka's eyes and saw that just talking about it provided some relief. "What time is it?" she asked. It was ten minutes to 2:00 p.m., which meant the workday was nearly over. Ivanka's eyes were red, but she smiled for the first time all day.

"Have you visited him?" I asked. She looked down, and I regretted the question immediately. "I don't have the courage, you know, the strength to see him like that," she said. "That's that. I don't have that courage. His father went to see him with my son's wife and his children." I nodded, imagining how painful it would be. I acknowledged that it must be very difficult to even find the time given her grueling work schedule. Ivanka agreed. She looked at me and told me that her head hurt. I had the feeling I should change the subject.

After thinking for a moment, she announced, "One day, before I die, I want to go somewhere, to travel, to go by foot. I would love that a lot." I asked what she meant. "To leave everything behind and just go away for a little," she continued, and then trailed off. Ivanka dreamed of escape but knew it would be impossible. Her family relied on her to survive.

Ivanka's son was still in prison when I left the sweeping crew in 2013. Her sadness, fear, and anger had not abated. But every day, she updated her closest friends at work on the status of her son's case and was bolstered by Petya's tireless support. They lived in different neighborhoods, their friendship forged on the job, but they had lived through similar circumstances. They endured labor that physically pained and at times humiliated them, but they made it through both work and life with respect created in common.[22] Individual pain became something to be lived through together. Intimate friendships transformed sadness, isolation, and fear into the shared experience of communal struggle, while making space to acknowledge the institutional issues that necessitated this struggle in the first place.

Ivanka told me that Donka's humor paled in comparison to what Petya could provide, and that she tended to stay quiet when Donka teased her. But for other sweepers, the ability to turn hardship into humor was just as crucial for connection as frank conversations about life. In both modes, sweepers collectively produce alternative ways of being amid conditions of no life. They create something else in which life is charged with the slight possibility for a future that is markedly different from their here

FRIENDSHIP 173

and now. That shared, cathartic power, which seemed almost alchemical, was made from the toil of daily life and transformed the workplace into a source of strength for many sweepers, however temporary it was.

At work, there were no needy children, unemployed husbands, or demanding mothers-in-law. Women could move with relative independence, smoke openly, take breaks when they wanted, enjoy each other's company, and only worry about feeding themselves and finishing their work detail. I would rush to make it to work on time each morning only to find that my colleagues were there ahead of me, already laughing and talking in the pitch black before dawn, drinking sweet coffee from plastic cups and waiting for the bosses to appear. Some of them arrived as much as an hour and a half early, which they told me was because they "didn't want to be late for the bosses." But they also told me that they enjoyed that time together as a group of women who, for the moment, did not need to report to anyone or be responsible for more than themselves.

The women formed workplace friendships, intimate solidarities that allowed them to change how they took up urban space. These solidarities led to humorous play on the bus and in the street and helped them to sustain one another in hard times, allowing workers to claim life in the face of no life. Their workplace friendships provide the space to stop for a minute and share what it's like to experience the loss of a child, whether to prison or death, while still having to keep "moving on." They turn the public space of the street into a place for negotiating close relationships—relationships that could *only* happen while at work on the street. These were the same streets where they alternatively were humiliated and feared violence.[23]

Cocktails Instead of Brooms

Once a year, for International Women's Day on March 8, sweepers told me they got the chance to live "like regular women." They said that sweeping had made them lose their femininity, but for one night, they celebrated one another *as* women. Dating back to a 1910 women's conference in Copenhagen, International Women's Day was established as an official Bulgarian holiday in 1945, soon after the Bulgarian Communist Party took power. Today, it is one of the most celebrated holidays in Romani communities in Bulgaria, observed by nearly all Romani women regardless of their religious background.[24]

174   CHAPTER FIVE

Immediately after the New Year, sweeping teams begin pooling money to reserve a table at one of Sofia's nightclubs on March 8. In preparation for the celebration, women buy new outfits and jewelry, and, since this might be the one night of the year when they can escape from family responsibilities, chip in for bottles of fruity alcohol. During the year that I swept, Rada, who was organizing the festivities, could only get a March 7 reservation at Onyx, a nightclub that hosted most International Women's Day events for Romani women's work teams (nearly all sweepers), so that's when the group would celebrate. As the day approached, I made plans to go home with Rada after work to get ready for the celebration, and to sleep there afterwards.

Work on the seventh seemed unending. That day, as we were cleaning in preparation for the opening of the new metro station elevator outside BILLA, Mimi explained that we would work "until you finish...whatever time that will be." She surveilled our labor with a warning: "You should work hard today instead of talking. When I tell you so, only then can you talk." I had been assigned to sweep with Viktor and Tosen, husbands of two other sweepers, and they told me to ignore Mimi. As they watched some passersby at the crosswalk, they warned, "If they see us here at the traffic light, they might think we were taking a break or making love or whatever." I rolled my eyes. I was used to these jabs and had learned that the most effective way to deal with them was to threaten to tell their wives later. But other remarks were more disturbing. Tosen warned me, "Those people are racist; if they see you with us, they might think you are a G*psy too, and you might get beaten." I nodded, at first unsure if he was serious, but then they explained that they had seen a news report about a murder that had happened in the area the day before, allegedly committed by a seventeen-year-old skinhead.

During our discussion, we looked up, and there was Mimi, standing next to me, smoking, and pointing to where we should clean next. She looked at me closely. "Come on, girl, you didn't learn at all to do this sweeping job properly.... You don't finish at all where you started. You need to finish the place where you started first before you move on." I nodded, still sweeping, trying to end the conversation as soon as possible. She continued, "You should put more effort into sweeping, so you can gather everything. Do you have work gloves? Whatever can't be swept away, use the gloves and remove it with your own hands." Most workers were never provided gloves, but I was given an oversized pair to use that day. My anger was boiling up, but I got down on my hands and knees and did as I was told.

The moment Mimi walked away, Tosen instructed me to stand up. "Don't touch it with your hands, even in gloves. I don't understand why that woman wants you to crawl on the ground picking up cigarette butts." It wasn't the first time it had happened. Viktor looked at Tosen and said, "That woman was harassing her because she doesn't hold the broom right." Tosen looked at me empathetically. "What does that supervisor know? She was telling you that you are not sweeping right, but she most probably doesn't know how to do it right either." I was angry. Viktor encouraged me. "Come on, Elanka, show us you can!" He joked, trying to make the mood lighter, "No one is slacking on my watch!" I gave in and laughed. But I was relieved when the day ended and I could return to the barracks, where other women gave me their support and where Rada was waiting for me to take the bus to her home together.

As soon as we got home and washed our hands, Rada served us bread and cheese and tomatoes. Then, she called one of her neighbors to come over and straighten my hair with a clothing iron. She assessed my all-black outfit and lent me big hoop earrings that were more sparkly than anything I owned. Her teenage daughter and husband laughed at us as we got dressed, but Rada told them to shut up, because this night was important. "For one night a year," she told me, "we are women." She had been preparing for International Women's Day for months. Over the last few weeks, she and the other sweepers had discussed what to wear, how to do their hair, and what they would drink. Rada explained that she bought a new outfit for the holiday every year. The rest of the time, her money went to supporting her husband's travel back and forth to his job in the Czech Republic, her daughter's clothing and makeup needs, her son's schoolbooks, household electricity and coal for heat, and her parents' medicine. But for International Women's Day, she took time for herself to dress up and wear something new. While she did her hair, she told me to look through her pictures from previous years' celebrations. As I flipped through the well-preserved pages of her photo album, I saw a smiling, carefree-looking young woman change over time to the still-young but now worried mother and responsible caretaker Rada had become.

We got ready quickly, then gathered with others from the sweeping team outside Rada's house to wait for taxis, most of which were driven by neighbors. During the ride, we checked our hair and makeup in our phones and laughed, realizing that we seemed like teenagers. We had each paid a cover charge of twenty leva for Onyx, but since that only covered food and soft drinks, everyone had stashed various types of alcohol in their purses, mostly small plastic bottles of apple-flavored vodka that would mix easily with whatever Onyx provided.

When we arrived, Onyx was filled with sweeping teams from across Sofia, each at a separate table. The sweepers on my team told me, "We are the blackest of the sweepers. Over there are the blonds; they sweep the center of Sofia." I nodded, as this division had been much discussed. The tables had traditional Bulgarian tomato-cucumber-cheese (*shopska*) salads at each place setting, along with big bottles of Fanta and Coca-Cola. There were neon green lights and poles for dancing. Pink and red balloons were tied to chairs and attached to the ceiling, where disco balls

FIGURE 5.5 Inside Club Onyx for International Women's Day celebrations. Photo by the author.

revolved in circles. As the women took their places and poured drinks, a DJ played music and called out to each team by name, prompting each group to scream and cheer in recognition.

The women on our team laughed, drank, ate, smoked cigarettes, and cried with joy and release. It was as though all the pent-up sadness, fear, stress, and worry had bubbled up and, for one night, had a place to be let go of.

During downtime at work, out of the bosses' earshot, I often heard sweepers remark that "in Bulgaria the poor feed the rich." It was linked to another phrase that many Romani activists, residents, and workers repeated: "Black people, we Roma, die for white people to live." Their sentiments suggest what Lauren Berlant calls "slow death" or "the physical wearing out of a population and the deterioration of people in that population that is very nearly a defining condition of their experience and historical existence."[25] Like the "slow violence" that Rob Nixon describes, it is not spectacular but "incremental and accretive."[26] But at Onyx, as on so many other occasions, I was reminded that even as Roma die so that white Bulgarians can live, Roma also find joyful moments of respite and build life for themselves and one another.[27]

When Romani women cultivate new kinds of relationality through their workplace friendships, they not only reveal the absurdity of both environmental sustainability initiatives and their own racialization but also produce alternative modes of world-making. Sweepers are expected to remain invisible as stewards of public space, cleaners of other peoples' trash, but instead they make themselves visible and audible, asserting their humanity on their own terms and outside of Europeanization frameworks.[28] They are not trying to become recognizably human—or "feminine"—in the terms of white European liberalism. Instead, they play with white femininity to denaturalize it as desirable and, in so doing, disrupt the expectations that such personhood would be an antidote to their racialized disposability. They do this with a shared intimacy that extends beyond the individual body to create "coalitional survival."[29] In this way, the friendships that sweepers build while cleaning city streets have a power, a purpose, and a politics that run on a different track than what liberal democracies define as political.

Romani women establish and maintain enduring and obligatory ties not just to their blood and affinal relations but also to people of their own choosing.[30] This helps catalyze a transformation of the status quo, if only temporarily.[31] Sweepers know they are structurally enmeshed in a death paradigm, but they refuse to be subsumed by it. Women who work together also love and soothe each other, tell jokes, and help each other achieve cathartic release. When Maya raised her pant leg to liken her sweeping work to prostitution, when Hristina teased me about my sexual desires on the bus, or when Donka catcalled a white man on the street, they called into existence an unruliness that felt freeing.[32] Their intimacy is a pressure release valve for stress and high blood pressure, the somatic effects of hard labor.

The sweepers I knew very rarely did things for themselves. There was only a single moment each month after payday when they would stop to buy themselves an ice cream on the way to the bus stop, a little treat before using the rest of their cash to pay for electricity, heating supplies, food, and overdue loan interest. But on International Women's Day, the sense of release was deeper and longer lasting. "Man hands" were converted back into "women's hands" with polished nails that held cocktails instead of brooms.

The team knew the night would end, and that the next morning everyone would be back in their uniforms at the barracks at 5:30 a.m., reporting to bosses who compared Romani women to animals and reminded them that their humanity is always in question. But no one spoke about that at Onyx. Instead, they held each other and laughed and cried as they drank fruit-flavored vodka and smoked freely under the scattered light of the disco ball. Romani women cannot transform workplace pain and humiliation away. They cannot ignore the demands of overdue bills, sick husbands, and dependent children; the threats of violence on the street and from the government; the racialized oppression that lumps them together with the very trash they clean. But they can, however temporarily, create the pleasure of something else, together.

CONCLUSION

Running Water in the Land of Spitting Dragons

Unable to travel to Bulgaria for research during the COVID-19 pandemic, I conducted a set of interviews for this book through Facebook Messenger, Skype, and Zoom. Simon, one of my closest friends and an organizer of the Sheraton protest, had moved to Belgium. We started by introducing one another to our children on the screen. I had had a child since conducting fieldwork and, although I would not share the news for a few more months, had another on the way. It was morning in California, and I was squeezing our talk into the few hours before my partner would hand off our toddler to me again.

It was evening for Simon, and he held his weighty laptop with two hands as he moved through different rooms of his apartment to find the best internet. Each spot provided a few minutes of uninterrupted conversation before his daughter would find him, crawl on him, and practice her English with me by singing children's songs. I watched him sweetly rub his daughter's wet, post-bath hair as he held his computer away from her grabbing hands and told me his thoughts in English. Simon said that it was interesting to be on this side of Europe: to observe its wealth, temporarily benefit from it, and know that these riches were tied to a long history of colonial extraction and violence.

It was different, Simon explained, from what he experienced in Bulgaria. But—and here he paused for a moment to remind his daughter that

179

180 CONCLUSION

it was time to say goodnight—it also helped him understand racism in new ways. It wasn't the same as Bulgaria, but the racial power dynamics were familiar. In Bulgaria he had become accustomed to being "black" and what that entailed in local power hierarchies. But in Western Europe, he had been working in the logistics sector among African immigrants and realized that he was higher in the racialized labor hierarchy than his colleagues, since his accent and skin color meant he could pass as "European." I thought back to the many times in Bulgaria when he was viewed as non-European, as a foreigner. I recalled when we first met in Sofia in 2003 and went to our favorite pizzeria, where the waitstaff, upon hearing us speaking English, would provide him with an English-language menu and me with the Bulgarian one. He explained to me that, because of his ease in English in conjunction with his dark skin, they assumed that he was the foreigner and I the bilingual (white) Bulgarian.

He turned our conversation to the two activist campaigns he was helping organize remotely. One was against a Sofia University professor who was using anti-Roma hate speech in his lectures. The second was against the European Commission, which was providing funds to Bulgaria for a new wave of Roma "integration" initiatives without monitoring how they were being used. In this case, they were financing a program to prevent alleged Islamic radicalization in Romani communities.[1] Simon had sent an official complaint letter to the European Commission and just received a written response that told him that, while they appreciated his concern, his only recourse was to work directly with the Bulgarian government. "But that is hopeless," I replied quickly, reiterating so many of our earlier discussions and aware that he knew better than I ever could. This route would fail.

I told him that, as I teach my students about the situation in Bulgaria and talk with colleagues in the United States about this book, I am repeatedly asked, "But what can be done? Where is the hope for the future?" People want something actionable, triumphant, or at least upbeat, to conclude the narrative. So, I put the question to him: "How do I conclude my book? Where is the hope?"

The Trash of Europe, or the World

Simon laughed. "I don't know about hope," he said, then continued, "but the answer, for me, is history." He thought aloud. "Roma need to know their past, a history of resistance and resilience, of poetry and politics." Little has changed in Europe's treatment of Roma in the last hundred years, Simon explained, but the expulsion of Roma from France in 2010 was a flashpoint for pushing back. I had asked if he thought the June 2011 Sheraton protest was as uniquely transformative as I remembered. "Yes, it was, but do you remember that first protest?" he responded. It was before the Sheraton protest, just weeks into my long-term fieldwork in the autumn of 2010, and I only heard about the gathering at the French embassy in Sofia after it had happened.[2] "That was the real beginning" of the current movement, he clarified.

France had deported Bulgarian and Romanian Roma to their "home" countries in flagrant violation of EU law permitting freedom of travel.[3] Bulgaria's approach to Roma, Simon said, depends on what happens to Roma in more established, "legitimate" European Union countries like France—richer countries, he explained, that have profited from a long history of colonial exploitation. If France could deport its Roma and treat them as disposable, Bulgaria could and would do so as well. If the EU did not sanction France, many believed, it surely would not sanction Bulgaria for similar actions.

EU policy after 2010 was not about human rights or integration, despite this rhetoric, but rooted in preventing inter-European Romani migration. That moment, Simon explained, normalized and codified Romani disposability, not just in Bulgaria but across Europe. What Roma already saw clearly was now apparent to the rest of the world (as much as they did not want to acknowledge it): For all its lofty claims, the EU was predicated not on inclusion or integration, but on a race regime that took shape through the institutionalized discardability of Roma—except when they are needed to bolster EU promises.

Bulgaria's relationship to Europe has been fundamentally asymptotic. The country approached but could never quite reach it. Bulgarians have long remained at the edges of both Europeanness and whiteness, especially in relation to the changing borders of Europe. And Roma are blamed for keeping Bulgaria from reaching true European status, as when an official from the Bulgarian Ministry of the Environment and Water claimed that their presence on city streets appears fundamentally anti-European. Yet, like other waste officials, she also noted that it was also Roma that kept Bulgaria in the running for Europeanness, as their racialized bodily labor helped the country approach, if not meet, this axis. Without Romani laborers, Bulgaria could never fulfill its EU waste mandates. But even this acknowledgment reinforces their positionality as only useful as a means to an end.

My Romani friends and colleagues refuse to sustain the momentum of Europeanization, but not in the way that so many white Bulgarians seem to believe. While they labor toward accomplishing certain EU goals, they subvert others at the same time—by finding pleasure in and despite the work, by organizing rare and pointed protests, and by forming solidarity networks in the face of institutional oppression. In the workplace and in daily life, this entails diagnosing the fundamental absurdity of Europeanization and refusing to sustain its status quo or play fully by its rules. In its midst, they create and, borrowing a phrase from Tina Campt, "embrace the possibility of living otherwise."[4] They point out how Bulgarians are as "naturally" white as Roma are nonwhite, denaturalizing Bulgarian whiteness. And they show that the definitions of white and European vs. Black and anti-European in Bulgaria arise from the same violent and absurdist processes of racial categorization that underlie Europeanization at large. In practice, as Roma refuse their discardability, they also unsettle the category of European as one of unmarked whiteness.

White Bulgarian friends often bemoaned that they are seen as "Europe's trash," especially while abroad. My Romani friends, aware of that common analysis, further remarked that in these recursive and enduringly unstable categorizations of racialized European expungeability, Roma are seen as the trash of Bulgaria. And to be the trash of Bulgaria, they explained, made them the trash of Europe, if not the world. As I noted at the start of this book, my Romani friends and colleagues told me more than a few times: "They respect dogs more than us." The first time I heard this, noted by a vendor at the Bitaka flea market, I asked who "they" were. My question was met with frustration at how obvious the answer was: "Everyone. Just everyone."

Sustainability and Change

A few days after we talked, Simon posted an image to his Facebook page from an 1891 edition of the French newspaper *Le Petit Journal* to show how far back dehumanization of Roma goes and for how long it has helped Europe to define itself. In the drawing, a group of caricatured cannibals gather around a bonfire, roasting a human on a spit. The men wear hats and bandanas and have dark, deep-set eyes. The women—barefoot, in head scarfs and big hoop earrings—appear like the caricatured ancestors of the cardboard cutout of the G*psy woman who greeted attendees in the Sheraton lobby for the 2011 Romani inclusion conference. The image is captioned "Cannibals Still Exist: 'a troop of bohemians in Czechoslovakia are convicted of eating human beings.'"[5] When I messaged with Simon, he asked if I had seen it, and I told him I had. "Good," he wrote back immediately. It was important for my book, he explained: "The years pass but the logic of Europe stays the same." For him, this story was as much about the enduring contours of Europe as it was about Roma's position in it.

Indeed, the commonplace understanding of Roma as disposable, as social "trash," has not fundamentally changed in centuries, let alone in the years since I concluded my longest period of fieldwork in Bulgaria in 2014. However, the waste sector has. Since the 1990s, Bulgaria had exported a great deal of its plastic waste to China, but in 2017, China outlawed this practice.[6] Bulgaria needed to identify new ways to meet EU targets; in line with ongoing practices, it thus required a new dumping ground or sink where waste could go that was outside of the purview of white Bulgarians.[7] Roma are still the people who tend to manage waste out in the open in urban space. And their own neighborhoods, waterways, and depopulating villages, inhabited primarily by those who cannot afford to go abroad, have become dumping grounds for both the rest of the country and the entire EU.[8]

Within liberal European frameworks of progressive environmentalism and Roma integration, even Romani waste is stigmatized and devalued. Their waste, as this chapter discusses, has been deemed categorically unrecoverable by officials.[9] The Romani workers and residents I have gotten to know reject the sustainability paradigm altogether to make space for something else. Donka, Rada, Sofka, Maya, and the rest of the street sweepers, along with Rosa, Simon, Maria, Baka, and others, make and remake their world outside of the disposability logics of the waste-race nexus.[10] The changes that Romani communities need may not be forthcoming if they rely on state structures. But, living within conditions not of their own making, including infrastructural state neglect, they find ways to cultivate small, temporary, resistive pleasures in their midst. Rather than push for state interventions, they draw on neighborhood solidarity to support one another's humanity, respect, and practical survival.

In its close attention to waste management policy and the people who implement it daily, this book has asked readers to consider the impossibility of extracting oneself from the waste-race nexus and yet still imagine the possibilities of life within, alongside, and in tension with it. And it shows how progressive environmentalism, in the guise of sustainability, may not alleviate but actually worsen racial and racializing conditions. This tension speaks to other places where both the waste-race nexus and racial sustainability infiltrate daily life, including communities across the world facing land dispossession and contamination, neighborhoods forced to fight off both toxic dumping and extraction for "green" energy, and stigmatized laborers who clean up postcolonial spaces. I hope this account offers an understanding of how people might turn "no life"—living under the conditions of racialized disposability—into new forms of living in which they continuously build a politics of possibility of "something else," of what is and what might be.

While the formulation of "no life" is useful for critiquing state neglect and materializing Europe's ongoing racial deniability, it may not fully account for how those involved experience the rhythms of waste and waste labor each day. Just as Europeanization pushes waste eastward and southward, toward ever-widening sinks, it also provides the policy and rhetoric for discard's "progressive" remediation. This progressivist model of sustainability lays the foundation for pervasive regimes of racialized disposability—those which Romani women note, critique, reject, and work hard to alter. This book has attended to how their labor of refusal leads to ways of living that cannot be subsumed by the conditions of the waste-race nexus.[11] This includes creating moments of respite and play that can happen in the space of temporary escape.[12] As such, I end this book not with waste but with respect, solidarity, love, and water. If not ways out of the waste-race nexus, these all provide sources of the something else that takes shape alongside, in reaction to, and in spite of it.

When Water Is Solidarity, Love, and Something Like Dignity

"Sweet girl, do you have hot water at home?" Violeta, a veteran sweeper, asked me, looking my uniformed body up and down. We were leaning against the painted wooden benches in the small public park where the sweeping team gathered in the midafternoon sun, waiting for the bosses to release us after the workday. I stared at her, exhausted and unsure how to respond. I usually did have plentiful hot water in my renovated apartment in downtown Sofia, but it was early autumn, and the water company was performing its annual system cleaning (*profilaktika*). Most Sofia residents, myself included, experience a two-week water outage during the preventative cleaning each year. But I knew many of my colleagues had no water at all. I started to explain: "Not right now, but it's okay..." when Violeta interrupted. "It's difficult without water. Come to my cousin's house with me. She has so much hot water and I go there in the evenings to wash up after work. It is nice and hot and you don't have to worry about losing water." She took me by the hand. "You need to come with me and clean up. You can't sit dirty."

I began to ask Violeta about why her cousin had hot water and she didn't, but Donka had overheard us and cut in, staring at my uniformed crotch: "Come on, Elanke, you are going to need to wash *that thing* if you are ever going to get a boyfriend. No man is going to want you after this work. After a hot day sweeping, you are going to stink." I raised my hands animatedly, covering my face in exaggerated shame. Donka got louder as my performance of discomfort egged her on. In moments like this, I felt the sad anticipation of returning home and just how much I would miss our rapport. When I took myself and my research too seriously, Donka would bring me back to earth, refusing any analytical gaze I shifted onto her and turning it back on me (and my body) with humor.

Violeta yelled at Donka to stop "ruining" me (*razvalya*), but Donka just leaned on her broom, laughing. Violeta pulled me aside. "Stop listening to Donka," she whispered. "Come with me, you can bathe anytime, and we don't need to talk about it with the others." I nodded, touched by her sincere care. I wasn't sure how to make it clear, yet again, that I typically did have running water at home.

Talking about water—worrying about it, laughing about it, offering each other (and visitors like me) access to it—was frequent among the Romani women I knew, especially those who worked with waste. Water is haphazardly provisioned in Bulgaria's Romani neighborhoods but has transformative potential. Its importance lies in not only its practical ability to sustain everyday domestic life (cooking, washing, drinking) but also its role in maintaining collective dignity, especially after a day of dirty labor. To take a hot shower after a long day of sweeping is not only practical but also just feels good.[13]

186 CONCLUSION

Knowing that water is inconsistent and scarce, Fakulteta residents were intensely concerned with the boundaries between the neighborhood, where roads were unpaved and trash went uncollected, and the city streets outside, where the roads were regularly cleaned (by themselves or their neighbors). My friends in Fakulteta would routinely clean their shoes, always keeping wet wipes in the car or their pockets to remove the dust that accumulated from walking around the neighborhood. When I started working with Martin and Anton at Romani Star in 2011, Anton told me that snow was a wonderful gift because it was the only time he could walk outside without worrying about getting his shoes dirty. Nevena, another Romani activist friend who worked part-time at Romani Star, explained that Roma "have been told for years that they need to prove themselves when it comes to hygiene…. So, he takes a bath three times [each day], because they say that he's a filthy G*psy."

The necessity of water for bathing is particularly important for street sweepers, who move daily between the dirt of city streets and caring for small children and elderly family members at home. Water is thus vital as a potential antidote to the waste with which Roma are structurally en-

FIGURE 6.1 Border of Fakulteta with nearby Krasna Polyana. Photo by the author.

meshed. Water also provides a way of socializing outside of the confines of labor, a way to tend to the body and take a much-needed break.[14] When the "jar shower" at home was not enough, Romani families would save up money to visit one of Sofia's few remaining public mineral bathhouses (*mineralni bani*). Taking a jar shower involved warming water in a glass jar set in the sun or on the stove, then going outside or into the bathroom with the repurposed jar to wash oneself. It was often accompanied by children playing outside and family members calling out for help; it was functional but not relaxing.

Rosa would often take her family from Fakulteta to the public bathhouse beside Sofia's Lake Pancherevo, inviting me along. They would go about once a month, making sure to visit before birthdays and the winter holidays. Upon entering and paying a fee to the bathhouse attendant, men and women went into separate locker rooms. There, they undressed and then took caddies of supplies into the large, dark single-sex baths where metal spouts came out of tiled walls at regular intervals and sulfuric steam filled the air. On the women's side, Rosa instantly recognized her neighbors who sat together, chatting over tubs of hot water, plastic boxes full of fruity-smelling soaps, shampoos, and conditioners, and the exfoliating loofah mitts purchased from door-to-door saleswomen in Fakulteta that they used to remove dead skin.

Rosa asked me if I knew how to scrub myself. "Of course," I replied. Rosa laughed when she saw me try and quickly took over, with a motherly exasperation. When Rosa scrubbed my body, as she did her daughters', she was expert and powerful. I was amazed at how much dirt she managed to get out of body parts I never knew could hold grime (my shoulders, my hips!). After we scrubbed and washed our hair, we went back to the locker room where we slathered lotion on our wet skin and tried to preserve the heavy warmth of the bathhouse. Rosa told me that she loved hot water and the feeling afterwards of being calm and clean, of becoming "brand new." Although she made the family trips to Panchevero special, often followed by going out to eat at a favorite Chinese restaurant, she declared it absurd that she *had* to go to a public bath in a European country in order to get clean. After all, she said, "having hot water at home is only human."

Water, access to it and its distribution, is deeply embedded in the racialization processes and resistant life-making projects I have addressed throughout this book. Over and against racist Bulgarian campaigns to "clean up and clean out" Roma from public space, waste workers and Romani neighborhood residents take pride in their ability to defy rampant stereotypes of the "dirty G*psy" and keep themselves and their homes pristine.[15] I understand these efforts not as falling under the sway of far-right discourses of racial purity and EU notions of urban "hygiene," but as refusing these terms altogether.[16]

Practically, water is different from other distributive urban infrastructures like electricity, gas, and cable. Whereas Romani neighborhood residents could access electricity by paying hefty turn-on fees or tapping into a neighbor's line, water was not as easy to manage, even in election periods when much else, such as street repairs and gifted satellite dishes, seemed temporarily possible. This is due to the materiality of water networks. Water pipes are deep underground and cannot be turned on and off remotely, so the provision and withdrawal of water are not easily tied to bill payments or debts in the way that other utilities are.

Water access, however, also reflects a fundamental sense of humanness, of what it means to be a "normal" person living in a "European" country, as Rosa noted.[17] And, since they cannot rely on the state to provide water to their homes, Romani women creatively marshal their own resources to make water flow, to enable life, on their own. They do so in community, like sharing water, as Violeta offered to do with me, or working together to repair pipes in a failing and neglected infrastructural network—an effort I turn to in this chapter. Both sharing and repairing allow Romani residents to meet their needs without relying on the state. Such solidarities helped the residents I met preserve what I understood, and they articulated, to be a sense of self-respect, or something like dignity.[18]

As I thought about Romani dignity, I remembered the many conversations I had with Simon, Rosa, Baka, Ivanka, Sofka, Maya, Rada, Donka, and their colleagues. I recalled how often they wanted to explain history to me, in terms of what they had held on to and what had been lost over the generations. Their analyses were about both the past and what a dignified future might look like. In an interview with Trayanka, a long-time resident of one of the poorest sections of Fakulteta known as "the jungle" (dzhunglata), she explained that, each election cycle, they are promised everything by politicians, but those assurances never materialize. She linked these unfulfilled promises to the "democratic generation," as she called it. "Before," she emphasized, making sure I knew she was referencing socialist times, "we had a sewer system, we had water, we had canals, pipes, everything...but those things aren't here anymore." She gestured with an outstretched arm to a small, abandoned lot: "After they tore down the water company's office right over there, everything else got torn down, and now this water goes there." She pointed to the dirt road outside her home covered in sloshing mud. "Yesterday it rained here and there was a flood. Now we are afraid to let our children out. There are different diseases we don't even know about. We live in a jungle, worse than a jungle. If the company would provide water legally [with meters], we would pay...[but] they don't give us any chance. They left us here like dogs." To live without water was to live without the possibility of a dignified future.

Trayanka never explicitly used the Bulgarian term for dignity (*dostoynstvo*). In fact, for most of my interlocutors, the term was tainted by the powers that have wielded "dignity" to insist on Romani disenfranchisement for decades. In a 1967 government memo about "work among the g*psy population," for example, the state socialist security forces focused on the need to restore Romani "dignity" to prevent resistance (Rafiev 1967). The memo claims that both mass media depictions of Roma and discriminatory hiring practices insulted their dignity, and that such anti-Roma practices needed to be stopped because they could lead to a Romani resistance movement.[19] It proposed, however, that the state could prevent Romani uprisings (termed "nationalistic manifestations") by appealing to their dignity.[20] Dignity was thus used as a tool for—and a technology of—state socialist political control.

Similar dynamics continue today. When Petar campaigned inside the Romani neighborhood in Vabrava, he reminded his audience not to sell their votes, telling them: "You are proud, maintain your dignity." That yet another white politician, in a long line of politicians telling them what to do, would insist that they maintain their dignity just made them guffaw. The residents saw Petar as an extension of the larger political system, of Bulgaria's decades-old but still-considered-new democracy, that gained power by preventing Roma from having any. White Bulgarian politicians have worked for decades to strip Roma of their political power and dignity but then tell them to work on their own to maintain it. Petar's declaration was just another example of the trite EU-approved terminology—*bryukselski*—that so many of my interlocutors called out as absurd.

Those same interlocutors cultivated an alternative regime of value, beyond the vacuous rhetoric of dignity and Europeanization. Inside

190 CONCLUSION

Romani neighborhoods, residents already knew what it meant to value themselves and one another. Through their relationships of collective care and neighborhood solidarities, as well as by offering water to those who cannot obtain it on their own and working together to repair pipelines, Roma have built life-giving material and affective networks. Water is critical to their world-making—the creation of "something else"—and they continually manage access to it with humor and critique.

An Imaginative Politics of Vivification

When I asked Rosa the best time to wash dishes at her home in Fakulteta, she thought for a moment, then laughed. "Well, the dragon only spits in the morning and at night." Krasi, her seven-year-old grandson, overheard us in conversation and nodded in agreement, laughing too. The figure of the dragon, for Rosa and her neighbors, playfully pointed to the absurdity of a monstrous system that provided water on stingy terms. The image reflects how she and her neighbors handle hardship, taming the dragon with imaginative humor. They invoke what I called in my field notes an "imaginative politics" of vivification: They comically animate otherwise decaying infrastructures to sustain life. Rosa said it was easier to try and tame the dragon than it was to appeal to municipal officials or local water firms for reliable service.

Fakulteta's water problems have a deep history. When Romani families were gifted or purchased formerly Jewish homes in Fakulteta at the end of WWII, the government changed its policy toward the neighborhood. Beginning in the 1950s, instead of providing repairs and network expansions, the government expected locals to restore and extend sewage and water pipelines themselves. According to Fakulteta residents who remembered this period or heard stories from their parents and grandparents, the municipality had provided the basic skeleton for the water system but did not provide water to individual homes as the neighborhood developed. Sometimes the municipality offered piping materials, but otherwise expected residents to obtain the necessary materials to extend the water network into their homes.[21] Ever since, as the neighborhood continues to expand, Fakulteta residents have been lengthening the stubs of these artery pipelines toward their homes on their own.[22]

Romani and white Bulgarians alike often described the socialist period to me as one in which personhood (or what they described as a sense of being human) was tightly linked with feeling like the state cared for them through providing both jobs and public infrastructures like roads, railroads, and, importantly, water. Many of my friends insisted that Romani neighborhoods, though segregated, had been part of a planned socialist system. You could cool your beer under a running tap in the kitchen, people throughout all of Sofia (including Fakulteta) told me, and not worry about the bill.[23] Echoing Trayanka's analysis, another long-time Fakulteta resident told me over coffee at her home, "after the changes [of 1989], the pressure stopped and so did the water bills. Now there are no bills, but there's also no pressure."

When Bulgarian socialism ended in 1989, the country's political-economic changes sent many Bulgarians abroad to seek education and work. At the same time, agricultural opportunities in the Bulgarian countryside dissipated, and the socialist residential registration requirements that had mandated that anyone who wanted to move to Sofia had to apply for formal permission were eliminated.[24] As a result, many Roma living in the countryside or in smaller towns without the linguistic or financial resources to go abroad moved to Sofia for work. Households grew as extended family members moved in and children had families of their own. When severe housing shortages emerged, people living in registered housing began creating additions to their homes, adding apartments above them or extending their house's footprint if their lot allowed. Others built on land that was not zoned for housing, such that entire Romani neighborhoods are now considered "semi-legal" at best. The city did not maintain pipelines in these growing neighborhoods, even the parts of the network for which they were responsible. With more people sharing water from pipes designed for a smaller community, pressure in some parts of the neighborhood significantly decreased.

In 2016, I met with one of Sofia's city architects, who told me that if the municipality were to do any repairs to the infrastructure in Fakulteta, they would need to tear most of the homes down. According to city regulations, homes need to be built a certain distance apart to allow for vehicles—he gave the example of an ambulance—to pass through. Even though Romani neighborhoods are notoriously underserved by emergency transport vehicles, he maintained this position as a justification for the lack of state-sponsored infrastructural maintenance. The only reason Sofia municipality did not destroy their homes, he told me matter-of-factly, was "because of [human rights] appeals from the Bulgarian Helsinki

Committee on their behalf." I asked if residents had lodged any protests about poor conditions themselves. He walked me over to a massive map of Sofia covering the wall in his office and pointed to Fakulteta, which I had come to recognize from the curvature of its streets. "No, you know, they are used to it," he said. Then he amended, "No matter if they protest. They are illegal anyway. They don't have a real street network. There are not regulated streets. They have water, but I do not know how. They have made it illegally. Everything in there is built in some illegal way."

I followed him back to his computer, where he brought up a PDF map of Fakulteta and zoomed in for more detail, pointing to a spot on the screen. "Here, it should be a street, but they have made a house. This house over here is also on the street. All these houses should be torn down so we can make a regulated street network." He further explained, "Sofia's water lines are only for legal streets. If, for example, there is a pipe on this street," he pointed to the map, "the water company puts the water meter there, and then residents pay for that locale. However, there are many houses that would be connected to that one meter. So instead, they deal with it inside. Inside, they make their own internal network."

When I asked him why the water pressure only came on haphazardly in the morning and at night, when Rosa told me the dragon spits, he smirked, and said he knew why. Although the water company does not turn the water off altogether because "it is too political" and it is impossible to isolate specific homes, it reduces water pressure during the day. The company understands this as a way to minimize water losses without public outcry. He explained that all water systems employ such measures, just typically to a lesser degree, but that those with regularly full pressure cannot feel these diurnal changes that are so consequential for Fakulteta residents. I checked his explanation with local water engineers, and they agreed that he was correct in his assessment.

When, during that same summer in 2016, I asked a local private water company representative about this fact, the conversation turned to not only the engineering of these changes but also how neighborhood geography matters. He explained that "when you regulate the pressure, or flow for instance...if you're situated downstream, you are not bothered by less." But if someone lives above the water source, he added, "they will suffer because there won't be enough pressure for them to easily access it."

Fakulteta has a reservoir within its boundaries, but most of the neighborhood cannot access it for their own needs.[25] It was built in such a way that those who could benefit from gravity would usually have steadily running water but those living at the top of the neighborhood, above the reservoir, would have completely dry taps for days. When I asked him about Fakulteta residents' insistence on getting water meters, he was flippant: "How can you legalize a meter, if you've got illegal house?" He then added, in line with the common stereotype, that the water meters wouldn't last in a Romani neighborhood anyway, because they were metal and would be sold as scrap. However, like Sofia's city architect, he insisted that the water situation in Fakulteta is "political," so it was better to speak with those in positions of political power, not only water company technocrats.

When I returned to Bulgaria the following year, in 2017, I took his insistence to heart and thought about who, exactly, was conducting the "politics" to which both he and the city architect referred. I decided to organize individual meetings with those in positions of overt political power, including multiple district mayors. During a long interview with an official of the district of Sofia that includes Fakulteta, he explained that he was working on the water situation there, but that any funds for Sofia's infrastructural development would be directed first to other neighborhoods that also lacked water and proper sewage systems. He referenced the wide array of unzoned homes in the elite neighborhoods that dotted the base of Sofia's Vitosha mountain. There, he explained, any financial investment would have financial returns because people paid taxes. His account echoed populist rhetoric, and invoked racial capitalist logics, about who were worthy citizens to invest in and who were fundamentally parasitic to the system.

Like the rich residents of Sofia's mountainside villas, my Romani coworkers and friends were accustomed to negotiating unstable water access at home. Romani neighborhood residents have learned to remedy gaps in water infrastructure on their own. They work hard at home to temporarily unsettle the waste-race nexus by bringing water back into the material infrastructures of long-term political neglect and, in doing so, providing the possibility of something more nourishing to take shape.

Repair As Care

The maintenance that Romani community members do on neighborhood water pipes is different from that which they do as part of their waste work when they clean up other peoples' trash. This is because water maintenance in Fakulteta is within their own neighborhood, not in spaces that, according to their bosses, they are not supposed to enjoy. This is also because the work they do in Fakulteta is a way to maintain life in conditions of no life. Romani residents both repair and extend failing state-provided water pipes, and in doing so generate a politics of social solidarity that refuses to abide by the logics of the racialized status quo.[26]

Bobi, the Romani pastor of Trayanka's church in Fakulteta, told me about how he helped his congregants get water. "I ask them, 'Do you want water? If you want it, then dig it yourself.... This is the hose, do it here and to there, and you'll have water.'" He installed a water pipe in his own home adjacent to the church. He confirmed that his congregation wants to pay for water but that, to pay, they need water meters that the city won't provide. Other pastors in Fakulteta told me that they too found alternative means of obtaining water. In some cases, the richest congregants, who had made their money as musicians or entrepreneurs abroad, allowed churches to tap into and share water from the pipes in their homes, where they had installed electric pumps that draw from the main water lines.

Although many Fakulteta residents took pride in joining together to build pipes and connect their homes to the neighborhood's main water channel (*kanal*), these intimate neighborly relations sometimes took other directions. Along with impressive acts of solidarity, I also witnessed how, when someone was using too much water for an event like a wedding, neighbors would insist that they reduce their water usage or clean the pipes afterwards because it negatively affected the adjacent homes.[27] Such collective attention to water was common as neighbors both enabled pipes to be built and necessitated the constant interpersonal management of those infrastructures.[28]

During our conversation, Bobi told me, "I've been to Germany, Italy, France.... Life there is completely different, it has nothing to do with Bulgaria." According to Bobi, it was when "democracy arrived" that the neighborhood became unbearably dirty. "Why?" I asked. "You know how many political parties have come here? The parties come tell us, 'We'll do this, we'll do that' while we're voting, and after [the elections] they move forward like they don't even know the neighborhood." Reiterating what I had learned on Petar's campaign trail, Bobi concurred that democratic politics failed Romani communities. "We are forgotten by everyone." I nodded and looked him in the eye, suddenly feeling the mood shift to something more solemn as he continued to speak slowly. "Sometimes I think we are forgotten by God here."

Despite being "forgotten," Fakulteta residents build on social ties to meet their needs.[29] Pastor Bobi showed me how residents in his area of Fakulteta, on the other side of town from Rosa and Baka, succeeded in bypassing municipal structures. "They agreed to work, to dig the asphalt... The issue is to have the material, to have the pipes, to connect the pipes up to here. And, from here, people have agreed to do it on their own for free." On any warm weekend day, residents of Fakulteta can be seen repairing their connections to the main pipelines without waiting for water company workers to help.

Once, a major pipe burst and the neighbors on one small street gathered to fix it, assisted by a private repair truck they had called. I asked a friend with a house on the street why they didn't call the water company. He said that the water company was just another agent of an always-surveilling government: "When you let *them* in, you never know what they might do." When I asked who "they" were, I was dismissed with a wave of the hand. I thought about who "they" were for a while. Sometimes it seemed they were politicians who were effectively useless, but who, during election periods, exploited Roma for their votes. But "they" also included police, municipal inspectors, company bosses, and others who had the power to destroy Romani livelihoods. Residents had become accustomed to being ignored, either placated by officials with empty words and no results or profiled and surveilled, as they made themselves known to those in power.

Indeed, when I asked friends in Fakulteta why they did not ask the municipality to repair broken pipes, they would look at me and roll their eyes at my ridiculous question. One friend told me flat out: "We, Roma, just don't do that." Residents recounted numerous stories of seeking assistance that ended up putting them at risk. Their experience was much like that of my sweeping coworkers who had children arrested without due process and the NGO leaders who were surveilled and imprisoned while attempting to fulfill EU integration goals. Many in Fakulteta spoke about the potential for their houses to be demolished if they appealed to authorities, reminiscent of other demolitions like the razing of the sweepers' homes to make space for the BILLA supermarket. Others in Fakulteta feared that their children could be taken away. In fact, drawing on stereotypes of "G*psy child theft," a child deemed too blond and white was removed in 2013 from a Romani family caring for her in Greece 2013.[30]

Fakulteta residents have learned to bypass the failure and disappointment of appealing to local authorities, opting instead to meet their needs themselves. They breathe life into broken water pipes not only through humorous images of a spitting dragon they must tame but also by sharing water and physically restoring decaying pipes. Their repair labor vivifies what the state has neglected since the neighborhood's inception and continues to neglect as part and parcel of Europeanization. Repair is a material, social, and political way to invigorate what is otherwise strategically disregarded, left to die.[31] Despite the racialized and gendered aspects of Romani repair work, these practices turn decaying water pipes into life-giving entities with the capacity to clean, soothe, and provide a sense of respect without having to appeal to state apparatuses.

FIGURE 6.2   The dragon that spits. Illustration by Izabela Ivanova.

From No Life to Something Else

When I visited Bulgaria in 2017, environmentalist friends told me that, since the country would no longer be able to export waste to China, it was frantically burning plastic at multiple sites "that did not meet EU incineration standards."[32] Two years later, during a month-long visit in 2019, I met with officials who told me that Sofia's waste was finally going to a European-standard installation site called Sadinata, just outside the city. I had the chance to visit the facility and meet a few of Sadinata's new employees. One evening, over green tea in a minimalist all-glass café located in one of Sofia's nicest parks, a young engineer working at the site, Valentina, explained that the Sadinata site was designed to increase the recovery of recyclable waste. This waste could be turned into profit. When the waste arrives at Sadinata, she explained, most of it moves along a conveyor belt where it is sorted by hand, mostly by Romani women, to separate what can be recycled from what cannot. It was like other recycling sites I had been to (as in Chapter 2), but it was municipally run. And like in those other sorting sites, the nonrecyclable components are dried out and then compacted into bale-like packages, some of which can be burned as refuse-derived fuel.

Valentina revealed that, according to unwritten policy, the trash that comes from Romani neighborhoods like Fakulteta or Filipovtsi goes directly to the landfill. "There's nothing to be recovered there," she explained, crinkling her nose as if smelling something foul, so "it's not worth anyone's time" to attempt to sort it. I was struck by the resemblance between Valentina's passing comment and the way most white Bulgarians speak about Romani people as discardable. The logics of Zero Waste continue to reinforce categorizations of white and nonwhite space, such that even in a Europeanizing system focused on waste recovery, segregated Romani garbage goes straight to the landfill. Valentina's explanation was focused on the consequent materiality of Romani refuse, not the conditions that led to it, for example, the fact that garbage trucks rarely enter their neighborhoods, that recycling companies refuse to install bins there, and that the roads inside haven't been paved well enough for garbage trucks to use.

This systemic neglect results in what Valentina sees as the unrecoverable waste from Romani neighborhoods, waste that in her view is too dirty, too contaminated, to ever turn a profit. Despite the actual composition of waste from Romani neighborhoods (whatever it might be—it's never been systematically studied), Valentina's comment serves as a telling metonymy: "not worth anyone's time" refers not only to the trash in question but also to the entire neighborhood, a common trope throughout popular media and my fieldwork conversations. The new EU-compliant waste facility of Sadinata refuses to sort Romani waste, just as the Bulgarian political system refuses to serve Romani communities with basic infrastructural access to things like water, waste collection, and safely paved roads.

And so, Romani neighborhood residents and workers live life with an eye and a feeling for something else. Sweepers cultivate loving friendships in the face of body-breaking labor. Romani neighborhood residents recuperate decaying water pipes through humor and material repair. These are life-claiming powers. So too is refusing to engage in ostensibly democratic elections. Their practices cannot undo the system of racial disposability that structures the conditions of everyday life, conditions upon which so many Romani livelihoods depend. Still, they continue to disrupt the liberal logics of racial sustainability and, with humor, assert other modes of living on their own terms. However, my interlocutors tended not to spend time talking about what the something else they were creating might be. They did not muse about a world in which their personhood was not constantly questioned, a world that somehow interrupted the ravages of racial capitalism and white supremacist Europeanization, a world in which they could reclaim their bodies from being used to propagate a race regime couched in terms of environmental progressivism.

I often asked questions about what such a future would look like, as I did with Simon. I sought explanations of the kinds of worlds people would make when they managed to succeed in refusing the status quo and disengaging from liberal democratic politics. The response, like that of Simon, was typically laughter. That would be fantasy, after all, and nobody has time for that. People have water to procure, leaves to sweep, laundry to do, kids to take care of, and bills to pay. But, amid a landscape of waste, they push forth in turning no life—the materialities of their "forgotten" neighborhoods, their racialized disposability, and an alienating political system—into abundant liveliness.

The kinds of care and repair that people do inside Romani neighborhoods stand in contrast to what they do on city streets. While working, they inevitably propagate the very system that subjugates them but, in Fakulteta or Filipovtsi, they work toward creating better infrastructural conditions that just might allow them to live a respectable life in the way they define it. On city streets, they clean up other people's waste so that Bulgaria can seek identification with a Europe in which Roma are considered "social waste." But at home, through neighborhood care-repair networks, they create alternatives to the landscape of dehumanization with which they must contend and in which they work for most of their waking hours.

My Romani interlocutors in this book, and those beyond the borders of Bulgaria, reconstitute waste outside the category of abject pollution. Waste both pollutes (especially when dumped or never picked up in Romani neighborhoods) *and* serves as a tool and material for moving on. When my Romani friends explained to me how urban Sofia's waste is dumped in their neighborhoods, strategically off the grid, they articulated waste in terms of disgust, displacement, and abjection. There were even cases in relatively recent memory of a nearby hospital calling Romani men with horse carts to pick up and dispose of hazardous medical waste because the hospital did not want to pay to incinerate it in compliance with EU hazardous-waste protocols. Fakulteta residents remember and feel the omnipresent pollution of their neighborhoods being used as sinks.

However, that is only one small part of their relationship to waste. Petko collects waste in ways that allow him to remember what it was like "before," when he lived a "normal" socialist life. As he moves his body through space and his mind through time, he encounters the pleasure of memory—of when he worked a daily bus route, his labor was deemed essential, and he was needed. In her quest for a livable life during her pensioner years, Baka savors the delight of discovering a fresh-baked, luxurious birthday cake in a dumpster. Still others, like Sofka, Ivanka, Maya, Rada, Donka, and the other women on the sweeping team, find that their work with waste enables intimate friendships and the life-giving sustenance of getting out of the house and into the female space of the street. They don't just survive; survival for them is not enough. Instead, they work to make life livable, pleasurable, something worth waking up for.

What lingers are the moments of love, neighborly care, workplace humor, and embodied practices of disruption and pleasure. Through these practices, Romani waste workers, activists, and neighborhood residents also reconfigure sustainability, liberal frameworks of dignity, and state infrastructural and political neglect in their own way. This remaking does not offer a prescriptive solution for what to do when one's entire being is seen as trash, when entire communities' labor, despite being crucial to so-called environmental sustainability, is undervalued and derided. However, it does present a different possibility, one concerning what it means to continually cultivate life amid waste, in discards not of one's own making. In doing so, Romani people disrupt the normalized framework of racial sustainability that pervades their lives, making space for something else in its place. If not a way out of the waste-race nexus, this might be a way to take a step back, see it for what it is, and laugh at the absurdity of its pervasive and shapeshifting logic.

As my street-sweeping colleague Sofka put it, "Roma die so that [white] Bulgarians can live."[33] But, as this book shows, Romani waste workers in Europe don't just die in abjection. They live. Theirs is not a story of resilience that provides a feel-good answer for those seeking hope amid climate change, environmental racism, and institutional oppression. It is a story of the hard labor of life-making amid both waste and environmental sustainability regimes, of reconfiguring the status quo in favor of something else, however enduring or fleeting, personal or collective, that something else might be.

NOTES

Note on Language and Terminology

1. Costache (2020).

2. The Bulgarian Transliteration Law: https://lex.bg/laws/ldoc/2135623667.

3. I use the "ya" spelling except in cases of common usage, like in the transliteration of "Bulgaria" or "Sofia," which employs "ia" instead of "ya."

Note on Illustrations

1. This accords with oral history interviews I conducted.

Introduction

1. Throughout my research, in interviews, media coverage, and public policy discourse, the term "Bulgarian" was used as a proxy for Orthodox Christian whiteness. Although Roma in Bulgaria are legally Bulgarian citizens, they are seen as perpetually outside the category of "Bulgarian." Many Romani friends used the term "white" to refer to non-Romani Bulgarians, but few non-Romani Bulgarians proclaimed their own whiteness in casual conversation. However, the (English) language of whiteness did become part of far-right politics and anti-Roma graffiti, as this chapter makes explicit. Also see Creed 2011 on the racialization of Bulgarianness as whiteness.

2. Police checks of Roma on city streets are a ubiquitous part of life and even more common for Roma collecting garbage, which I witnessed multiple times.

3. This dates to when Sofia was named the capital city in 1879 and Romani communities living in the center were moved to make space for major downtown sites like the current-day Parliament.

NOTES TO THE INTRODUCTION

4. By "progressive," I'm drawing on Savannah Shange's discussion of the term, which, at least in the United States, has "come to mean anyone to the left of the Democratic Party platform. The term can reference an incredibly diverse group of communities and individuals, some of whom have conflicting political imaginaries" (2019, 11). Across Europe, the designation "progressive" tends to point to similar kinds of "left-leaning," forward-thinking platforms.

5. See Boatcă 2021 on "Europe as a creolized space, or Europe Otherwise" as well as Böröcz's 2006 and Herzfeld's 2005 critical analyses of the invocation of "Europe." Rucker-Chang addresses the "conflation of 'whiteness' with 'European'" as crucial to the nationalist imaginary in the "European Union South" (2018, 190).

6. In this book I use multiple terms synonymously: waste, discard, garbage, trash. I do so with Myra Hird's approach in mind, "partly in an attempt to signify the variability of the terms themselves: different scholars, government documents, industry reports, people working with waste, and so on use these terms in various ways that in turn affect the ways in which these phenomena are understood" (2013, 28). Practically, my focus is on domestic waste (*bitovi otpadatsi*, or, more colloquially, *bokluk*, in Bulgarian) and its collection, recycling, recovery, and processing. The related body of literature is too large to include in one note. Some key texts that accompanied me as I wrote include Ahmann 2018, 2024; Alexander and O'Hare 2020; Alexander and Reno 2012; Butt 2023; Chalfin 2014, 2023; Checker 2011, 2020; Doherty 2021; Fredericks 2018; Giles 2021; Gille 2007; Hawkins and Muecke 2002; Hecht 2018, 2023; Liboiron 2021, Liboiron and Lepawsky 2022; Melosi 2004; Millar 2018; Moore 2012; Nagle 2013; O'Neill 2019; Reno 2014, 2015, 2016; Stamatopoulou-Robbins 2019; Strasser 1999; Solomon 2019, 2022; and Zhang 2020, 2024; among others.

7. One might even say they are "thingified" in the terms of Aimé Césaire: "Between colonizer and colonized there is room only for forced labor, intimidation, pressure, the police, taxation, theft, rape, compulsory crops, contempt, mistrust, arrogance, self-complacency, swinishness, brainless elites, degraded masses. No human contact, but relations of domination and submission which turn the colonizing man into a classroom monitor, an army sergeant, a prison guard, a slave driver, and the indigenous man into an instrument of production. My turn to state an equation: colonization = 'thingification'" ([1955] 1972, 21). The story of Bulgarian Roma does not end with being rendered into things; in the words of Damani Partridge, their shared life experiences are rooted in solidarity and life-making, and because of that, they can link "mutual struggle to political possibility" (2022, 2).

8. "Racialized" refers to the processes by which people are hierarchically categorized to maintain social orders of power that we understand as "race." I use the terminology of "disposability" here to highlight the effects of racialization, not to suggest that there are "really disposable people" (Denning 2010, 80). Also see Millar (2018, 7) on the problematic use of metaphors of human disposability.

9. My thinking about racial sustainability has been fortified by writings about racial capitalism, by discard studies' approaches to waste and power (Liboiron

and Lepawsky 2022), and by critical analyses of sustainability, including Melissa Checker's account of how sustainability became "capitalism's darling" (2020, 22; also Isenhour 2015). The racial capitalism scholarship that I refer to includes Cedric Robinson's ([1983] 2000) work and Jodi Melamed's analysis that asserts "the term 'racial capitalism' requires its users to recognize that capitalism is racial capitalism" (2015, 77). "Capital can only be capital when it is accumulating, and it can only accumulate by producing and moving through relations of severe inequality among human groups—capitalists with the means of production/workers" (77). I suggest that racial sustainability requires a similar kind of recognition.

10. The 1997 EU Commission Opinion on Bulgaria's Application of Membership to the European Union highlighted the role of environmentalism and minority/human rights, among other pressing issues. Regarding sustainability, the document states: "The Union's environmental policy, derived from the Treaty, aims towards sustainability based on the integration of environmental protection into EU sectoral policies, preventive action, the polluter pays principle, fighting environmental damage at the source, and shared responsibility." And in regard to Roma, it states: "The g*psies (Romanies) continue to suffer considerable discrimination in daily life and are the target of violence either directly by the police or by individuals whom the police do not always prosecute. Their social position is difficult, though here sociological factors play a part alongside the discrimination they suffer from the rest of the population.... The government should take appropriate steps to ensure that the specific difficulties of these people are genuinely taken into account. In this connection, it would be useful to carry out a reliable survey of the numbers of g*psies resident in Bulgaria and of their social situation (levels of unemployment, statistics on their health and educational level): no precise statistics of this kind are available at present" (https://ec.europa.eu/commission/presscorner/detail/en/DOC_97_11). Nearly a decade later, in a report from November 2006 about Bulgaria's upcoming (January 1, 2007) EU accession, it highlights how intersectional injustice, pertaining to Romani women, remains a critical issue (https://www.europarl.europa.eu/doceo/document/A-6-2006-0420_EN.html).

11. This aligns with what Gidwani and Maringanti call the "waste-value dialectic," in which "the conditions of possibility of capitalist value lie in bodies, places, and things that come to be designated at the front end and back end of capitalism as waste" (2016, 125).

Regarding the term *boklutsi*, *bokluk* can be defined as garbage or waste, and *boklutsi* is the plural form of the noun but also the term used to refer to people categorized as waste.

12. See the European Environment Agency's 2013 report on municipal waste management in Bulgaria: https://www.eea.europa.eu/publications/managing-municipal-solid-waste/bulgaria-municipal-waste-management.

13. I have previously written about this articulation of *neshto drugo* and defined it as "anything else" (Resnick 2023). However, upon rethinking it and in conversation with others (especially Martin Fotta), I translate it now as "something else" in order to better capture the sensibility with which it is used.

204 NOTES TO THE INTRODUCTION

Laurence Ralph's (2014) analysis of "alternative forms of existence" (17) and the force of people's "renegade will" (145) first inspired my thinking on this point. In revisions, I turned to Marisa Solomon's work on race and waste, especially Solomon's commitment to avoid "reproducing scenes of suffering for white environmental spectatorship." Instead, Solomon focuses on "how Black livingness is circumscribed by, yet is also an intervention into, environments of white supremacy" (2022, 568).

14. Weheliye 2014, 3. Also see Vaughn 2022.

15. Rucker-Chang and West Ohueri 2021, 216.

16. Bonilla-Silva 2006. Also see van Baar 2011, 2019 and Pulay 2018 on the "Europeanization of Roma representation."

This book thus brings together work on postsocialist and post-Soviet racialization (Atanasoski 2006, 2013; Baker 2018; Baldwin 2015; Balogun 2020; Cervinkova 2012; Chari and Verdery 2009; Fikes and Lemon 2002; Imre 2005, 2014; Kocze 2018; Lemon 2000, 2002; Owczarzak 2009; Rainbow 2019; Rucker-Chang and West Ohueri 2021; Todorova 2021; Trehan and Kóczé 2009; Weitz 2002) with analyses of Europe as both geographic and metaphysical space (Boatcă 2010, 2021; Bonilla-Silva 2006; Böröcz 2001; De Genova 2016; El-Tayeb 2011; Gilroy 1993; Goldberg 2002; Hesse 2007; Mills 1997). Like racialization itself, the legacies of its disavowal and erasure have taken shape differently in different contexts, including other socialist and postsocialist/post-Soviet spaces like Latvia (Dzenovska 2018), Russia (Lemon 2000), the former Yugoslavia (Baker 2018), and Albania (West Ohueri 2021), as well as outside of postsocialist rhetoric and policy. Across Europe, key examples of racialization processes include in the Netherlands (Wekker 2016), Greece (Cabot 2014), Portugal (Fikes 2009), England (Brown 2009), France (Arkin 2020; Beaman 2017; Fernando 2014; Kleinman 2019; Lie 2021), and Germany (Campt 2004; Florvil 2020; Partridge 2022).

17. I thank Deborah Thomas for helping clarify this point.

18. I am grateful that many years ago Bruce Grant pointed me to Susan Buck-Morss's (2000) essay on the interconnections of Enlightenment ideas of human freedom and realities of ongoing slavery.

19. Also see Jung 2010.

20. See https://blogs.worldbank.org/en/europeandcentralasia/why-we-need-talk-about-roma-inclusion.

21. See data gathered by the European Commission: https://commission.europa.eu/strategy-and-policy/policies/justice-and-fundamental-rights/combatting-discrimination/roma-eu/roma-equality-inclusion-and-participation-eu-country/bulgaria_en.

22. The World Bank has collected these statistics: https://documents1.worldbank.org/curated/en/727791642521506054/pdf/Bulgaria-Systematic-Country-Diagnostic.pdf. Also see Matache 2017a.

23. The 2021 census notes that 84.6% defined themselves as Bulgarians (*bulgari*), 8.4% as Turks (*turtsi*), and 4.4% as Roma (*romi*) (https://www.nsi.bg/census2011/PDOCS2/Census2011final_en.pdf). However, other statistics,

NOTES TO THE INTRODUCTION

including from the Council of Europe note that Roma comprise approximately 10.33% of the Bulgarian population (https://commission.europa.eu/strategy-and -policy/policies/justice-and-fundamental-rights/combatting-discrimination/ roma-eu/roma-equality-inclusion-and-participation-eu-country/bulgaria_en). It is important to acknowledge the inaccuracies and effects of such census information: Surdu 2019 provides an analysis of why census numbers regarding Romani populations might be far from actual numbers and "calls for a critical scrutiny of how Roma ethnicity is crafted through practices of ethnic quantification" (486).

24. Roma in Bulgaria are also not romanticized in the same way they have been in other places, like in Russa via Pushkin's poetry, among other cultural artifacts (Lemon 2000).

25. Rosa 2019, 3, draws on the work of Barnor Hesse 2007.

26. See Tlostanova 2010; Todorova 2018.

27. See Turda and Weindling 2007. Also, Miglena Todorova 2018, writing about the work of Bulgarian anthropologist Metodii Popov, notes that "a leading Bulgarian anthropologist explicitly staked a claim on European origin and Whiteness after studying the blood types and body shapes of thousands of subjects in Bulgaria" (120).

28. This was documented in state security archives, including "Informatsiya za Izpalnenieto na Reshenie №1360 na Sekretariata na TsK na SGNS ot 9.10.1978" [Information on the Execution of Decision No. 1360 of the Secretariat of the Central Committee of Sofia City People's Council from October 9, 1978] and "Ordinance No. 7 of the Councils of Ministers from January 26, 1979" (Trichkov 1980) and told to me repeatedly during oral history interviews and by friends who echoed the stories of their parents and grandparents (http://comdos.bg).

29. Gerald Creed notes something similar, explaining that, unlike other racial exclusions across Europe, "the presence of, and interaction with, G*psies is an essential part of being Bulgarian" (2011, 193). He analyzes how "this close association increasingly serves as a means of racial/ethnic Europeanization by highlighting Bulgarians' whiteness" in contrast to "explicitly nonwhite, non-European G*psies" (193).

30. As Frantz Fanon showed, racialization cannot be encapsulated by the "epidermalization" of race (1952). In other words, race is not innately of the body, but it can materialize through its social ramifications on and in the body. Street sweepers' bodies provide one site of this materialization, which can be studied in relation to other accounts of racialization vis-à-vis labor (cf. Amrute 2016; Blanchette 2020; Díaz 2020; Holmes 2013; Lemon 2000; Solomon and Wool 2021).

31. Here see the scholarship on the racial dimensions of the category of "human" (Jackson 2020; Weheliye 2014; Wynter 2003) in dialogue with work about the racialization of the Soviet (or socialist) Man (Bardziński 2013).

32. Todorova 2021, 63.

33. Kalmar 2023; Lewicki 2023. Also see Grill 2018.

34. Even though Bulgaria did join the Schengen Zone on March 31, 2024, its borders were initially only opened by air and sea, but not by land. Many believe

this reflected a prominent Western European policy concern with Bulgaria's challenges (rule of law, corruption) and fears that the country cannot manage its external borders and therefore cannot prevent migrants from outside of Europe from moving through Bulgaria westward to countries like Germany, the Netherlands, and Austria (https://www.euronews.com/my-europe/2022/10/24/whats-keeping-bulgaria-and-romania-out-of-schengen).

35. Also see West Ohueri 2024 on "peripheral whiteness."

36. They see their whiteness along the lines of what Anikó Imre describes as "alleged innocence preserved by a claim of exception to the history of imperialism" (2014, 130). Also see Lentin 2004, 2011 on race and postracialism.

37. For key examples, see: Agard-Jones 2013; Bullard [1990] 2008; Chen 2012; Harper, Steger, and Filčák 2009; Liboiron 2021; Murphy 2017; Park and Pellow 2011; Pellow 2017; Pulido 2017; Sze 2006; and Voyles 2015.

38. The EU policies I focus on in this book primarily concern domestic or municipal solid waste (MSW), which represents a relatively small percentage of waste, especially when compared to industrial solid waste (ISW) (Gille and Lepawsky 2022).

39. For thinking about postsocialist racial capitalism, I draw on foundational work about racial capitalism (Robinson [1983] 2000) as well as the postsocialist capitalist growth that Harper 2006 calls "wild capitalism." For Jodi Melamed and Cedric Robinson's essential insights that inform my analysis, see note 9 in this introduction.

40. See work by Andrew Graan on the dual potentiality of Europeanization in Eastern Europe to promise both "prosperity" and the threat of "neoimperialism" (2010, 836). Savannah Shange's examination of "a series of successful progressive reforms, and what they cost Black communities," influenced my thinking on so-called progressive reform (2019, 3).

41. Gabrys 2009; Liboiron 2021.

42. Liboiron 2021, 64.

43. The 2009–2013 edition of the Bulgarian National Waste Management Programme (NWMP) states that its main purpose, sustainable development, is to be accomplished through "an integrated framework which will lead to reduction of the harmful impact upon the environment caused by the waste generation, to improvement of the effectiveness of the natural resources consumption, to increase the producer responsibilities, and to encourage the investments in waste management" (7). The NWMP describes sustainable development as "a model for social and structural economic transformations that optimize the present economic and social benefits without compromising the potential for their existence in future" (66), https://www.strategy.bg/StrategicDocuments/View.aspx?lang=bg-BG&Id=495.

44. I see this approach as in conversation with scholars addressing life-making in contexts not related to waste (e.g., Cox 2015; Povinelli 2002; Thomas 2019) and in the context of life-making amid waste (e.g., Fredericks 2018; Millar 2018; Nagle 2013; Solomon 2022; Stamatopoulou-Robbins 2019).

NOTES TO THE INTRODUCTION

45. Rorke 2023.

46. Buchanan 2002, 3.

47. I think alongside scholars who "analyze how late liberal power appears" when encountered from particular perspectives (Povinelli 2016, 42; Shange 2019; also Appel 2019)—in this case, the perspectives of Romani activists, waste workers, and NGO leaders, as well as white Bulgarian bureaucrats, politicians, and waste officials. As the (late) liberal forces of European progressivism move through both everyday Romani life and the waste sector, they constitute Bulgaria's contemporary race regime of disposability and sustainability.

48. Greenhouse 2018, 2. I also draw on Audra Simpson's analysis of "the political" as "distributions of power, of effective and affective possibility, the imagination of how action will unfold to reach back to that distribution for a re-sort, but also for a push on what should be" (2016, 326). Defining "politics" or "the political" is a daunting task. I began by thinking through different concepts and critiques of power, including disengagement (Sojoyner 2017), retreat (Robinson [1983] 2000), repair (Thomas 2019), disruption (Fernando 2014), infrapolitics (Scott 1990), refusal (Campt 2019; Fredericks 2018; Simpson 2016), resistance (Abu-Lughod 1990), and defiance (Shange 2019). Tina Campt's 2019 definition of refusal as "a rejection of the status quo as livable and the creation of possibility in the face of negation" has resonated most with what I saw taking shape among Roma in Bulgaria.

49. A history of "furtive politics" in Bulgaria dates back to at least late-Ottoman-era revolutionaries, who used covert operations to resist the Ottomans (Methodieva 2021), and continued throughout the socialist period in Bulgaria and within the broader East European region (Berdahl 1999b; Buchanan 2006; Creed 2011; Verdery 1996). While these socialist resistive politics have their own historical trajectory, I see them also in dialogue with Robin D. G. Kelley's account of infrapolitics as "daily acts that have a cumulative effect on power relations" (1993, 78).

50. In doing so they enable a range of "possibilities for creative self-making" (Cox 2015, 185). These possibilities allow for "living in ways that honor individual humanity" and the potential to develop transformative politics "capable of building and creating what neoliberalism dehumanizes and destroys" (9).

51. Vincze 2014, 444.

52. This aligns with Hannah Arendt's analysis of race in Europe: "The historical truth of the matter is that race-thinking, with its roots deep in the 18th century, emerged during the nineteenth century simultaneously in all Western countries. Racism has been the powerful ideology of imperialistic policies since the turn of our century" (1944, 36). Also see El-Tayeb 2011; Goldberg 2006; and Hesse 2007, 2009 for analyses of Europeanization as a racial project.

53. Kelley 2017, para. 5, emphasis in original. Robin D. G. Kelley builds on Cedric Robinson's pioneering ([1983] 2000) work on racial capitalism. But we can expand Robinson's focus to other economic orders that also depend upon racial hierarchy to function—including Bulgarian state socialism (especially its reliance on racialized labor).

NOTES TO THE INTRODUCTION

54. Some examples of work about specifically this kind of expendability: in relation to chattel slavery and its aftermaths (King 2019; Sharpe 2016), in settler-colonial systems (la paperson 2017; Liboiron 2021), in conditions of genocide (Mamdani 2001; Raffles 2007), and in relation to liberal infrastructure projects (Anand, Gupta, and Appel 2018; Chari 2013; Stoler 2013; and von Schnitzler 2016).

55. I thank Jessica Greenberg who suggested this framing of "racial socialism." The concept of "racial socialism" departs from Cedric Robinson's Marxist approach, highlighting the lived experiences of inequality in East European socialism (as opposed to underscoring Marxist ideology). On "surplus" in multiple modalities, see Chahim 2023; Gidwani and Reddy 2011; Gilmore 2007; Grant 2014; and Vincze 2023.

56. I am grateful for Orhan Tahir thinking through this analysis with me. For examples, see https://documents1.worldbank.org/curated/en/509711468261335080/pdf/622560BRI0Roma0Box0361475B00PUBLIC0.pdf; https://documents.worldbank.org/en/publication/documents-reports/documentdetail/196921468261335364/roma-inclusion-an-economic-opportunity-for-bulgaria-czech-republic-romania-and-serbia.

57. This body of work includes da Silva 2007; Florvil 2020; Kóczé 2018, 2020; Pierre 2012; Rana 2011; Rexhepi 2022; Rucker-Chang 2020; Thomas 2004, 2019; Thomas and Clarke 2006, 2013; Waseem 2023; and West Ohueri 2021.

58. Romani feminist scholarship that fortified my research includes (but is not limited to) work by Nicoleta Bițu n.d.; Nicoleta Bițu and Enikő Vincze 2012; Ethel Brooks 2012; Ioanida Costache 2018, 2020; Petra Gelbart 2012; Angéla Kóczé 2011, 2015, 2018; Margareta Matache 2017a, 2017b; Anna Mirga-Kruszelnicka 2015, 2018, 2022; Alexandra Oprea 2004, 2009, 2012; Jelena Savić 2018, 2022; and Enikő Vincze 2014, 2023. Black feminist epistemologies and analyses of both "the political" and refusal have further helped ground my analysis. These include Tina Campt 2012, 2019 (see also Coleman 2018); Cathy Cohen 1997, 2004; Aimee Meredith Cox 2015; Saidiya Hartman 1997; Savanah Shange 2019; Christina Sharpe 2016; Marisa Solomon 2019, 2022; Deborah Thomas 2004, 2016, 2019; and Gloria Wekker 2016. Although this project has been inspired by many Black feminist approaches to race both within and outside of Europe, I do not mean to suggest that Romani life is tidily analogous to Black life. However, racialization in both the United States and Europe has been shaped by global forces of capitalist white supremacy that constitute historical and contemporary European expansion, imperialism, and dehumanization.

59. Angela Kóczé and Nidhi Trehan, drawing on the work of Patricia Hill Collins, write: "Black feminist epistemologies also offer us a pathway towards achieving emancipatory knowledge" (2020, 189). Jelena Savić "draw[s] the conceptual connecting lines between global structure of racism relying primarily on the American authors like Mills, McIntosh, and Feagin (Mills 2003; McIntosh 1988; Feagin 2013) and the situation of Roma in the European context" in order to foster a critical Romani perspective (2022, 3).

NOTES TO THE INTRODUCTION

60. See https://romarchive.eu/en/about/context-project/.

61. I cannot do justice to the five-hundred-year history of Romani life in Ottoman Empire Bulgaria here, and sources on the topic are limited. Elena Marushiakova and Veselin Popov's 2001 history provides much of my knowledge. There are also accounts, primarily from foreign travelers, of Roma being sold into slavery during the Ottoman period.

62. Marushiakova and Popov 2001, 58.

63. Neuburger 2004, 8.

64. Among these groups, Roma often faced the worst conditions, as they were "frequently treated with contempt by Bulgarians and Turks alike" (Methodieva 2021, 39).

65. Tahir 2020.

66. Pashov 2023; Stanoeva 2010.

67. Marinov 2020.

68. Shakir Pashov published the first Bulgarian Romani newspaper, *Terbie* [Upbringing], and was instrumental in developing Romani civil society, which grew steadily stronger until his work was banned in 1934 (Tahir 2020).

69. This trope of "spreading disease" was evoked again during the COVID-19 pandemic when political parties surrounded Romani neighborhoods, including Fakulteta, under the premise of protecting the Bulgarian population from Romani contagion (Matache and Bhabha 2020; Resnick 2020).

70. The exact number of Romani Holocaust victims has been debated; five hundred thousand has come to stand as the symbolic number of Romani and Sinti people murdered: https://www.romarchive.eu/en/voices-of-the-victims/the-number-of-victims/.

71. This includes the infamous studies done by anthropologist Eva Justin, a member of the Nazi-run Racial Hygiene Research Center, who learned Romani and worked with Sinti/Romani children to write her dissertation, "Biographical Destinies of Gypsy Children and Their Offspring Who Were Educated in a Manner Inappropriate for Their Species." Upon completion of her research, the children were sent to a family camp for Roma in Auschwitz II-Birkenau, where they were subjected to the experiments of Josef Mengele and later killed. In these "family camps," men were also often used for forced construction labor.

72. Leon Mitrani explains: "Jews did not have access to state administrative or executive positions. They could not own land or work in agriculture. Their access to army leadership posts was also limited.... Though there was no explicit ban, Jews could not teach in Bulgarian schools; they were not allowed in the courts except as lawyers. It was impossible to imagine a Jewish policeman, and truly inconceivable that a Jew should be mayor or prefect of a district" (1991, 2, cited in Ragaru 2023).

73. See factsheet: https://www.coe.int/en/web/roma-genocide/virtual-library/-/asset_publisher/M35KN9VVoZTe/content/bosnia-and-herzegovina-recognition-of-the-genocide?inheritRedirect=false.

74. Dimitrov 2001; Emen-Gökatalay 2021.

NOTES TO THE INTRODUCTION

75. Primary sources from the period, including the writing of Shakir Pashov himself, note that Georgi Dimitrov's policy toward Roma between 1946 and 1949 was linked to their personal relationship. See Marushiakova and Popov 2015.

76. Marushiakova and Popov 1997, 175.

77. Todorova 2006. Also see Popov 1938.

78. This information comes from the socialist State Security Archives compiled in 2015 by the Committee for Disclosing the Documents and Announcing Affiliation of Bulgarian Citizens. The documents in this archive related to the "State Security Policing of Minorities" often refer to anti-Roma "discriminatory attitudes" as leftovers from the pre-1944 Bulgarian capitalist past or as a sign of external Western influence. See Communist Party Council of Ministers, June 17, 1959. "Pismo №809 do Okrazhnite, Gradski i Rayonni Komiteti na BKP" [Letter No. 809 to the District, City and Regional Committees of the BCP (Bulgarian Communist Party)].

79. Neuburger 2004, 183. This was a continuation of when, in the 1920s through the 1940s, Muslim leaders claimed that "G*psies are not Turks, and Turks are not G*psies" and that Roma had no rights to land because they were "illegally meddling" (189).

80. Romani Archive, TsDA, Fond 1B, Inv. 55, Arch. 1344, pp. 42–51.

81. Znepolski et al. 2018, 315.

82. Marushiakova and Popov 2000, 6. Also, Mary Neuburger explains in a footnote that from 1960 to 1962, Roma were "encouraged to take on either Bulgarian or Turkish names, the latter as a transitional measure for eventual integration into the Bulgarian nation" (2004, 154).

83. Eminov 1997, 230. As these examples show, the problematic conflation of language with identity is part of ethnoreligious racialization in Bulgaria.

84. While this group is commonly called "Turks" in Bulgaria, when in Turkey they refer to themselves as *Bulgaristanlı,* referencing Bulgaria as a geographic location. This is distinct from the term "Bulgar" (Bulgarian), which implies ethnic identity (Parla 2019).

85. Eminov 1997, 230.

86. Kamusella 2018, xv.

87. Evidence for this comes from two different archives: an online collection of state socialist security documents about minorities (http://comdos.bg/media/DVD%20SBORNIK%2032_Minorities%20opt.pdf), and the DA-Sofia, Fond 1659, Komunalno Stopansko Predpriyatie "Chistota" – Sofia (1936–1999) [Communal Economic Company "Chistota" – Sofia (1936–1999)].

88. DA-Sofia, F. 1659, Inv. 1, Arch. 21, pp. 62–63.

89. DA-Sofia, F. 1659, Inv. 2, Arch. 23, pp. 12–13.

90. DA-Sofia, F. 1659, Inv. 2, Arch. 23, pp. 12–13.

91. The (Rafiev 1967) report declares: "Now there are over 18,000 g*psies working in production. In utility companies such as Chistota and 'Utility Services': 7,250 people, in construction 6,300 and in agriculture [there are] 56,400

NOTES TO THE INTRODUCTION

211

people." It links "permanent work" with the "overcoming of vagrancy," calling these the "biggest success of the Party with the g*psy population...[which serves as] a solid premise for fast resolution of other tasks connected to the further economic and cultural development of that population."

92. Romani Archive, TsDA, Fond 1B, Inv. 55, Arch. 1344, pp. 42–51.

93. For an example, see Lecerf 2024.

94. See Lemon 1995; Chang and Rucker-Chang 2020; and Creed 2011 for similar observations.

95. See Fikes and Lemon 2002 on accounts of "African presence" in the former USSR that are available or have been cited primarily in English. Also see Apostolova 2017 and Dragostinova 2021 on internationalism in Bulgaria.

96. These dormitories are now called "the Vietnamese dorms" (*Vietnamskite obshtezhitiya*) or simply "the Vietnamese" (*Vietnamskite*).

97. News stories of Ghanaian and other African students leaving Bulgaria were used in the United States as fodder for anticommunist sentiment and include students citing racism as a primary reason for leaving. One such quotation that begins a February 16, 1963, *Chicago Daily Tribune* article was from Robert Kotey, the twenty-five-year-old secretary of the Ghana Students' Union in Bulgaria: "We have been called black monkeys and jungle people and we were treated like dirt."

98. This included bringing in lawyers from civil rights cases in the United States, including Jack Greenberg, one of the leading lawyers who argued *Brown vs. the Board of Education* before the US Supreme Court. During my first trip to Bulgaria in 2003, I accompanied Romani NGO leaders on a trip with Greenberg, who spoke to Romani activist audiences about his experience. See Chang and Rucker-Chang 2020 and Resnick 2009.

99. I draw on the work of Kimberly Simmons on historical colorization, or "intragroup racial and color-naming practices," in the context of Dominicans in the United States and African Americans in the Dominican Republic (2008, 96).

100. Cf. Partridge 2008, 2022.

101. Over the years, many of my friends in Fakulteta attempted to provide evidence of how they are treated as trash so that I could document it. This included insistence that I photograph water infrastructures that were falling apart (as discussed in the Conclusion), overflowing waste bins that never got picked up, expired food that was sold in the neighborhood, and the *mente*, or counterfeit, products that they had to purchase (Jung 2019). As Jung notes, there is a correlation between *mente* goods and things categorized as "trash" (*bokluk*) or "garbage products" (2019, 27). Jung notes how "poor, ordinary Bulgarian consumers" "became dismayed" by these products in the postsocialist period (27). However, my Romani friends did not see this as a ubiquitous issue. Instead, they observed that ordinary Bulgarians could afford "nice stuff" while they were left to pick up and consume trash (e.g., *mente* cigarettes) because they were racially categorized as such. Also see Fehérváry on the "materialization of political subjectivity" in state socialism (2009, 429).

NOTES TO THE INTRODUCTION

102. This points to a form of recursive racialization, with Bulgarians categorized as not-quite-white in a pan-European framework but white within Bulgaria itself (Resnick 2024a). Also see Lewicki (2023).

103. See Weinberg, Schnaiberg, and Pellow 2000 on recycling and ecological modernization. Also see Gregson and Crang 2015 and Gregson et al. 2016 for analyses of the EU green economy's reliance on "dirty labor."

104. This comes from DA-Sofia, F. 1659 and oral history interviews (conducted in 2011, 2012, and 2013).

105. Oral histories and archival data from the DA-Sofia, F. 1659 and state security reports on minorities indicate that during socialism, Sofia's street sweepers were predominantly Roma.

106. During my first trip to Bulgaria in 2003, I worked at an NGO that was developing an educational pilot project that coordinated desegregation in six towns throughout Bulgaria. Most of their funding came through the Open Society Institute (OSI) and other private donors. Pre-accession (PHARE) EU funding officers would often come to the office to discuss the role of Romani integration in Bulgaria's Europeanization process. When I returned in 2009, former activists talked constantly about their disappointment (cf. Greenberg 2010, 2014): in 2003 they had had high hopes for what Europeanization would bring for the "Romani movement," but as the years went by, they told me, "it was just more of the same, in different form, with fancy conferences."

107. There were other hurdles in the then-thirty-one chapters of acquis communautaire, the accumulated rules and laws of the European Union, but as accession neared, the primary points for remediation were those listed here. See the Copenhagen, or EU accession, criteria: https://neighbourhood-enlargement.ec.europa.eu/enlargement-policy/glossary/accession-criteria_en.

108. I use the terms "formal" and "informal" here as a shorthand but with the understanding that the concept of informality is problematically linked to ideas of "lack" and "scarcity" without any attention to, as Kathleen Millar puts it, "how form is made" (2018, 28).

109. See Ghertner 2015 on aesthetic rule.

110. I first noticed this in 2012, five years since Bulgaria had joined the European Union. The way that "Europe" was always imagined as somewhere *over there* can be analyzed in terms of what Alexei Yurchak 2005 calls the "imaginary West" and in line with how Katherine Verdery describes speaking about "Europe" in postsocialist Romania as both "a statement of political intentions and a statement of national identity" (1996, 105). Also note what Donna Buchanan calls the place of an asymptotic and "amorphous" Europe in a postsocialist Bulgarian framework (2006, 37–38).

111. Beliso-De Jesus and Pierre 2020, 66; also Szombati 2018 and Shoshan 2016. Neda Atanasoski explains that "postsocialism marks the emergence of novel modes of interpreting the imperatives of the world map set in place by European imperial rule" (2013, 5).

NOTES TO THE INTRODUCTION AND CHAPTER 1

112. Goldstein 2003, 5. An important body of literature on humor in socialist and postsocialist spaces engages the absurdity of life (e.g., Boyer and Yurchak 2010; Klumbytė 2014; Nadkarni 2007; and Yurchak 2005).

113. Tuck and Yang 2014, 230.

114. Tuck and Yang 2014. 231.

115. Resnick 2021; Roberts 2017.

116. I am inspired deeply by the work of Aimee Meredith Cox (2015, 2022).

117. See, for example, Díaz and Rosa 2020; Hale 2005; Muehlebach 2012; Povinelli 2002; Rosa 2019; Shange 2019; and Speed 2005.

118. The coedited 2015 issue of *Roma Rights* covers the ongoing debate about the role of non-Romani scholars in Romani studies: http://www.errc.org/uploads/upload_en/file/roma-rights-2-2015-nothing-about-us-without-us.pdf. Also see work by Brooks 2012; Brooks, Clark, and Rostas 2022; Costache 2018; Kóczé 2015; Mirga-Kruszelnicka 2018; and Silverman 2018.

119. Matache 2017b.

120. Larkin 2008, 7.

121. I use an asterisk (*) in the word "G*psy" because the term has been used as a racial slur, and I do not want to replicate it in this text (Costache 2020; also see "Note on Language and Terminology"). It is important to also understand the history of the word and the contemporary usage of "Roma" (Fremlova 2022).

Chapter One

1. In other European cities, waste work is done by differently racialized groups and using different technologies. In Paris, for example, streets are still largely swept by hand and most garbage collectors are first- and second-generation immigrants from North and sub-Saharan Africa. In Athens, Greece—a country with a relatively high official unemployment rate (20.8% vs. the 9.2% average across the Euro area)—machines sweep the streets and most garbage collectors, like those on the back of trucks, are white Greek men. Waste work is also racialized differently across the globe. For comparative processes of waste-based racialization, dispossession, and colonialism see Ahmann 2024; Butt 2023; Dillon 2013; McKee 2015; Millar 2020; Reno and Halvorson 2021; Solomon 2019, 2022; Stamatopoulou-Robbins 2019; Vasudevan 2019; and Zimring 2016.

2. There is a well-established body of work on personhood and social categorization through socialist and postsocialist labor (Creed 1998; Dunn 2004; Fehérváry 2013; Grant 1995; Kideckel 2008; Kurtović 2020; Lampland 1995).

3. The minimum wage in Bulgaria when I began sweeping in October 2012 was 290 leva (160 dollars) per month. It was raised to 310 leva (170 dollars) per month in January 2013.

4. A privatizing contract between the Sofia metropolitan privatization agency and Chistota-Privat AD concluded on February 24, 1999, resulting in 75% of

Chistota shares being sold to private firms. The other 25% remained municipally owned. Over the next ten years, these cleaning companies were bought out by larger firms, many of which were owned by one or two conglomerate umbrella companies. Throughout the 2000s and during the time of my research, the conglomerates were reprimanded for failing to comply with Bulgaria's anti-monopolization laws.

5. To be eligible for unemployment benefits in Bulgaria, one needs to work twelve out of the previous eighteen months, be officially registered as unemployed, and have not yet earned the right to a pension. The benefit amount is then calculated as 60% of one's average daily income over the last twenty-four months (https://ec.europa.eu/social/main.jsp?catId=1103&langId=en&intPageId=4441#:~:text=The%20minimum%20amount%20for%202023,minimum%20benefits%20for%204%20months).

6. See Atanasoski and Vora 2019 on labor, race, and technoliberalism.

7. They were also deeply concerned with intergenerational debt accumulation. When a person dies in Bulgaria, their closest family members inherit the rights and responsibilities of the dead person, including the responsibility to pay any outstanding debts to physical persons, banks, and other legal entities.

8. According to Marushiakova and Popov 2021, the first Roma organization in Sofia was founded on May 7, 1929, and incorporated former *londzhi* (pl.) into the *Organisation Istikbal* (Future), which started with fifteen hundred members. Also in 1929, *Association Vzaimopomosht* (Mutual Aid) was founded by former members of *londzhi* (122). Krastev, Ivanova, and Krastev 2020 explain: "In references from the mid-70s about nationalist manifestations among the g*psy population of the country, it is written that *londzhas* are one of the forms of legal g*psy organizations. Their number in the different neighborhoods of Sofia is stated—18 of them were created in 1972, and in 1973, just on the territory of the Dimitrovski region, there were 12. In 1975–1976, in the neighborhoods 'Fakulteta,' 'Hr. Mihaylov,' and 'Druzhba,' there were 50 *londzhi*, each one of them with 10 to 30 members."

9. Stefchev 1979.

10. After the collapse of socialism, Roma struggled again to take out loans because they lacked the correct identification documents or enough documented income since so many Roma, particularly men, work as day or noncontracted laborers.

11. See Fanon 1952; James (1938) 2001; and Patterson (1982) 2018 on the role of labor in racial oppression.

12. Lisa Lowe explains, "The social inequalities of our time are a legacy of these processes through which 'the human' is 'freed' by liberal forms, while other subjects, practices, and geographies are placed at a distance from the 'human'" (2015, 2).

13. This sentiment connects to literature on nostalgia (Berdahl 1999a; Buchanan 2010; Grant 2010; Nadkarni and Shevchenko 2004) and its links with neoliberalism (Creed 2010) and a future yet to come (Boyer 2006). Parla's 2009, 2019 works, which document Turkish immigrants noting similar things about socialist Bulgaria, are particularly relevant.

NOTES TO CHAPTER 1

14. This could be seen as a kind of workplace infrapolitics, a surreptitious resistance to the daily rules and exploitative labor practices of the company (Kelley 1993, 1994; Scott 1990). But it was not quite so oppositional and was certainly not a "one-up event," but rather it maintained "sociality through time" (Simpson 2016, 329). This refusal was generative, creative, and relationship-building, with sweepers invoking their quiet "capacity to undermine, disrupt, or destabilize the logic of the dominant" by "dwelling in" the space of both disruption and absurdity (Campt 2017, 162).

15. Other scholars have framed such somatic experiences as signs of fungibility (Hartman 1997; King 2019), in which, as la paperson explains, "'life' is reduced to just another state of matter, to plug and play into machines of re/production" (2017, 15). Or, as Deborah Thomas puts it, workers become "objects in the midst of other objects" (2019, 4).

16. This speaks to what Catherine Fennell refers to as "bodily dispositions built through institutional segregation, neglect and abandonment" (2015, 130). Such bodily dispositions made it so that most of my Romani coworkers talked about needing to work in order to feel good. Also see West Ohueri 2021 on embodied racism in Albania.

17. Resnick 2021, 4.

18. See the European Parliament Fact Sheet on resource efficiency and the circular economy: https://www.europarl.europa.eu/factsheets/en/sheet/76/resource-efficiency-and-the-circular-economy. Also see O'Neill (2019) on global instantiations of Zero Waste and the circular economy and Gille (2010) on how postsocialism intersects with EU regulations.

19. See https://eur-lex.europa.eu/legal-content/EN/TXT/PDF/?uri=CELEX :32008L0098&from=EN.

20. 2008/98/EC, https://eur-lex.europa.eu/legal-content/EN/TXT/HTML/ ?uri=CELEX%3A32008L0098.

21. 2008/98/EC.

22. These sanctions, however, have been critiqued as too soft to be effective, such that the reduced landfill tax is the only real incentive to meet targets (https://www.eea.europa.eu/publications/many-eu-member-states/bulgaria). Sosna 2024 writes about lived, everyday effects of the EU's hierarchization of "different means of waste management," including how "landfilling became a target for elimination" (322).

23. See https://ec.europa.eu/environment/eir/pdf/factsheet_bg_en.pdf; also https://unece.org/DAM/env/epr/epr_studies/Synopsis/ECE_CEP_181_Bulgaria _Synopsis.pdf. Very little progress has been made since I began tracking this in 2008.

24. See Ghodsee 2005 on gendered labor in the tourism sector in Bulgaria as well as Brooks 2012; Kóczé 2020; Kóczé et al. 2018; and Oprea 2004 on intersectional Romani feminisms.

25. This and the following quotes are drawn from Rafiev 1967.

26. See Aroyo 1974.

216 NOTES TO CHAPTERS 1 AND 2

27. Krisztina Fehérváry explains that "social identity and the construction of self were profoundly tied to the act of transformation of the material world and the display of the products of this labor" (2013, 63). In this way, socialist-era industrialization and beautification projects "were based on the contention that physical labor (especially collective labor) had transformative powers and could rehabilitate even the most morally corrupt person from class enemies to Roma (g*psies)" (63).

28. DA-Sofia, F. 1659, Inv. 2, Arch. 2, pp. 4–6. In a December 5, 1946, document, it states that two-fifths of the positions in the cleaning sector of Sofia are vacant and that the main reasons for this are the bad working conditions and low wages, which were later increased to attract more workers.

29. The word *m*ngal*, according to Bulgarian dictionaries, is translated as "brazier" or a vessel that holds hot coals for heating a home or cooking outdoors. The word is wielded as a racist slur because of the association of dark skin with the blackness of coal soot. One widely shared, video-recorded use of the term occurred in 2007, when Bulgarian soldiers handing out water to children at the Ashraf refugee camp in Iraq called them this slur and "G*psy" (*ts*gani*) interchangeably.

30. Website accessed on the morning of July 19, 2012, before it was removed.

31. See Lemon 1995, 1998, 2000 on the racialization of Roma in terms of both embodied labor and material proximities. Lie 2021 might analyze this through a "raciosemiotic approach," emphasizing how semiotic modalities "contribute along with language to the generation of ideologies about racialized groups" (10).

32. For more about the race-technology interface, see Atanasoski and Vora 2019 and Chun 2009.

33. DA-Sofia, F. 1659.

34. Todorova 2018, 120. Todorova draws on the work of Turda and Weindling 2007 to make this argument.

35. This point is a nod to Homi Bhabha's analysis of mimicry ([1994] 2012).

36. Aesthetic Europeanness relies upon the racialized power hierarchies that have undergirded Europeanization for centuries. Racial categorization and "Europeanness" emerged through, and continue to facilitate, settler and nonsettler colonialisms, chattel slavery, and genocide (Hesse 2007; Liboiron 2021; Wolfe 2006). As part of the ongoing legacy of Europeanization-as-racialization, EU expansion relies on the "organizing grammar of race" to establish its aesthetic regimes and propel itself forward (Wolfe 2016, 387).

37. I thank Savannah Shange for helping me frame this insight.

38. This concords with what Mayanthi Fernando writes regarding how "Muslim French disrupt the tight relation between contemporary republican politics and Frenchness" (2014, 61).

Chapter Two

1. During my research, packs of stray dogs attacked and killed multiple people, including professor and writer Botyo Tachkov in 2012.

2. In Bulgaria a "centralized collection system with outlets in all municipalities where people were able to sell used paper, metals, glass and textiles was

NOTES TO CHAPTER 2

established back in 1949" (Velkova 2003, 9). By the 1990s "there was one outlet for every 8,000 inhabitants with the intention of achieving one outlet for every 5000 inhabitants" (9–10).

3. The Treaty on European Union (TEU) details the European Union's purpose, principles, institutions, governance framework, and common foreign and security policy: https://eur-lex.europa.eu/summary/chapter/20.html. The other critical treaty is the Treaty on the Functioning of the European Union (TFEU).

4. Cf. Lavergne 2010.

5. The height of the Bulgarian hyperinflation crisis was in late 1996 and early 1997. See Balyozov 1999 and analyses from the International Monetary Fund: https://www.imf.org/external/pubs/ft/fandd/1999/09/gulde.htm.

6. See https://www.washingtonpost.com/archive/opinions/1997/02/15/a -humanitarian-effort/8924a81f-d98a-451b-a060-1a0f2fcf452d/. Also see Jung 2019 on the role of socialist, postsocialist, and EU-era consumption in how Bulgarians understood their relationships to state structures and Europeanness.

7. "Bulgaria's economy contracted dramatically after 1989 with the collapse of the Eastern Bloc's COMECON (Council for Mutual Economic Assistance) system and the loss of the Soviet market, to which the Bulgarian economy had been closely tied. The standard of living fell by about 40%. In addition, UN sanctions against Yugoslavia and Iraq took a heavy toll on the Bulgarian economy" (https:// 2009-2017.state.gov/outofdate/bgn/bulgaria/19088.htm). For inflation rate documentation, see https://www.nsi.bg/en/content/2539/inflation-rate-calculator.

8. For a deep dive into Bulgaria's hyperinflation, see Charles and Marie 2017.

9. Cellarius 2000. The anthropologist Barbara Cellarius noted that during this time barter became a primary means of exchange in the Bulgarian Rhodope Mountain village where she was conducting research. Since currency was so hard to come by, families found it nearly impossible to meet household demands through monetary means alone; potatoes thus began to serve as a proxy for cash.

10. This was months before Bulgaria positively concluded its negotiations to join the EU. See Stanchev 2004 and World Bank time-series data for indices of economic development: https://data.worldbank.org/indicator/NY.GDP.PCAP.CD ?locations=BG.

11. In the 1990s and early 2000s organized crime groups had a stronghold throughout Bulgaria, resulting in a great deal of violence, theft, and smuggling that some argue began during the state socialist regime (Kenarov 2009).

12. Gulde 1999.

13. See "Agenda 2000 - Commission Opinion on Bulgaria's Application for Membership of the European Union": https://ec.europa.eu/commission/ presscorner/detail/en/DOC_97_11.

14. DA-Sofia, F. 1659, Inv. 2, Arch. 2, pp. 14–15. Throughout the 1940s and '50s, Chistota attempted to bring men to the city from villages, supplying them with dormitories and other benefits, but this practice proved ineffective.

15. DA-Sofia, F. 1659, Inv. 1, Arch. 21, p. 33.

16. One example of EU green economy policy: https://www.eea.europa.eu/ publications/earnings-jobs-and-innovation-the.

218 NOTES TO CHAPTER 2

17. Gille 2000, 204.

18. Reuse had racial dimensions as well as recycling. For example, there are entire towns in northwestern Bulgaria in which Romani communities still live in solid brick houses that they report were built with leftover (waste) bricks from the brick factories where they worked during socialism.

19. Gille 2007.

20. Recycling officials widely refuted this common refrain by explaining that, although it might appear that all waste goes to the same place, this is only because the waste installation site uses the same conveyor belt (where Romani women sort by hand) for all waste streams. Alexander and O'Hare 2020 similarly write about a waste politics of "ignorance."

21. The tension between volunteer cleaning and underpaid waste labor was evident throughout my research. While street sweepers worked according to a contract, they told me repeatedly that they also had to work weekends and holidays "for the state." They were not paid overtime but explained that it was as "voluntary" as it was in socialist times—meaning compulsory. They also sometimes worked alongside cleaning campaigns sponsored by famous television stations, like the annual bTV "Clean Bulgaria in One Day" campaign. At these events, they see that their paid labor is considered less important than volunteers, who are often well-off white Bulgarians with prestigious jobs who want to publicly help clean up Bulgaria. A group of young Romani activists who took part in the 2012 campaign and cleaned up Fakulteta wore matching T-shirts to distinguish themselves as volunteers, knowing that they would otherwise be televised and naturalized as just another group of "G*psy cleaners."

22. This is according to the 1990 Bulletin of Phoenix Resource that I was given by Professor Nadezhda Davcheva-Ilcheva, who created one of Bulgaria's first laboratories for the research and utilization of metal (copper, steel, aluminum) industrial waste products.

23. Mauch 2016.

24. MacBride 2011, 126.

25. Cf. Gabrys 2009; Liboiron 2021.

26. Zero Waste, at its core, relies on the concept of resources, which is rooted in colonialist approaches to Land, specifically Land's transformation into a commodity to be used, profited from, and privatized (Liboiron 2021).

27. Discussions with waste officials about the Bulgarian adoption and adaptation of Zero Waste brought up what Christina Schwenkel calls the "productive tensions between hope and fantasy that coalesced around traveling technologies" (2020, 20). These conversations reminded me of others throughout my fieldwork about Bulgaria's adoption of "Western" plastic technologies of the 1970s that promised to revolutionize consumption and, inevitably, would transform discard as well (see Rubin 2008 on socialist plastics in the GDR).

28. PRO (Packaging Recovery Organisation) Europe outlines the green dot financing symbol: https://www.pro-e.org/the-green-dot-trademark.

29. The European Union's EUR-lex site provides the full list of criteria: https://eur-lex.europa.eu/summary/glossary/accession_criteria_copenhague.html.

NOTES TO CHAPTER 2

30. Christina Schwenkel writes about a similar indexing of economic reform by waste accumulation in Vietnam (2018, 2020). Also see Jung 2019 on the "co-existing conditions of material abundance and growing inequality" of postsocialism (6).

31. I am grateful for Marisa Solomon's help in formulating this point.

32. See Kristen Ghodsee's account of the decline of Bulgaria's massive zinc-mining operation, GORUBSO, and the role of former miners (2010).

33. This reliance resonates with Rosalind Fredericks's work in Dakar on the role of human labor in neoliberal waste infrastructures: "Garbage illuminates the ways that material matters in its encounter with human bodies and the intersecting precarities that are bred when infrastructures rely increasingly on laboring bodies" (2018, 95).

34. See https://ec.europa.eu/transport/sites/default/files/media/publications/doc/modern_rail_en.pdf.

35. See Creed 1998; Jung 2010; and Resnick 2017 on ideas of "normal" in Bulgaria, as well as Greenberg 2010, 2014; and Fehérváry 2002 on "a normal life" in Serbia and Hungary, respectively.

36. Gerald Creed addresses stereotypes of Romani criminality in Bulgaria. Creed analyzes the essentialization of Romani criminality through the claims of a friend who states that "Bulgarians steal, but G*psies cannot *not* steal" (2011, 179).

37. During the 2012 campaign to "Clean Bulgaria in One Day," I traveled to the touristed Black Sea town of Sozopol where a group of wealthy and well-traveled scuba divers were filmed by bTV as they dove into the water to collect garbage. I watched from a dinghy as they prepared for the dive and expressed concern that there wouldn't be enough nearby trash to make the story worthwhile for the TV crew. Once in the water, they surfaced every now and then, reaching their arms out to show what they had collected—mostly debris from boats, like tire parts used as boat bumpers and stray pieces of metal. Afterwards, the divers joined me back in the boat and held up the metal scraps they had found as though trash trophies, declaring themselves "G*psies of the sea."

38. The report can be found online: https://ipen.org/sites/default/files/documents/19ceh_zero_waste_as_bep_in_cee_countries-en.pdf.

39. The report was organized by International POPs Elimination Project in partnership with the United Nations Industrial Development Organization, the United Nations Environment Program, and the Global Environment Facility. Also see Velkova 2003 on the lack of information about *kloshari* labor.

40. This report cites "MEW (2003a)" as the source of this information. However, I have not been able to identify this source or locate any statistics on the percentage of people who work as *kloshari* (scavengers) in Bulgaria. I asked Stoyanova, who had shared the report with me, for this documentation, but it was from so long ago that she could not find it. However, I trust these details, as they accord with my own interviews.

41. See Neuburger 2012 on the history of cigarettes as currency in Bulgaria.

42. The report specifically notes that local residents can help divert waste from being incinerated, aligning with goals laid out in the Stockholm

Convention (accepted on May 22, 2001), which "regards waste management as a big source of emissions of persistent organic pollutants."

43. This also causes problems with mail delivery. Daniela Mihaylova explained this to me via personal communication and pointed me to the Bulgarian Civil Registration Act (paragraph 1, point 1 of the Supplementary Provisions [*Dopalnitelni Razporedbi*]).

44. I think the visible presence of both me and my visiting friend, who was filming the ride as part of a collaborative project we were working on, also contributed to us being stopped by the police.

45. Most EU documents about waste management in Bulgaria do not include any mention of collection points (*punktove*), recyclers (*kloshari*), or the human labor that it takes to meet EU recycling targets.

46. Bulgaria is just one example of the many places that Western Europe stores, burns, or hides its waste beyond the watchful eyes of European Union monitors. Bulgaria and Romania have served as EU dumping sites for years; see https://www.europeandatajournalism.eu/eng/News/Data-news/Why-and-how -Bulgaria-imports-waste-from-other-EU-countries and https://emerging-europe .com/news/the-eu-needs-to-regulate-waste-exports-to-central-and-eastern -europe/. The EU also exported over thirty-two million tons of waste to non-EU countries in 2020—nearly twice the amount traded within the EU that same year. The four largest non-EU importers of EU waste are Turkey, India, Indonesia, and Pakistan (https://ec.europa.eu/eurostat/web/products-eurostat-news/-/ddn -20210420-1).

47. See https://voxeurop.eu/en/how-bulgaria-is-becoming-europes-lucrative -landfill/.

48. See Sosna, Stehlíková, and Mašek 2024 on the practices, politics, and possibilities of quantification in the waste sector.

49. These two principles were the basis of the 1990s Environmental Protection Law (EPL) (publ. in the Official Gazette, n. 86/1991; amend. n.90/1991; add. and correc., n.100/1992; n.31, 63/1995; n.13/1997; n.85, 86/1997), which was replaced by the Environmental Protection Act in 2002 (https://www.moew.government .bg/en/environmental-protection-act-7628/).

50. Materially, this reuse has extended to shoddily built socialist-era buildings, like the dorms built for Vietnamese guest workers (*Vietnamskite obshte-zhitiya*) that were owned by the Sofia municipality and rented to low-income Romani residents. (This housing complex has since been partially demolished, starting in 2017.) Luciana Aenasoaie 2016 describes similar conditions in Romania, including how Roma in Piatra Neamt were relocated to a former communist chicken farm outside the city using EU funds.

51. Zero Waste is a case of when "clean up becomes a civilizing project to ensure a better, whiter, gentrified future" (Solomon 2019, 77). Bulgarian discussions about Zero Waste reminded me of Anya Bernstein's description of Russian immortalism: "an attempt to bring the future into the present by advocating and exemplifying certain modes of being and acting in the world" (2019, 10).

NOTES TO CHAPTERS 2 AND 3

52. Resnick 2024a. Also see https://www.nytimes.com/2011/09/28/world/europe/anti-roma-demonstrations-spread-across-bulgaria.html.

53. "Bulgaria for Bulgarians" was a common chant throughout a series of 2010–2011 protests, serving as both an anti-refugee and anti-Roma declaration. For example, see https://www.state.gov/wp-content/uploads/2019/01/Bulgaria-1.pdf.

54. For example, in Devecser, Hungary, infamous for its toxic, red sludge flood in 2010, far-right protesters called on community members to fight back against "G*psy criminality" and to "sweep out" and "exterminate" the "rubbish" of the country (https://www.errc.org/news/far-right-violence-against-roma-in-hungary-victory-in-strasbourg-for-the-helsinki-committee).

Chapter Three

1. See Sarafian 2023 on "the politics of childbearing" and how images of Romani women's reproduction "feed obsessive discussions of G*psiness in media, policy, state, and nonstate areas" (101).

2. See https://ec.europa.eu/esf/home.jsp.

3. Resnick 2009 addresses transnational affiliations that Romani activists use to ground a sense of legitimacy *within* Bulgaria.

4. Guiraudon 2009; Chang 2018; and Stenroos 2018 provide further analyses of the role of Roma within "minority integration" initiatives in Europe.

5. This isn't well documented in official reports, but this was a constant topic of conversation in the Romani Star office, which was provided condoms through an EU program to distribute to neighborhood residents in Fakulteta.

6. One can look to examples from the Council of Europe (https://www.coe.int/en/web/children/roma-children) and the European Commission (https://commission.europa.eu/strategy-and-policy/policies/justice-and-fundamental-rights/combatting-discrimination/roma-eu/roma-equality-inclusion-and-participation-eu_en).

7. See "Post-monitoring dialogue with Bulgaria" from the Council of Europe Parliamentary Assembly: https://assembly.coe.int/nw/xml/XRef/Xref-XML2HTML-en.asp?fileid=19402&lang=en.

8. Over time, as skilled Romani leaders were pushed out in favor of "experts," they either were employed as low-paid consultants to add legitimacy to white Bulgarians' projects or weren't paid at all because it was assumed that they would want to "help" for free. See Jung 2010 for another discussion of such experts taking over the NGO arena in Bulgaria.

9. These conditions could be considered what Lauren Berlant calls "compromised conditions of possibility" (2011, 21).

10. Such subversions were often discussed, with humor, over casual conversation and included things like figuring out ways during socialism to access contraband music, import prohibited consumer goods, and use personal connections to bypass state structures.

11. Documentation from state socialist surveillance of minority groups like Roma, states that directions had been given "from the Ministry of Interior and

NOTES TO CHAPTER 3

the Directorate of the National Police for reenforcing the explicit control and the operational surveillance over the criminal contingent among the Bulgarian citizens of G*psy origin" (Katsamunski 1982). Also, Surdu and Kovats 2015 and Rostas and Moisă 2023 address EU-era racial police profiling.

12. According to an informational report from Ali Rafiev (1967), head of the Department "for Work with Mass Organizations and the Turkish Population" of the Bulgarian Communist Party's Central Committee: "Another set of issues to keep in mind when working within the g*psy population is the efforts amongst the capitalist propaganda to create hesitation and disbelief towards the party and their politics. Effort towards creating nationalistic attitudes within the more woke g*psies. For this purpose they spread rumors about the creation of g*psy country in Africa, texts about putting the g*psy issue in front of the UN and the formation of a World g*psy organization, about the India origin of the g*psies and so on."

13. Krastev, Ivanova, and Krastev 2020.

14. See http://roma-swu.weebly.com/uploads/9/1/1/0/91107766/ds_plan-1950 .pdf.

15. Communist Party Council of Ministers, June 17, 1959. "Pismo №809 do Okrazhnite, Gradski i Rayonni Komiteti na BKP" [Letter No. 809 to the District, City and Regional Committees of the BCP (Bulgarian Communist Party)].

16. This quote is from the Archive of the Ministry of the Interior, F. 26, Inv. 2, Arch. 436, p. 3, cited in Ivanova and Krastev 2019, "The G*psies/Roma in Bulgaria in the Years of Socialism—Forced Migration and Population." Proceedings of the conference (Re)thinking Socialism: Knowledge, Memory and the Oblivion of the Socialist Past. Bulgarian Academy of Sciences, Institute of Ethnology and Folklore Studies with Ethnographic Museum (IEFSEM – BAS), November 7–9, 2019.

17. Bulgarian state surveillance of Roma resonates with what Simone Browne, writing about the trans-Atlantic slave trade, calls "racializing surveillance" (2015, 8).

18. This was even documented in Bulgarian state socialist security archives. A 1967 memorandum outlines the threat of foreign journalists visiting Romani neighborhoods, claiming that "because of their bad hygiene, lack of water and sewage systems, and the huge overcrowding, these neighborhoods are a place of outbreaks of infectious diseases and subject to the cameras of unscrupulous tourists and journalists" (Rafiev 1967).

19. Anthropologists Richard Thurnwald and Eugen Fischer, founders of Nazi eugenic "science," sponsored and supported Justin's doctoral research. See Benedict, Shields, Holmes, and Kurth (2018) for more on Eva Justin.

20. It is rumored that socialist leaders went abroad before socialism's collapse in November 1989 to avoid lustration and potential prosecution—and to make sure their money was safe in non-Bulgarian banks.

21. New political leaders emerging at the end of socialism focused on the environment to leverage anticommunist sentiment, and some of these same leaders went on to lead Romani rights movements in the early 1990s. This includes leaders of the oppositional, prodemocracy environmental group Ecoglasnost, who

NOTES TO CHAPTER 3

went on to lead human rights organizations focusing on Romani issues in the early 1990s, such as Krassimir Kanev of the Bulgarian Helsinki Committee and Dimitrina Petrova of the now-defunct Human Rights Project. See also Krastanova 2019 and Petrova 1992.

22. At the time, George Soros's Open Society Institute (OSI) was promoting democracy in postsocialist states, leading to strong relationships between Roma NGOs and programs that sent Romani students to English-language and other educational and activist programs abroad.

23. See https://eur-lex.europa.eu/EN/legal-content/glossary/accession-criteria -copenhagen-criteria.html. These priorities were made clear in pre-accession PHARE funding. Also see Babül 2017 on human rights and EU accession criteria.

24. Dzenovska 2018 analyzes related issues of tolerance, inclusion, and political liberalism.

25. This proposal was posted to the website of the Bulgarian Council of Ministers, the main authority of the executive branch of Bulgarian government, and promoted widely on social media.

26. See http://www.strategy.bg/PublicConsultations/View.aspx?lang=bg-BG &Id=4289.

27. http://www.strategy.bg/PublicConsultations/View.aspx?lang=bg-BG&Id =4289.

28. "Cleaning up" the past to make way for a new material and ideological regime is not new to Bulgaria. After Ottoman liberation in 1878, mosques were converted into churches, and Sofia was drastically transformed to forge a sense of European legitimacy (Gigova 2011). Socialist purges used a similar logic, focusing on the human dimension of political change and killing former leaders to clean out the old regime (Fitzpatrick 1994). Cleaning out also took place in the postsocialist transition as street names were changed and communist infrastructures and monuments removed or destroyed (Vukov 2015).

29. The European Commission provides a website that explains its funding programs and regulations: https://ec.europa.eu/regional_policy/en/funding/, cf. Kóczé and Rövid 2012; Sigona and Trehan 2009.

30. Also see Chang 2018 regarding the populist backlash against Roma integration initiatives.

31. This data comes from the European Union Agency for Fundamental Rights 2014 report "Poverty and Employment: The Situation of Roma in 11 EU Member States" (https://fra.europa.eu/sites/default/files/fra-2014-roma -survey-employment_en.pdf).

32. This information comes from the 2020 European Commission report "Youth Guarantee Country by Country" (https://ec.europa.eu/social/BlobServlet ?docId=13631&langId=en#:~:text=While%20the%20overall%20unemployment %20rate,the%20EU%20rate%20of%2010.5%25).

33. One such study is that of the UNDP about "Roma and non-Roma in the Labour Market in Central and South Eastern Europe" (O'Higgins 2012).

NOTES TO CHAPTER 3

34. I provide these statistics to give a sense of how quantitative analyses address issues of workplace discrimination and racialized labor. However, it is also important to note that in places like Bulgaria and beyond (e.g., Czech Republic), there has been a general oversimplification of "interpretations of Roma underemployment, which assume that the Roma are 'unemployed' despite the fact that the majority of Roma engage in waged labor, albeit often in informal arrangements that national employment statistics do not account for" (Černušáková 2021, 49).

35. This is according to the European Union Agency for Fundamental Human Rights (https://fra.europa.eu/sites/default/files/fra-2014-roma-survey-employment_en.pdf).

36. See https://nsi.bg/sites/default/files/files/pressreleases/SILC2021_en_6IY8TD4.pdf.

37. Cf. Resnick 2017.

38. Robinson [1983] 2000.

39. The idea that Roma who protested must be paid by others who capitalized on their protest was a common assertion in conversation and on social media platforms but has no veracity.

40. Under the expulsion program, Roma adults were given "300 euros and children 100 euros to return to Romania or Bulgaria." In 2011 Human Rights Watch noted that, "according to government figures, 4,714 Romanians and Bulgarians were expelled from France in the first three months of the year. Just over 9,500 were expelled in all of 2010" (https://www.hrw.org/news/2011/09/29/france-one-year-new-abuses-against-roma). And, according to Human Rights Watch, by February 2011, the French government confirmed "that 70 percent of the 741 unlawful Roma camps identified in July 2010 had been dismantled" (https://www.hrw.org/news/2011/09/28/frances-compliance-european-free-movement-directive-and-removal-ethnic-roma-eu).

41. Bertossi 2010. In France, Law no. 2011–672 on Immigration, Integration and Nationality ("2011 Immigration Law") was enacted on June 16, 2011, and was used to expel Roma from France.

42. It was reported that France deported 19,380 Roma migrants in 2013, a much higher number than in 2012 (9,404) and 2011 (8,455) (https://www.rfi.fr/en/europe/20140114-french-socialists-double-roma-evictions).

43. Although this was not explicitly stated, many European scholars and activists read between the lines to make this same analysis, including my interlocutors in this chapter. See the edited volume by Magazzini and Piemontese 2019.

44. The article can be found here: https://www.24chasa.bg/Article/622490.

45. This interview was quoted and reposted by various international organizations, including the Open Society Institute.

46. This accords with Jane Hill's work on (racist) "real talk" and white supremacist politics (1998).

47. While at the time I worried about my ability to complete research because of this, the more lasting effect has been to question how the US embassy imagined

NOTES TO CHAPTERS 3 AND 4

the role of the United States in Romani communities. This later became clear to me when an effort to quell Islamic extremism in Romani neighborhoods became a main concern of the US embassy and local officials. See https://wikileaks.org/plusd/cables/05SOFIA1729_a.html; https://balkaninsight.com/2016/01/11/the-roma-and-the-radicals-bulgaria-s-alleged-isis-support-base-01-10-2016-1/.

48. For an example of EU-policy terminological loopholes see Lecerf 2024.

49. Not much has been published on these events except by a few foreign journalists, including Chuck Sudetic, who was writing for the Open Society Foundation at the time. I discussed these issues with him in Bulgaria while he was conducting interviews in 2013 and then via a phone call in 2020. After the call he generously provided me with his interview notes, which I draw on here.

50. Sudetic 2013.

51. Stefan explained that the post-1989 years could be organized into stages. He called the final stage, after EU accession, the "totalitarian period," in which "institutions, the government, undertook strong measures against Romani organizations...they were closing chapters for EU accession. [They] closed chapters for industry, energy...and one of the chapters was Roma...and after that, you know, it left room free for torture."

52. Resnick 2009. Also see Chang and Rucker-Chang 2020.

53. See accounts of this event: https://www.novinite.com/articles/141465/Bulgarian+President%27s+Website+Stirs+Outrage+with+Ethnic+Slur; https://www.bghelsinki.org/en/news/bulgarian-presidential-employee-reprimanded-over-racial-slur.

54. Or, following Christina Sharpe, it was "the Weather" (2016, 105).

Chapter Four

1. This was also confirmed in post-election meetings with the Danish delegation, the OSCE, and the Bulgarian Helsinki Committee that I attended. A 2012 Council of Europe report on the 2011 Bulgarian elections states: "Whilst evidence of vote-buying is difficult to trace—it is by nature a secret activity, transactions are in cash or in kind—and Congress observers found nobody who admitted personal experience of it, there was widespread belief that the problem is a real one.... In addition, a survey conducted by Transparency International Bulgaria (TI) dated 21 October 2011 found that 10% of the respondents declared that they, or a friend of theirs, were offered money to vote for a particular party or candidate in the elections" (§29). The report goes on to note that survey respondents identified poverty as a reason people sold their votes, and that "accusations and counter-accusations of pressure, undue influence and selling/buying of votes are issues in Bulgaria that divide and fragment communities. These accusations were particularly aimed at the most vulnerable in those communities—often Romani ones—who, through political campaigns intolerant to minorities, may also be presented as the source of the problem" (§31) (https://rm.coe.int/168071b0c9).

2. Sudetic 2013.

NOTES TO CHAPTER 4

3. This is mandated in the Election Code of Bulgaria, adopted on March 5, 2014: https://www.venice.coe.int/webforms/documents/default.aspx?pdffile=CDL-REF(2014)025-e.

4. Mishev 2023.

5. Weiss 2016, 355.

6. Robinson (1983) 2000, 310. Retreat, Robinson posits, makes room for something new in former spaces of oppression. Locating retreat, refusal, and disengagement in my friends' ostensibly mundane abstention illuminates how the most obvious form of democratic politics fails entire communities.

7. See Pasieka 2017 on transnationalism and far-right groups.

8. I first learned of this phrase during the mass protests of 2013–2014, when my roommate explained why so many Bulgarians were spending day after day protesting the government for over a year (Resnick 2017).

9. This refusal also leads them to "imagine...other ways of organizing the polity and other ways of practicing politics" (Fernando 2014, 61–62). See Channell-Justice 2022; Kurtović 2019; and Razsa 2015 on multiple political "otherwises" being fought for in Southeastern Europe and post-Soviet places.

10. See https://www.novinite.com/articles/170724/Demolition+of+Illegal+Roma+Buildings+in+Bulgaria%27s+Garmen+Continues.

11. See https://www.bghelsinki.org/en/news/appeal-voivodinovo/.

12. This connects to debates about acceptable and unacceptable forms (and definitions) of neighborhood razing, gentrification, and urban renewal around the globe (Alves 2019; Checker 2011, 2020; Potuoğlu-Cook 2006) as well as notions of eventfulness (Ahmann 2018).

13. See https://novini.bg/bylgariya/obshtestvo/670744.

14. See Atanasova 2023 on this phenomenon in the 2023 elections. Also see Krasteva 2016.

15. May and Czymara 2024 analyze this phenomenon.

16. See Atanasova 2023, which explains that out of 705 representatives in European Parliament in 2023, only three were Roma. At the national level in Bulgaria, representation is equally poor, if not worse.

17. Conflating Roma with state structures was common in everyday white Bulgarian conversation and in media accounts; see Lemon 2000 and Sigona and Trehan 2009.

18. It even became a US State Department concern: https://2009-2017.state.gov/documents/organization/186548.pdf.

19. See Resnick 2011.

20. See Kaneff 2004.

21. Yuson Jung writes about *mente*, or "fake," low-quality products in Bulgaria that also came to signify all that "was not right in the aftermath of socialism" (2019, 1). I also thank Krisztina Fehérváry for pointing me to debates over lower-quality food products, like lower-quality Nutella, being sold in postsocialist countries and higher-quality versions sold in Western Europe:

https://www.economist.com/europe/2017/06/29/eastern-europeans-think -western-food-brands-are-selling-them-dross.

22. This anti-corruption cleanup metaphor extends beyond Bulgaria, having also been used in protests in Egypt, Russia, and elsewhere (Reeves 2013; Winegar 2016).

23. The #DANSWITHME protests began in 2013 and continued for over a year (Koycheva 2016; O'Brien 2019; Resnick 2017).

24. These protests articulate with Manning's 2007 analysis of the representation and reception of Georgia's "Rose Revolution" due to the historical semiotic reverberations of this chant. The rhyme was both new to many protesters (who were too young to remember the protests of the 1990s) and old enough for a legitimate place in a longer Bulgarian protest history, including the late-1989/1990s anti-communist protests that also centered on "red trash."

25. See https://www.segabg.com/hot/nakazvat-spas-gurnevski-samo-poricanie -zaradi-obidi-kum-kolegi.

26. For other examples of this, see Chalfin 2023; Doherty 2021; and Fredericks 2018.

27. See Lavergne 2010 on genealogies of power in postsocialist Bulgaria.

28. I witnessed similar dynamics taking place in villages throughout the Bulgarian countryside, even where residents were not Roma but (primarily elderly) white Bulgarians.

29. Although Petar is a public official, I use a pseudonym for him here of my own accord in order to protect his privacy, since so much of this chapter was off the official record.

30. Due to the relatively small size of this neighborhood, I use a pseudonym to anonymize it.

31. Shange 2019, 3–4.

32. This is a pseudonym.

33. While the typical day-laborer wage in Sofia was twenty leva per day at the time, the going rate for labor outside Sofia was usually much lower.

34. The systemic discrimination against Roma in hiring practices is something that has been well documented since the 2000s (https://www.errc.org/ roma-rights-journal/systemic-exclusion-of-roma-from-employment).

35. See work by Alves 2018 on the state's role in producing the urban living conditions that Black Brazilians are then criminalized for.

36. Simpson 2016, 326.

37. Here I draw primarily on two substantial reports from this election period. The first is the 2012 monitoring report from the Civil Society in Action Association: "The Katunitsa Impact on Bulgarian Presidential and Local Elections 2011 Transition from Social Populism Towards National Populism: Possible Risks of Ascribing Ethnic Character to Social Conflicts During Elections in Bulgaria." Monitoring for this report was part of the project Roma Observation Mission on Presidential and Local Elections in Bulgaria, supported by the Open Society Institute-Budapest (OSI) Roma Initiative Program and the Sofia-based Open Society

NOTES TO CHAPTER 4

Foundation (OSF) Roma Program. The second is an OSCE report, which states: "All interlocutors met by the OSCE/ODIHR NAM expressed concerns over possible vote-buying and voter intimidation, particularly in the municipal elections, which are considered crucial by most interlocutors. Minority groups, especially Roma, are perceived as most vulnerable in terms of such possible electoral irregularities and interlocutors commented that particular attention should be paid to this issue.... Further, it was noted that schemes for vote buying are becoming more sophisticated; particular concerns were expressed as to some contestants bribing election commissioners" (https://www.osce.org/odihr/elections/81779).

38. In fact, the report from Civil Society in Action explains that because what was happening in the country after Katunitsa, many Roma did not sell their votes at all during this election. Instead, "using threats and force" was the more popular tactic in the 2011 election and included the following:

- Attacks against Roma neighborhoods and media hate speech during the pre-election period created fear and made people vulnerable to pressure and manipulations by the political parties.
- The strong dependency of workers on their employers, of debtors on their creditors, and of people relying on social benefits in an acute economic crisis with a high unemployment rate and massive impoverishment of society forced many of the voters to cast their vote not in line with what they believed in, but in the name of their survival.

39. Roma are also criminalized for many other crimes they don't commit. As multiple international tribunals have found, Roma regularly deal with police profiling and state-sanctioned violence (https://www.refworld.org/docid/50a9ed2f2.html).

40. Many Romani elected officials have been manipulated by political opportunists in ways that make the white public assume that either Roma have enough representation or all Roma are as corrupt as the few that have successfully run for office for various parties.

41. Scott 1990, 198; Kelley 1994. But who is the "we" to which Scott alludes? Marche 2012 and Simpson 2016 also approach this question in their analyses.

42. The metaphor of the octopus is widespread in Bulgaria. The octopus, imagined as a "predatory sea creature," has come to symbolize Bulgaria's mafia-government network because its tentacles can reach everywhere (https://duma.bg/partiyata-oktopod-n247220).

43. Simpson 2016, 329. Also see Povinelli 2011 on "social projects."

44. Cohen 2004, 40. Cohen here is writing about how some scholars of infrapolitics, like James Scott (1990) and Robin D. G. Kelley (1994, 2002), "have ignored the distinction of defiant or resistant acts and acts of politicized resistance, misdiagnosing the resources that exist and the resources needed for political mobilization" (41). Cohen explains, "It might be that marginal subjects with a politicized consciousness choose localized attempts at control and autonomy because they have no mobilized outlet to confront the larger political context. Or they reject politics because they believe that the mobilized organizations that do

exist have no interest in and commitment to the issues that animate their lives" (41). I have thought long and hard about whether what the Romani people in this book do is "political," and I have landed on the idea that sometimes it is, sometimes it might not be, but it still shifts the landscape of power at different levels of scale and with differing temporalities (sometimes it's a long-term shift, other times it's fleeting, temporary, or even fantastical).

Chapter Five

1. In line with my general approach, I have used a pseudonym for this neighborhood to preserve the anonymity of the workers, not to obscure the corporate history of land dispossession.

2. This information comes from a 2001 appeal letter written by the now-defunct Human Rights Project and from personal communication with Krassimir Kanev of the Bulgarian Helsinki Committee.

3. The act became effective on June 1, 1996: https://faolex.fao.org/docs/pdf/bul18536.pdf.

4. Reports of this displacement are mired in violence: "In September 2004, the Ministry of Defense donated part of its former barracks, located on the periphery of the city, to the Sofia municipality for housing the Roma from the [municipality] as well as other Roma from different parts of Sofia who were not eligible for municipal housing. News of this allocation of housing was met with protests from non-Roma in [a nearby village], which is part of the Sofia municipality, who threatened with civil disobedience if the Roma were placed in their municipality" (https://rm.coe.int/no-31-2005-european-roma-rights-center-errc-v-bulgaria-case-document-n/16807408dd).

5. Church leaders also worked with residents as liaisons with the local mayors and even asked me to invite representatives from the United States Embassy in Bulgaria, which I did, resulting in an official visit to the neighborhood. The neighborhood has since been demolished (in 2012), and residents have been re-housed.

6. Cf. Resnick 2021.

7. Elsewhere (Resnick 2023), I write about the "intimacy of labor," which is rooted in the relationships between workers themselves. This is distinct from "intimate labor," which includes care work, domestic labor, and sex work (Bakker 2007; Boris and Parreñas 2010).

8. Simpson 2014, 107 on "endless play." Also see Shange 2019.

9. Cohen 1997, 455. Cohen notes that what society categorizes as "nonnormative heterosexuality" include that of single moms, teen moms, and many women from communities of color, which results in the "demonization of poor women" altogether (465).

10. In the sense described by Mankekar and Gupta, this field of relationality is one of affect, not emotion, because it exists in a collective plane of solidarity and "transgress[es] binaries of mind versus body, and private feeling versus collective sentiment" (2016, 24). Sweeping enables the kind of sensibility that surfaces

NOTES TO CHAPTER 5

in the fight to dictate life on one's own terms, given labor and living conditions designed to dehumanize and humiliate. In other words, sweepers continually make and remake their own world, together. See Kondo 2018 on "worldmaking" and "reparative creativity."

11. This "something else" intersects with what Michelle Murphy calls an "alterlife," a way to understand how people figure "life and responsibilities beyond the individualized body" (2017, 497).

12. I have been inspired by the interview with Tina Campt on "refusing refusal" (Coleman 2018) and Elizabeth Grosz's work (2012) on "possibilities for being otherwise" (14). Also see Emejulu and Sobande (2019) for other examples of feminist resistance and refusal in Europe.

13. Workers often took home their brooms and other equipment if they worked late or if they had to start very early the next morning.

14. See Willen (2019) for a comparative example of how people living amid experiences of expungeability and criminalization (in this case, at the hands of the Israeli government) cultivate dignity in their indignation.

15. Boris 2019, 81.

16. See Beeman 1999 on humor and surprise.

17. Seizer 1997, 63.

18. See Menninghaus 2003 and Kristeva 1982 for analyses of abjection in relation to laughter.

19. Cf. Rubin 2011. Similarly, Jennifer Robertson 1991 finds that possibilities for gender subversion among Takarazuka performers in Japan are, as Rosalind Morris puts it, "contained by other identity structures—in particular class—that are gendered without being reducible to gender" (1995, 583).

20. See Simmons 2008 on "historical colorization" among Dominicans in the United States and African Americans in the Dominican Republic.

21. Council of Europe Commissioner for Human Rights: https://www.coe.int/en/web/commissioner/-/ethnic-profiling-a-persisting-practice-in-europe.

22. This shared dignity went "beyond the individualized body" (Murphy 2017, 497).

23. Although contemporary conditions precipitate these particular intimate relations, this kind of intimacy in public workspaces has a socialist legacy. One goal of the communist regime in Eastern Europe was to eliminate a felt sense of "the private" "through the extension of state control into activities, spaces, and relations deemed 'private'" (Gal 2002, 86). See also Yurchak 2005 on "public" vs. "private" work and Bren 2002 on the politics of private life.

24. Many socialist-era holidays have been rejected by increasingly popular evangelical Christian movements that are strong in Romani communities throughout Europe, including among the sweepers with whom I worked, but Women's Day has been widely accepted.

25. Berlant 2007, 754.

26. Nixon 2011, 2. And in the words of Ruth Wilson Gilmore, as noted in Chapter 3, it is also a "premature" death (2007).

NOTES TO CHAPTERS 5 AND THE CONCLUSION

27. And, as Jackson writes in analyzing how Black women deal with animalization, they do so without reinvesting in or "reestablish[ing] 'human recognition' within liberal humanism as an antidote to racialization" (2020, 1). In response to their positionality within the waste-race nexus, Romani women generate "a critical praxis of being, paradigms of relationality, and epistemologies that alternately expose, alter, or reject" their racialization (2).

28. It might also be said that they ascribe life to themselves through "unruly yet generative conceptions of being" (Jackson 2020, 4).

In this framing, I invoke the language of stewardship from a 2019 exhibition at the Queens Museum curated by my colleague and collaborator, Christina Freeman: https://queensmuseum.org/2019/03/who-takes-care-of-new-york.

29. Hobart and Kneese 2020, 5, drawing on the work of Lorde 1988.

30. If we think of sweepers' empathy as alternative kin-making, of an enduring and life-making coming together, we can understand the process of "feeling with, rather than a feeling for, others" as a "critical survival strategy" (Hobart and Kneese 2020, 2).

31. This kind of alchemical intimate kin-making forges "alternative worlds" that "maintain the otherwise that stares back at us" (Povinelli 2011, 10).

32. See Robin D. G. Kelley on Black women in the racialized workplace: "Women, unlike their black male co-workers had to devise a whole range of strategies to resist or mitigate the daily physical and verbal abuse of their bodies, ranging from putting forth a sort of 'asexual' persona, to posturing as a 'crazy' person, to simply quitting" (1994, 27).

Conclusion

1. See https://balkaninsight.com/2016/01/11/the-roma-and-the-radicals-bulgaria-s-alleged-isis-support-base-01-10-2016-1/. Also see Ghodsee 2010.

2. Protests in 2010 against the expulsion in France took place in Bulgaria but also in Paris (https://www.bbc.com/news/world-europe-11186592).

3. See EU legislation on free movement of EU citizens: https://commission.europa.eu/strategy-and-policy/policies/justice-and-fundamental-rights/eu-citizenship-and-democracy/free-movement-and-residence_en#:~:text=Digital%20COVID%20Certificate-,The%20right%20to%20free%20movement,EU%20Charter%20of%20Fundamental%20Rights.

4. Campt 2019, 83.

5. Roma in France were historically called "bohemians" (in French, *bohemién*) because of the widespread misunderstanding that they came from current-day Czech Republic (then Bohemia). See Seigel 1999.

6. China was the main importing country for much of the world's plastic waste and, until 2017, its plastic waste imports reached 8.88 million tons. On July 27, 2017, China issued the "Prohibition of Foreign Garbage Imports: The Reform Plan on Solid Waste Import Management," which banned the import of twenty-four types of solid waste, including plastics (https://www.nature.com/articles/s41467-020-20741-9).

NOTES TO THE CONCLUSION

7. Cf. Gabrys 2009; Liboiron 2021.

8. Despite dumping waste from places like Italy and the UK in Bulgaria and then dumping Bulgarian waste in Romani neighborhoods, Roma are blamed for the "degenerate qualities" of Bulgaria's waste system (Pandian 2009, 20). This accords with what Anand Pandian describes in South India: the "worthlessness of these [waste] landscapes [is] easily attributed to the indolence of their native residents" (20). Also see articles on international waste dumping in Bulgaria: https://www.dw.com/en/my-europe-illegal-garbage-dumps-reflect-eus-east-west-divide/a-52480168.

9. Resnick 2024b.

10. See Campt 2012, 2019. And, as Tiffany Lethabo King notes, "decolonization is not just about the ascetic project of giving things up but fundamentally about creating new and pleasurable ways of living" (2015).

11. This concept of refusal has been informed by Rosalind Fredericks's account of members of a trash-workers' union in Dakar, Senegal who engage in a "refusal to be refuse which inverts the stigma of trash work" (2018, 143) and Sharad Chari's discussion of the "refusal to be detritus" (2013, 133).

12. Cathy Cohen reminds us that "parties, dances, and other leisure pursuits" are not "merely guises for political events" or "clear acts of resistance" (2004, 40). The importance of these "escapes" is "to leave momentarily the individual and collective battles against racism, sexism and material deprivation" (40).

13. I am grateful to Anand Pandian for pointing me to the work of Astrida Neimanis on the feminist embodiment of water. Neimanis writes of how "the flow and flush of waters sustain our own bodies, but also connect them to other bodies, to other worlds beyond our human selves" (2017, 2). As Fakulteta residents and sweepers focus on water access, they also engage their "always more-than human embodiment" (3). See Anand 2017; Ballestero 2019; Barnes 2014; Cattelino, Drew, and Morgan 2019; Farmer 2023; and Muehlebach 2023 for other discussions of water mediating life.

14. For comparison, see Melissa Caldwell's 2011 work on post-Soviet/postsocialist urban breaks in Russian dachas as a way to escape from routine, grime, and industrialized labor.

15. As Sophia Stamatopoulou-Robbins puts it, "Management and maintenance are more apt terms for thinking human interactions with disorderly and toxic materials, as humans constantly engage with waste in order to approximate cleanliness or a sense of control over their environment. The perpetual need to maintain spaces free of refuse and to engage with it means humans constantly engage in incomplete acts" (2019, 170).

16. "Hygiene" has a long history in scholarly and policy approaches to Romani neighborhoods and still appears in policy reports and recommendations from the Council of Europe, including recent work on COVID-19's impact: https://www.coe.int/en/web/commissioner/-/governments-must-ensure-equal-protection-and-care-for-roma-and-travellers-during-the-covid-19-crisis.

17. See Fehérváry 2013; Greenberg 2014; and Resnick 2018 on ideas of postsocialist "normal."

NOTES TO THE CONCLUSION

18. See Gidwani and Maringanti 2016 on waste labor and "the right to dignity."

19. This document (Rafiev 1967) states that in order to pay attention to the "nationalistic tendencies" among Roma, it is important to combat "the existence of a problematic, dismissive attitude towards the g*psy population, which insults their dignity and their feelings as equal citizens of the country" because it increases "anti-Bulgarian attitudes amongst the g*psy population."

20. Despite pointing out anti-Roma discrimination in Bulgaria, the memo (Rafiev 1967) emphasizes that such anti-Roma prejudice is due to the influence of "the enemy's" propaganda from the West and is to blame for strengthening "the anti-Bulgarian sentiments among the g*psy population."

21. Most of my data about this history comes from oral history interviews with multigenerational families in the neighborhood.

22. For comparison, see Tessa Farmer's 2023 work on the sociality of water in Cairo, Egypt, and projects of connection.

23. Christina Schwenkel writes about a similar post–Cold War dynamic in Vietnam, where water relations reveal a "problematic materiality—one that emerged as a signifier both of the promise of state care in a system of centralized distribution of goods and services, and of an enduring condition of neglect tied to the state's inability to adequately provide for its citizens" (2015, 521). These experiences with water have affective corollaries in other places with people living under very different conditions, including how residents of public housing complexes in Chicago have dealt with "abundant heat" (Fennell 2015).

24. During socialism, one needed special permission to live in Sofia based on employment or schooling, and getting official Sofia registration was difficult and highly coveted. Many Roma who have lived in Sofia for generations remain proud of their roots as "true *Sofiyantsi*," a status those who moved there from the villages could never attain.

25. The Konyovitsa reservoir supplies water to many parts of Sofia outside of Fakulteta: https://bnr.bg/sofia/post/100251279/golyama-chast-ot-sofiya-bez-voda -dnes-i-utre-zaradi-rekonstrukciya-na-vodoprovodi-pri-rezervoar-konaovica.

26. This practice aligns with critiques of 1970s feminist approaches to care, which normalize the stewardship of public (white) space that sweepers are effectively forced to perform as part of the waste-race nexus. This labor can be viewed in dialogue with other kinds of labor across a neoliberalizing Europe, including in Italy's "voluntary labor regime" (Muehlebach 2012). In contrast, Joan Tronto and Berenice Fisher define "care" as "everything that we do to maintain, continue, and repair 'our world' so that we can live in it as well as possible. That world includes our bodies, ourselves, and our environment, all of which we seek to interweave in a complex, life sustaining web" (1990, 40). Also see Corwin and Gidwani's "Repair Work as Care," in which they explore how "maintenance and repair reveal the interdependence of humans on each other and with non-humans" (2021, 3).

27. For example, if 150 families use a pipe originally intended only for fifty, nobody gets the pressure they desire (or, sometimes, any water at all) because it becomes so diffused.

28. See Collier 2011; Khalvashi 2019; and Tuvikene, Sgibnev, and Neugebauer 2019 on related infrastructural issues.

29. This connects with Nikhil Anand's 2017 work on "hydraulic citizenship" as well as Clara Han's observations in neoliberal Chile regarding how "care manifests and takes shape in intimate relations," the limits of which "are intimately discovered in the midst of institutional responses to disease, distress, and need" (2012, 22). My framing also draws on Josh Lepawsky's 2018 work on electronic waste and repair, Christina Schwenkel's work on crumbling housing infrastructures in Vietnam (2015, 2020), and Shannon Mattern's 2018 and Steven Jackson's 2014 analyses of maintenance, repair, and care.

30. See https://www.npr.org/sections/thetwo-way/2013/10/25/240791734/case-of-little-maria-is-solved-bulgarian-romas-are-her-parents; this also comes up in Susan Lepselter's unpublished manuscript "Rescuing the Blonde Angel: The Global Captivity Narrative and the Panic of 2013." Maria was a Romani Bulgarian child who was unofficially adopted by the Greek family she was found living with.

31. Though I do not wish to overly romanticize repair, this might be seen as an attempt at refusing death (cf. Mattern 2018).

32. These sites include thermal power plants and cement factories (such as "Devnya Tsiment" in Northeastern Bulgaria). According to a 2022 European Environmental Agency report on Bulgaria's municipal and packaging waste targets, "three cement plants and one thermal power plant have permits to incinerate waste, with a total annual capacity of nearly 500 thousand tonnes, both for refuse-derived fuel (RDF) from domestic sources and imported RDF" (https://www.eea.europa.eu/publications/many-eu-member-states/bulgaria). During my research there were also much-debated plans to build an EU-funded cogeneration unit in Sofia that would produce heat and electricity from refuse-derived fuel for its urban heating grid (https://ec.europa.eu/regional_policy/en/projects/Bulgaria/cogeneration-unit-in-sofia-to-produce-heat-and-electricity-from-refuse-derived-fuel). However, as of 2024, Bulgaria's Supreme Administrative Court canceled this decision.

33. Statistics certainly back her up, revealing institutional racism through Romani infant mortality rates, early onset of debilitating diseases, and significantly shorter lifespans. But, as noted earlier, statistics are not nearly enough to portray the entirety of anti-Roma racism in Bulgaria and across Europe.

REFERENCES

ARCHIVAL SOURCES CONSULTED AND CITED
TsDA (Tsentralen Darzhaven Arhiv): Central State Archive, Sofia, Bulgaria

Fond 1B: Central Committee of the Communist Party.
Inv. 6, Arch. 4749, pp. 7–10. 1962. "Protiv Turcheeneto na Tsigani, Tatari i Balgari s Mohamedansko Veroizpovedanie" [Against the Turkification of Gypsies, Tatars, and Bulgarians Professing the Mohammedan Religion]. Sofia, Bulgaria.

Inv. 6, Arch. 4749, pp. 11–17. April 5, 1962. "Reshenie 'A' №101 na Politbyuro na TsK na BKP" [Decision "A" No. 101 of the Political Office of the Central Committee of the BCP (Bulgarian Communist Party)]. Sofia, Bulgaria.

DA-Sofia (Regionalen Darzhaven Arhiv - Sofia): State Archive-Sofia (Regional State Archive - Sofia)

Fond 1659: Communal Economic Company "Chistota"—Sofia (1936–1999).
Inv. 1, Arch. 21, p. 33. Velinova, M. September 4, 1956. "Zapoved Otnosno Nagrazhdavane na Parventsi v Proizvodstvoto" [Order for Rewarding the Best Production Workers]. Sofia, Bulgaria.

Inv. 1, Arch. 21, pp. 62–64. 1956. "Plan za Rabotata s Kadrite v KPS 'Chistota' pri SGNS za 1956 Godina" [Plan for the Work with the Staff of CEC "Chistota" of the SCPC (Sofia City People's Council) for 1956]. Sofia, Bulgaria.

Inv. 2, Arch. 2, pp. 1–18. Stavrev, Stavri. December 5, 1946. "Doklad ot Nachalnika na Otdelenie 'Chistota' pri Stolichnata Narodna Obshtina—Stavri

Zafirov Stavrev" [Report by the Head of the Cleanliness Department of Sofia People's Municipality—Stavri Zafirov Stavrev]. Sofia, Bulgaria.

Inv. 2, Arch. 23, pp. 12–15. Stefanov, N. November 18, 1970. "Informatsiya za Zabolevaemostta za I-vo Shestmesechie na 1970 i Prostudnata Zabolevaemost i Merki za Predpazvane na Rabotnitsite i Sluzhitelite prez Zimniya Period" [Information on Morbidity in the First Six Months of 1970 and Cold Morbidity and Measures to Protect Workers During the Winter Period]. Sofia, Bulgaria.

Fond 4005: Single Owner Limited Liability Company (Ltd) "Phoenix Elite"— Sofia (1977–1999).

ONLINE ARCHIVAL SOURCES CONSULTED AND CITED
Archive of the Committee for Disclosing the Documents and Announcing Affiliation of Bulgarian Citizens to the State Security and the Intelligence Services of the Bulgarian National Armed Forces. http://comdos.bg.

Documents Regarding State Security and Minorities

Communist Party Council of Ministers. 1959. "Pismo №809 do Okrazhnite, Gradski i Rayonni Komiteti na BKP" [Letter no. 809 to the District, City, and Regional Committees of the BCP (Bulgarian Communist Party)]. Sofia, Bulgaria, June 17. Document no. 74, 269–272. https://comdos.bg/media/DVD %20SBORNIK%2032_Minorities%20opt.pdf.

Council of Ministers. 1958. "Postanovlenie №258 na Ministerskiya Savet za: Urezhdane na Vaprosite za Tsiganskoto Naselenie v Bulgaria" [Decree no. 258 of the Council of Ministers About: Settling the Issues Concerning the Gypsy Population in Bulgaria]. Sofia, Bulgaria, December 17. Document no. 73, 262–268. https://comdos.bg/media/CD_SBORNIK%2032_Minorities %20opt.pdf.

Head of the Criminal Department. 1967. "Belezhki na Otdel Kriminalen—DNM" [Memo of the Criminal Department—DPM (Directorate of the People's Militia)]. Sofia, Bulgaria, February 21. Document no. 76, 290–294. https://comdos .bg/media/CD_SBORNIK%2032_Minorities%20opt.pdf.

Katsamunski, L. 1982. "Pismo do Sofiyskoto Gradsko i Okrazhnite Upravleniya na MVR v Stranata i otdel Transportna Militsiya—DNM" [Letter to the Sofia City and District Departments of the Ministry of Interior and the Transport Police Department—DPM (Directorate of the People's Militia)]. Sofia, Bulgaria, August 16. Document no. 148, 516–519. https://comdos.bg/media/DVD %20SBORNIK%2032_Minorities%20opt.pdf

Peev, G. 1950. "Spravka za Sastoyanieto na Tsiganskoto Maltsinstvo i Agenturno-Operativnata Rabota Vsred Sashtoto" [Reference of the State of the Gypsy Minority and the Agency and Operative Work Among It]. Sofia, Bulgaria. Document no. 71, 249–255. https://comdos.bg/media/CD_SBORNIK%2032 _Minorities%20opt.pdf.

REFERENCES

Rafiev, Ali. 1967. "Informatsiya za Rezultatite ot Izpalnenieto na Resheniyata na TsK na BKP i Pravitelstvoto po Rabotata sred Tsiganskoto Naselenie" [Information About the Results of the Implementation of the Decisions of the Central Committee of the BCP and the Government on the Work Among the Gypsy Population]. Sofia, Bulgaria, February 2. Document no. 75, 273–289. https://comdos.bg/media/CD_SBORNIK%2032_Minorities%20opt.pdf.

Selimov, Tair. 1950. "Informatsionen Doklad za Deynostta na Tsiganskoto Maltsinstvo v Bulgaria" [Information Report About the Activity of the Gypsy Minority in Bulgaria]. Sofia, Bulgaria. Document no. 72, 256–261. https://comdos.bg/media/CD_SBORNIK%2032_Minorities%20opt.pdf.

Sixth State Security Department. 1972. "Spravka Otnosno Proyaven Interes ot Zadgranichni Tsentrali kam Tsiganskoto Naselenie v NRB i Tendentsii na Turcheene" [Reference About the Interest of Foreign Headquarters Towards the Gypsy Population in PRB and Tendencies of Turkification]. Sofia, Bulgaria, October 13. Document no. 78, 305–309. https://comdos.bg/media/CD_SBORNIK%2032_Minorities%20opt.pdf.

Stefchev, G. 1950. "Strogo Poveritelen Plan za Agenturno-Operativna Rabota po Liniyata na Tsiganskoto Maltsinstvo" [Strictly Confidential Plan for Intelligence and Operational Work with the Gypsy Minority]. Sofia, Bulgaria, March 28. Document no. 70, 347–350. https://comdos.bg/media/CD_SBORNIK%2032_Minorities%20opt.pdf.

Stefchev, N. 1979. "Strogo Sekretna Spravka Otnosno Natsionalisticheskite Proyavi i Tendentsii Sred Balgarskite Tsigani" [Strictly Confidential Reference About the Nationalistic Manifestations and Tendencies Among the Bulgarian Gypsies]. Sofia, Bulgaria, January 22. Document no. 140, 463–471. https://comdos.bg/media/DVD%20SBORNIK%2032_Minorities%20opt.pdf.

Trichkov, Krastyu. 1980. "Informatsiya ot Krastyu Trichkov, Predsedatel na Komiteta za Darzhven i Naroden Kontrol otnosno Izpalnenieto na Razporezhdane 7 na Ministerskiya Savet ot 21.1.1979" [Information from Krastyu Trichkov, Chairman of the Committee for State and People's Supervision About the Implementation of Ordinance No. 7 of the Council of Ministers]. Sofia, Bulgaria, July 6. Document no. 86, 347–354. https://comdos.bg/media/CD_SBORNIK%2032_Minorities%20opt.pdf.

Endangered Archive Program, British Library. https://eap.bl.uk/.

Ganchev, G. 1984. "Informatsiya za Izpalnenieto na Reshenie №1360 na Sekretariata na TsK na SGNS ot 9.10.1978" [Information on the Execution of Decision No. 1360 of the Secretariat of the Central Committee of Sofia City People's Council from October 9, 1978]. Sofia, Bulgaria, December 5. https://eap.bl.uk/archive-file/EAP285-13-4.

Romani Archive. https://roma-swu.weebly.com/.

Communist Party Council of Ministers. 1973. "Nyakoi Problemi na Rabotata Sred Tsiganskoto Naselenie u Nas" [Some Problems of the Work Among the Gypsy

Population in Our Country"]. Sofia, Bulgaria. TsDA, Fond 1B, Inv. 55, Arch. 1344, pp. 42–51. https://roma-swu.weebly.com/uploads/9/1/1/0/91107766/%D0%98%D0%BD%D1%84%D0%BE%D1%80%D0%BC%D0%B0%D1%86%D0%B8%D1%8F_%D0%BE%D1%82_%D0%98%D0%BD%D1%84%D0%BE%D1%80%D0%BC%D0%B0%D1%86%D0%B8%D0%BE%D0%BD%D0%BD%D0%BE11.pdf.

PUBLISHED WORKS

Abu-Lughod, Lila. 1990. "The Romance of Resistance: Tracing Transformations of Power Through Bedouin Women." *American Ethnologist* 17 (1): 41–55.

Aenasoaie, Luciana. 2016. "Weaving and Unraveling the Factory Town: Social Alterations and European Belonging in the Aftermath of Romanian Industrial Collapse, 1950–2015." PhD diss., University of Michigan.

Agard-Jones, Vanessa. 2013. "Bodies in the System." *Small Axe: A Caribbean Journal of Criticism* 17 (3): 182–192.

Ahmann, Chloe. 2018. "'It's Exhausting to Create an Event Out of Nothing': Slow Violence and the Manipulation of Time." *Cultural Anthropology* 33 (1): 142–171.

———. 2019. "Waste to Energy: Garbage Prospects and Subjunctive Politics in Late Industrial Baltimore." *American Ethnologist* 46 (3): 328–342.

———. 2024. *Futures After Progress: Hope and Doubt in Late Industrial Baltimore.* University of Chicago Press.

Alexander, Catherine, and Joshua Reno, eds. 2012. *Economies of Recycling: The Global Transformation of Materials, Values and Social Relations.* Zed Books.

Alexander, Catherine, and Patrick O'Hare. 2020. "Waste and Its Disguises: Technologies of (Un)Knowing." *Ethnos* 88 (3): 1–25.

Alves, Jaime Amparo. 2018. *The Anti-Black City: Police Terror and Black Urban Life in Brazil.* University of Minnesota Press.

———. 2019. "Refusing to Be Governed: Urban Policing, Gang Violence, and the Politics of Evilness in an Afro Colombian Shantytown." *PoLAR: Political and Legal Anthropology Review* 42 (1): 21–36.

Amrute, Sareeta. 2016. *Encoding Race, Encoding Class: Indian IT Workers in Berlin.* Duke University Press.

Anand, Nikhil. 2017. *Hydraulic City: Water and the Infrastructures of Citizenship in Mumbai.* Duke University Press.

Anand, Nikhil, Akhil Gupta, and Hannah Appel, eds. 2018. *The Promise of Infrastructure.* Duke University Press.

Apostolova, Raia. 2017. "Duty and Debt Under the Ethos of Internationalism: The Case of the Vietnamese Workers in Bulgaria." *Journal of Vietnamese Studies* 12 (1): 101–125.

Appel, Hannah. 2019. *The Licit Life of Capitalism: US Oil in Equatorial Guinea.* Duke University Press.

Arendt, Hannah. 1944. "Race-Thinking Before Racism." *The Review of Politics* 6 (1): 36–73.

REFERENCES

Aroyo, Zhak. 1974. *Ikonomicheskata Politika na Balgarskata Komunisticheska Partiya* [The Economic Policies of the Bulgarian Communist Party]. Partizdat. https://www.marxists.org/bulgarsky/aroyo/1974/Zhak_Aroyo_red_ _Ikonomicheskata_Politika_Na_Blgarskata_Komunisticheska_Partia_1974 .pdf.

Atanasoski, Neda. 2006. "'Race' Toward Freedom: Post-Cold War US Multiculturalism and the Reconstruction of Eastern Europe." *The Journal of American Culture* 29 (2): 213–226.

——. 2013. *Humanitarian Violence: The U.S. Deployment of Diversity.* University of Minnesota Press.

Atanasoski, Neda, and Kalindi Vora. 2019. *Surrogate Humanity: Race, Robots, and the Politics of Technological Futures.* Duke University Press.

Atanasova, Maria. 2023. "Bulgarian Political Parties: An Exploration of Roma Representation in Online Electoral Campaigns." MA thesis, Central European University.

Babül, Elif. 2017. "Morality: Understanding Police Training on Human Rights (Turkey)." In *Writing the World of Policing: The Difference Ethnography Makes,* edited by Didier Fassin. University of Chicago Press.

Baker, Catherine. 2018. *Race and the Yugoslav Region: Postsocialist, Post-conflict, Postcolonial?* Manchester University Press.

Bakker, Isabella. 2007. "Social Reproduction and the Constitution of a Gendered Political Economy." *New Political Economy* 12 (4): 541–556.

Baldwin, Kate A. 2015. *The Racial Imaginary of the Cold War Kitchen: From Sokol'niki Park to Chicago's South Side.* Dartmouth College Press.

Ballestero, Andrea. 2019. *A Future History of Water.* Duke University Press.

Balogun, Bolaji. 2020. "Race and Racism in Poland: Theorising and Contextualising 'Polish-Centrism'." *The Sociological Review* 68 (6): 1196–1211.

Balyozov, Zdravko. 1999. *The Bulgarian Financial Crisis of 1996–1997.* Bulgarian National Bank.

Bardziński, Filip. 2013. "The Concept of the 'New Soviet Man' as a Eugenic Project: Eugenics in Soviet Russia After World War II." *Ethics in Progress* 4 (1): 57–81.

Barnes, Jessica. 2014. *Cultivating the Nile: The Everyday Politics of Water in Egypt.* Duke University Press.

Beaman, Jean. 2017. *Citizen Outsider: Children of North African Immigrants in France.* University of California Press.

Beeman, William O. 1999. "Humor." *Journal of Linguistic Anthropology* 9 (1/2): 103–106.

Beliso-De Jesus, Aisha, and Jemima Pierre. 2020. "Anthropology of White Supremacy." *American Anthropologist* 122 (1): 65–75.

Benedict, Susan, Linda Shields, Colin Holmes, and Julia Kurth. 2018. "A Nurse Working for the Third Reich: Eva Justin, RN, PhD." *Journal of Medical Biography* 26 (4): 259–267.

Berdahl, Daphne. 1999a. "'(N)Ostalgie' for the Present: Memory, Longing, and East German Things." *Ethnos* 64 (2): 192–211.

—. 1999b. *Where the World Ended: Re-Unification and Identity in the German Borderland*. University of California Press.

Berlant, Lauren. 2007. "Slow Death (Sovereignty, Obesity, Lateral Agency)." *Critical Inquiry* 33 (4): 754–780.

—. 2011. *Cruel Optimism*. Duke University Press.

Bernstein, Anya. 2019. *The Future of Immortality: Remaking Life and Death in Contemporary Russia*. University of Chicago Press.

Bertossi, Christophe. 2010. "France and Deporting the Roma: How Did We Get There?" Elcano Royal Institute. https://www.realinstitutoelcano.org/en/analyses/france-and-deporting-the-roma-how-did-we-get-there-ari/.

Bhabha, Homi K. (1994) 2012. *The Location of Culture*. Routledge.

Bițu, Nicoleta. n.d. "Roma: Who Are We?" RomArchive. https://www.romarchive.eu/en/about/context-project/.

Bițu, Nicoleta, and Enikő Vincze. 2012. "Personal Encounters and Parallel Paths Toward Romani Feminism." *Signs: Journal of Women in Culture and Society* 38 (1): 44–46.

Blanchette, Alex. 2020. *Porkopolis: American Animality, Standardized Life, and the Factory Farm*. Duke University Press.

BNE IntelliNews. 2012. "Hungary's Village of Despair." https://www.intellinews.com/hungary-s-village-of-despair-500016677/?archive=bne.

Boatcă, Manuela. 2010. "Multiple Europes and the Politics of Difference Within." In *The Study of Europe*, edited by Hauke Brunkhorst and Gerd Grözinger. Nomos.

—. 2021. "Thinking Europe Otherwise: Lessons from the Caribbean." *Current Sociology* 69 (3): 389–414.

Bonilla-Silva, Eduardo. 2006. *Racism Without Racists: Color-Blind Racism and the Persistence of Racial Inequality in the United States*. Rowman & Littlefield Publishers.

Boris, Eileen. 2019. *Making the Woman Worker: Precarious Labor and the Fight for Global Standards, 1919–2019*. Oxford University Press.

Boris, Eileen and Rhacel Salazar Parreñas. 2010. *Intimate Labors: Cultures, Technologies, and the Politics of Care*. Stanford University Press.

Böröcz, József. 2001. "Introduction: Empire and Coloniality in the 'Eastern Enlargement' of the European Union." In *Empire's New Clothes: Unveiling EU Enlargement*, edited by József Böröcz and Melinda Kovács. Central Europe Review.

—. 2006. "Goodness Is Elsewhere: The Rule of European Difference," *Comparative Studies in Society and History* 48 (1): 110–387.

Boyer, Dominic. 2006. "*Ostalgie* and the Politics of the Future in Eastern Germany." *Public Culture* 18 (2): 361–381.

Boyer, Dominic, and Alexei Yurchak. 2010. "American Stiob: Or, What Late-Socialist Aesthetics of Parody Reveal About Contemporary Political Culture in the West." *Cultural Anthropology* 25 (2): 179–221.

REFERENCES

Bren, Paulina. 2002. "Weekend Getaways: The Chata, the Tramp, and the Politics of Private Life in Post-1968 Czechoslovakia." In *Socialist Spaces: Sites of Everyday Life in the Eastern Bloc*, edited by David Crowley and Susan E. Reid. Berg.

Brooks, Ethel C. 2012. "The Possibilities of Romani Feminism." *Signs: Journal of Women in Culture and Society* 38 (1): 1–11.

Brooks, Ethel, Colin Clark, and Iulius Rostas. 2022. "Engaging with Decolonisation, Tackling Antigypsyism: Lessons from Teaching Romani Studies at the Central European University in Hungary." *Social Policy and Society* 21 (1): 68–79.

Brown, Jacqueline Nassy. 2009. *Dropping Anchor, Setting Sail: Geographies of Race in Black Liverpool.* Princeton University Press.

Browne, Simone. 2015. *Dark Matters: On the Surveillance of Blackness.* Duke University Press.

Buchanan, Donna A. 2002. "Soccer, Popular Music and National Consciousness in Post-State-Socialist Bulgaria, 1994–96." *British Journal of Ethnomusicology* 11 (2): 1–27.

———. 2006. *Performing Democracy: Bulgarian Music and Musicians in Transition.* University of Chicago Press.

———. 2010. "Sonic Nostalgia: Music, Memory, and Mythography in Bulgaria, 1990–2005." In *Post-Communist Nostalgia*, edited by Maria Todorova and Zsuzsa Gille. Berghahn Books.

Buck-Morss, Susan. 2000. "Hegel and Haiti." *Critical Inquiry* 26 (4): 821–865.

Bullard, Robert D. (1990) 2008. *Dumping in Dixie: Race, Class, and Environmental Quality.* Avalon Publishing (Westview Press).

Butt, Waqas H. 2020. "Waste Intimacies: Caste and the Unevenness of Life in Urban Pakistan." *American Ethnologist* 47 (3): 234–248.

———. 2023. *Life Beyond Waste: Work and Infrastructure in Urban Pakistan.* Stanford University Press.

Cabot, Heath. 2014. *On the Doorstep of Europe: Asylum and Citizenship in Greece.* University of Pennsylvania Press.

Caldwell, Melissa L. 2011. *Dacha Idylls: Living Organically in Russia's Countryside.* University of California Press.

Campt, Tina M. 2004. *Other Germans: Black Germans and the Politics of Race, Gender, and Memory in the Third Reich.* University of Michigan Press.

———. 2012. *Image Matters: Archive, Photography, and the African Diaspora in Europe.* Duke University Press.

———. 2017. "Performing Stillness: Diaspora and Stasis in Black German Vernacular Photography." *Qui Parle* 26 (1): 155–170.

———. 2019. "Black Visuality and the Practice of Refusal." *Women and Performance: A Journal of Feminist Theory* 29 (1): 79–87.

Canut, Cécile. 2019. "Tell Me That I Am Not a *Ciganin*, Damn Your Mother! The Social and Political Consequences of Enregisterment in Bulgaria." *Signs and Society* 7 (3): 398–426.

Cattelino, Jessica R., Georgina Drew, and Ruth A. Morgan. 2019. "Water Flourishing in the Anthropocene." *Cultural Studies Review* 25 (2): 135–152.

Cellarius, Barbara A. 2000. "'You Can Buy Almost Anything with Potatoes': An Examination of Barter During Economic Crisis in Bulgaria." *Ethnology* 39 (1): 73–92.

Černušáková, Barbora. 2021. "Roma Workers Under Czech Racial Capitalism: A Post-Socialist Case Study." *Journal of Law and Political Economy* 2 (1): 48–69.

Cervinkova, Hana. 2012. "Postcolonialism, Postsocialism and the Anthropology of East-Central Europe." *Journal of Postcolonial Writing* 48 (2): 155–163.

Césaire, Aimé. (1955) 1972. *Discourse on Colonialism*. Monthly Review Press.

Chahim, Dean. 2023. "The Logistics of Waste: Engineering, Capital Accumulation, and the Growth of Mexico City." *Antipode*: 1–25. https://doi.org/10.1111/anti.12864.

Chalfin, Brenda. 2014. "Public Things, Excremental Politics, and the Infrastructure of Bare Life in Ghana's City of Tema." *American Ethnologist* 41 (1): 92–109.

———. 2023. *Waste Works: Vital Politics in Urban Ghana*. Duke University Press.

Chang, Felix B. 2018. "Roma Integration 'All the Way Down': Lessons from Federalism and Civil Rights." *Critical Romani Studies* 1 (1): 62–85.

Chang, Felix B., and Sunnie T. Rucker-Chang. 2020. *Roma Rights and Civil Rights: A Transatlantic Comparison*. Cambridge University Press.

Channell-Justice, Emily. 2022. *Without the State: Self-Organization and Political Activism in Ukraine*. University of Toronto Press.

Chari, Sharad. 2013. "Detritus in Durban: Polluted Environs and the Biopolitics of Refusal." In *Imperial Debris*, edited by Ann Laura Stoler. Duke University Press.

Chari, Sharad, and Katherine Verdery. 2009. "Thinking Between the Posts: Postcolonialism, Postsocialism, and Ethnography after the Cold War." *Comparative Studies in Society and History* 51 (1): 6–34.

Charles, Sébastien, and Jonathan Marie. 2017. "Bulgaria's Hyperinflation in 1997: Transition, Banking Fragility and Foreign Exchange." *Post-Communist Economies* 29 (3): 313–335.

Checker, Melissa. 2011. "Wiped Out by the 'Greenwave': Environmental Gentrification and the Paradoxical Politics of Urban Sustainability." *City and Society* 23 (2): 210–229.

———. 2020. *The Sustainability Myth: Environmental Gentrification and the Politics of Justice*. New York University Press.

Chen, Mel Y. 2012. *Animacies: Biopolitics, Racial Mattering, and Queer Affect*. Duke University Press.

Chun, Wendy Hui Kyong. 2009. "Introduction: Race and/as Technology; or, How to Do Things to Race." *Camera Obscura 70* 24 (1): 7–35.

Cohen, Cathy J. 1997. "Punks, Bulldaggers, and Welfare Queens: The Radical Potential of Queer Politics?" *GLQ* 3 (4): 437–465.

———. 2004. "Deviance as Resistance: A New Research Agenda for the Study of Black Politics." *Du Bois Review: Social Science Research on Race* 1 (1): 27–45.

REFERENCES

Coleman, Kevin. 2018. "Practices of Refusal in Images: An Interview with Tina M. Campt." *Radical History Review* 2018 (32): 209–219.

Collier, Stephen J. 2011. *Post-Soviet Social: Neoliberalism, Social Modernity, Biopolitics.* Princeton University Press.

Corwin, Julia E., and Vinay Gidwani. 2021. "Repair Work as Care: On Maintaining the Planet in the Capitalocene." *Antipode*: 1–20. https://doi.org/10.1111/anti.12791.

Costache, Ioanida. 2018. "Reclaiming Romani-ness: Identity Politics, Universality and Otherness Or, Towards a (New) Romani Subjectivity." *Critical Romani Studies* 1 (1): 30–43.

———. 2020. "The Power of Racism, Its Trauma, and the Road to Healing." DoR. https://www.dor.ro/roma-and-the-ethnicization-of-covid-19-in-romania/.

Cox, Aimee Meredith. 2015. *Shapeshifters: Black Girls and the Choreography of Citizenship.* Duke University Press.

———. 2022. "Worldmaking and the Ethnographic Possibilities for an Abolitionist Anthropology." *Cultural Dynamics* 34 (1–2): 100–105.

Creed, Gerald W. 1998. *Domesticating Revolution: From Socialist Reform to Ambivalent Transition in a Bulgarian Village.* Penn State Press.

———. 2010. "Strange Bedfellows: Socialist Nostalgia and Neoliberalism in Bulgaria." In *Post-Communist Nostalgia*, edited by Maria Todorova and Zsuzsa Gille. Berghahn Books.

———. 2011. *Masquerade and Postsocialism: Ritual and Cultural Dispossession in Bulgaria.* Indiana University Press.

Da Silva, Denise Ferreira. 2007. *Toward a Global Idea of Race.* University of Minnesota Press.

De Genova, Nicholas. 2016. "The European Question: Migration, Race, and Postcoloniality in Europe." *Social Text* 34 (3): 75–102.

Denning, Michael. 2010. "Wageless Life." *New Left Review* 66 (6): 79–97.

Detchev, Stefan. 2009. "Who Are the Bulgarians? 'Race,' Science and Politics in Fin-de-Siècle Bulgaria." In *We, the People: Politics of National Peculiarity in Southeastern Europe*, edited by Diana Mishkova. Central European University Press.

Díaz, Vanessa. 2020. *Manufacturing Celebrity: Latino Paparazzi and Women Reporters in Hollywood.* Duke University Press.

Dillon, Lindsey. 2013. "Race, Waste, and Space: Brownfield Redevelopment and Environmental Justice at the Hunter's Point Shipyard." *Antipode* 46 (5): 1205–1221.

Dimitrov, Vesselin. 2001. "In Search of a Homogeneous Nation: The Assimilation of Bulgaria's Turkish Minority, 1984–1985." *JEMIE: Journal of Ethnopolitics and Minority Issues in Europe* 2 (2).

Doherty, Jacob. 2021. *Waste Worlds: Inhabiting Kampala's Infrastructures of Disposability.* University of California Press.

Dragostinova, Theodora K. 2021. *The Cold War from the Margins: A Small Socialist State on the Global Cultural Scene.* Cornell University Press.

Dunn, Elizabeth Cullen. 2004. *Privatizing Poland: Baby Food, Big Business, and the Remaking of Labor.* Cornell University Press.

Dzenovska, Dace. 2018. *School of Europeanness: Tolerance and Other Lessons in Political Liberalism in Latvia.* Cornell University Press.

El-Tayeb, Fatima. 2011. *European Others: Queering Ethnicity in Postnational Europe.* University of Minnesota Press.

Emejulu, Akwugo, and Francesca Sobande. 2019. *To Exist Is to Resist: Black Feminism in Europe.* Pluto Press.

Emen Gökatalay, Gözde. 2021. "A Crisis of Legitimacy or a Source of Political Consolidation? The Deportation of Bulgarian Turks in 1950–1951 and the Democratic Party." *Middle Eastern Studies* 57 (6): 920–934.

Eminov, Ali. 1997. *Turkish and Other Muslim Minorities in Bulgaria.* Routledge.

Eurostat. 2021. "Where Does EU Waste Go?" April 20. https://ec.europa.eu/eurostat/web/products-eurostat-news/-/ddn-20210420-1.

Fanon, Frantz. 1952. *Black Skin, White Masks.* Grove Press.

Farmer, Tessa. 2023. *Well Connected: Everyday Water Practices in Cairo.* Johns Hopkins University Press.

Fehérváry, Krisztina. 2002. "American Kitchens, Luxury Bathrooms, and the Search for a 'Normal' Life in Postsocialist Hungary." *Ethnos* 67 (3): 369–400.

——. 2009. "Goods and States: The Political Logic of State-Socialist Material Culture." *Comparative Studies in Society and History* 51 (2): 426–459.

——. 2013. *Politics in Color and Concrete: Socialist Materialities and the Middle Class in Hungary.* Indiana University Press.

Fennell, Catherine. 2015. *Last Project Standing: Civics and Sympathy in Post-Welfare Chicago.* University of Minnesota Press.

Fernando, Mayanthi L. 2014. *The Republic Unsettled: Muslim French and the Contradictions of Secularism.* Duke University Press.

Fikes, Kesha. 2009. *Managing African Portugal: The Citizen-Migrant Distinction.* Duke University Press.

Fikes, Kesha, and Alaina Lemon. 2002. "African Presence in Former Soviet Spaces." *Annual Review of Anthropology* 31 (1): 497–524.

Fitzpatrick, Sheila. 1994. *Stalin's Peasants: Resistance and Survival in the Russian Village After Collectivization.* Oxford University Press.

Florvil, Tiffany N. 2020. *Mobilizing Black Germany: Afro-German Women and the Making of a Transnational Movement.* University of Illinois Press.

Fotta, Martin. 2019. "'Only the Dead Don't Make the Future': Calon Lives Between Non-Gypsies and Death." *Journal of the Royal Anthropological Institute* 25 (3): 587–605.

Fredericks, Rosalind. 2018. *Garbage Citizenship: Vital Infrastructures of Labor in Dakar, Senegal.* Duke University Press.

Fremlova, Lucie. 2022. *Queer Roma: Transforming LGBTQ Lives.* Routledge.

Gabrys, Jennifer. 2009. "Sink: The Dirt of Systems." *Environment and Planning D: Society and Space* 27 (4): 666–681.

REFERENCES

Gal, Susan. 2002. "A Semiotics of the Public/Private Distinction." *Differences: A Journal of Feminist Cultural Studies* 13 (1): 77–95.

Gelbart, Petra. 2012. "Either Sing or Go Get the Beer: Contradictions of (Romani) Female Power in Central Europe." *Signs: Journal of Women in Culture and Society* 38 (1): 22–29.

Ghertner, D. Asher. 2015. *Rule by Aesthetics: World-Class City Making in Delhi.* Oxford University Press.

Ghodsee, Kristen. 2005. *The Red Riviera: Gender, Tourism, and Postsocialism on the Black Sea.* Duke University Press.

——. 2010. *Muslim Lives in Eastern Europe: Gender, Ethnicity, and the Transformation of Islam in Postsocialist Bulgaria.* Princeton University Press.

Gidwani, Vinay, and Anant Maringanti. 2016. "The Waste-Value Dialectic: Lumpen Urbanization in Contemporary India." *Comparative Studies of South Asia, Africa and the Middle East* 36 (1): 112–133.

Gidwani, Vinay, and Rajyashree N. Reddy. 2011. "The Afterlives of 'Waste': Notes from India for a Minor History of Capitalist Surplus." *Antipode* 43 (5): 1625–1658.

Gigova, Irina. 2011. "The City and the Nation: Sofia's Trajectory from Glory to Rubble in WWII." *Journal of Urban History* 37 (2): 155–175.

Giles, David Boarder. 2021. *A Mass Conspiracy to Feed People: Food Not Bombs and the World-Class Waste of Global Cities.* Duke University Press.

Gille, Zsuzsa, 2000. "Legacy of Waste or Wasted Legacy? The End of Industrial Ecology in Hungary." *Environmental Politics* 9 (1): 203–234.

——. 2007. *From the Cult of Waste to the Trash Heap of History: The Politics of Waste in Socialist and Postsocialist Hungary.* Indiana University Press.

——. 2010. "Is There a Global Postsocialist Condition?" *Global Society* 24 (1): 9–30.

Gille, Zsuzsa, and Josh Lepawsky. 2022. "Introduction: Waste Studies as a Field." In *The Routledge Handbook of Waste Studies*, edited by Zsuzsa Gille and Josh Lepawsky. Routledge.

Gilmore, Ruth Wilson. 2007. *Golden Gulag: Prisons, Surplus, Crisis, and Opposition in Globalizing California.* University of California Press.

Gilroy, Paul. 1993. *The Black Atlantic: Modernity and Double Consciousness.* Verso Books.

Goldberg, David Theo. 2002. *The Racial State.* Wiley.

——. 2006. "Racial Europeanization." *Ethnic and Racial Studies* 29 (2): 331–364.

Goldstein, Donna. 2003. *Laughter Out of Place: Race, Class, Violence, and Sexuality in a Rio Shantytown.* University of California Press.

Graan, Andrew. 2010. "On the Politics of *Imidž*: European Integration and the Trials of Recognition in Postconflict Macedonia." *Slavic Review* 69 (4): 835–858.

Grant, Bruce. 1995. *In the Soviet House of Culture: A Century of Perestroikas.* Princeton University Press.

—. 2010. "Cosmopolitan Baku." *Ethnos* 75 (2): 123–147.

—. 2014. "The Edifice Complex: Architecture and the Political Life of Surplus in the New Baku." *Public Culture* 26 (3): 501–528.

Greenberg, Jessica. 2010. "'There's Nothing Anyone Can Do About It': Participation, Apathy, and 'Successful' Democratic Transition in Postsocialist Serbia." *Slavic Review* 69 (1): 41–64.

—. 2014. *After the Revolution: Youth, Democracy, and the Politics of Disappointment in Serbia.* Stanford University Press.

Greenhouse, Carol J. 2018. "Political Anthropology." In *The International Encyclopedia of Anthropology*, edited by Hillary Callan and Simon Coleman. John Wiley & Sons.

Gregson, Nicky, and Mike Crang. 2015. "Waste, Resource Recovery and Labour: Recycling Economies in the EU." In *Why the Social Sciences Matter*, edited by Jonathan Michie and Cary Cooper. Palgrave Macmillan.

Gregson, Nicky, Mike Crang, Julie Botticello, Melania Calestani, and Anna Krzywoszynska. 2016. "Doing the 'Dirty Work' of the Green Economy: Resource Recovery and Migrant Labour in the EU." *European Urban and Regional Studies* 23 (4): 541–555.

Grekova, Maya, Veronika Dimitrov, Nevena Germanova, David Khjuranov, and Jana Markova. 2008. *Romite v Sofia: ot Izolatsiya kam Integratsiya* [The Roma in Sofia: From Isolation to Integration]. Istok-Zapad.

Grill, Jan. 2018. "'In England, They Don't Call You Black!' Migrating Racialisations and the Production of Roma Difference Across Europe." *Journal of Ethnic and Migration Studies* 44 (7): 1136–1155.

Grosz, Elizabeth. 2012. "The Future of Feminist Theory: Dreams for New Knowledges." In *Undutiful Daughters: New Directions in Feminist Thought and Practice*, edited by Henriette Gunkel, Chrysanthi Nigianni, and Fanny Söderbäck. Palgrave Macmillan.

Guiraudon, Virginie. 2009. "Equality in the Making: Implementing European Non-Discrimination Law." *Citizenship Studies* 13 (5): 527–549.

Gulde, Anne-Marie. 1999. "The Role of the Currency Board in Bulgaria's Stabilization." *Finance and Development* 36 (3). https://www.imf.org/external/pubs/ft/fandd/1999/09/gulde.htm.

Hale, Charles. 2005. "Neoliberal Multiculturalism: The Remaking of Cultural Rights and Racial Dominance in Central America." *PoLAR: Political and Legal Anthropology Review* 28 (1): 10–28.

Han, Clara. 2012. *Life in Debt: Times of Care and Violence in Neoliberal Chile.* University of California Press.

Harper, Krista. 2006. *Wild Capitalism: Environmental Activism and Postsocialist Political Ecology in Hungary.* East European Monographs.

Harper, Krista, Tamara Steger, and Richard Filčák. 2009. "Environmental Justice and Roma Communities in Central and Eastern Europe." *Environmental Policy and Governance* 19 (4): 251–268.

Hartman, Saidiya V. 1997. *Scenes of Subjection: Terror, Slavery, and Self-Making in Nineteenth-Century America.* Oxford University Press.

REFERENCES

Hawkins, Gay, and Stephen Muecke. 2002. "Introduction: Cultural Economies of Waste." In *Culture and Waste: The Creation and Destruction of Value*, edited by Gay Hawkins and Stephen Muecke. Rowman & Littlefield Publishers.

Hecht, Gabrielle. 2018. "Interscalar Vehicles for an African Anthropocene: On Waste, Temporality, and Violence." *Cultural Anthropology* 33 (1): 109–141.

——. 2023. *Residual Governance: How South Africa Foretells Planetary Futures.* Duke University Press.

Herzfeld, Michael. 2005. *Cultural Intimacy: Social Poetics in the Nation-State.* Routledge.

Hesse, Barnor. 2007. "Racialized Modernity: An Analytics of White Mythologies." *Ethnic and Racial Studies* 30 (4): 643–663.

——. 2009. "Afterword: Black Europe's Undecidability." In *Black Europe and the African Diaspora*, edited by Darlene Hine, Tricia Clark, and Danielle Keaton. University of Illinois Press.

Hill, Jane. 1998. "Language, Race, and White Public Space." *American Anthropologist* 100 (3): 680–689.

Hird, Myra J. 2013. "Is Waste Indeterminacy Useful? A Response to Zsuzsa Gille." *Social Epistemology Review and Reply Collective* 2 (6): 28–33.

Hobart, Hi'ilei Julia Kawehipuaakahaopulani, and Tamara Kneese. 2020. "Radical Care: Survival Strategies for Uncertain Times." *Social Text* 38 (1): 1–16.

Holmes, Seth M. 2013. *Fresh Fruit, Broken Bodies: Migrant Farmworkers in the United States.* University of California Press.

Imre, Anikó. 2005. *Whiteness in Post-Socialist Eastern Europe: The Time of the Gypsies, the End of Race.* State University of New York Press.

——. 2014 "Postcolonial Media Studies in Postsocialist Europe." *boundary 2* 41 (1): 113–134.

International Bank for Reconstruction and Development/The World Bank. 2021. *Bulgaria Systematic Country Diagnostic.* https://documents1.worldbank.org/curated/en/727791642521506054/pdf/Bulgaria-Systematic-Country-Diagnostic.pdf.

Isenhour, Cindy. 2015. "Sustainable Consumption and Its Discontents." In *Sustainability: Key Issues*, edited by Helen Kopnina and Eleanor Shoreman-Ouimet. Routledge.

Isenhour, Cindy, Gary McDonogh, and Melissa Checker, eds. 2015. *Sustainability in the Global City: Myth and Practice.* Cambridge University Press.

Ivanova, Evgeniya, and Velcho Krastev. 2019. "The Gypsies/Roma in Bulgaria in the Years of Socialism—Forced Migration and Population." In *Proceedings of the Conference (Re)Thinking Socialism: Knowledge, Memory and the Oblivion of the Socialist Past*. Bulgarian Academy of Sciences, Institute of Ethnology and Folklore Studies with Ethnographic Museum (IEFSEM–BAS), November 7–9.

Jackson, Stephen J. 2014. "Rethinking Repair." In *Media Technologies: Essays on Communication, Materiality, and Society*, edited by Tarleton Gillespie, Pablo J. Boczkowski, and Kirsten A. Foot. MIT Press.

Jackson, Zakiyyah Iman. 2020. *Becoming Human: Matter and Meaning in an Antiblack World*. New York University Press.

James, Cyril Lionel Robert. (1938) 2001. *The Black Jacobins: Toussaint L'Ouverture and the San Domingo Revolution*. Penguin UK.

Jung, Yuson. 2010. "The Inability Not to Follow: Western Hegemonies and the Notion of 'Complaisance' in the Enlarged Europe." *Anthropological Quarterly* 83 (2): 317–353.

———. 2019. *Balkan Blues: Consumer Politics After State Socialism*. Indiana University Press.

Kalmar, Ivan. 2023. "Race, Racialisation, and the East of the European Union: An Introduction." *Journal of Ethnic and Migration Studies* 49 (6): 1465–1480.

Kamusella, Tomasz. 2018. *Ethnic Cleansing During the Cold War: The Forgotten 1989 Expulsion of Turks from Communist Bulgaria*. Routledge.

Kaneff, Deema. 2004. *Who Owns the Past? The Politics of Time in a 'Model' Bulgarian Village*. Berghahn Books.

Kelley, Robin D. G. 1993. "'We Are Not What We Seem': Rethinking Black Working-Class Opposition in the Jim Crow South." *The Journal of American History* 80 (1): 75–112.

———. 1994. *Race Rebels: Culture, Politics, and the Black Working Class*. The Free Press.

———. 2002. *Freedom Dreams: The Black Radical Imagination*. Beacon.

———. 2017. "What Did Cedric Robinson Mean by Racial Capitalism?" Review of *The Terms of Order: Political Science and the Myth of Leadership*, by Cedric Robinson. *Boston Review*, January 12. http://bostonreview.net/race/robin-d-g-kelley-what-did-cedric-robinson-mean-racial-capitalism.

Kenarov, Dimiter. 2009. "Chronicle of a Death Foretold." Dimiter Kenarov Freelance Journalist, April 29. https://dimiterkenarov.com/2009/05/chronicle-of-a-death-foretold/.

Khalvashi, Tamta. 2019. "A Ride on the Elevator: Infrastructures of Brokenness and Repair in Georgia." In *Repair, Brokenness, Breakthrough: Ethnographic Responses*, edited by Francisco Martinez and Patrick Laviolette. Berghahn Books.

Kideckel, David A. 2008. *Getting by in Postsocialist Romania: Labor, the Body, and Working*. University of Indiana Press.

King, Tiffany Lethabo. 2015. "Interview with Dr. Tiffany Lethabo King." Interviewed by Shaista Patel, Ghaida Moussa, and Nishant Upadhyay. *Feral Feminisms*, no. 4: 64–68. https://feralfeminisms.com/lethabo-king/.

———. 2019. *The Black Shoals: Offshore Formations of Black and Native Studies*. Duke University Press.

Kleinman, Julie. 2019. *Adventure Capital: Migration and the Making of an African Hub in Paris*. University of California Press.

Klumbytė, Neringa. 2014. "Of Power and Laughter: Carnivalesque Politics and Moral Citizenship in Lithuania." *American Ethnologist* 41 (3): 473–490.

Kóczé, Angéla. 2011. "Gender, Ethnicity, and Class: Romani Women's Political Activism and Social Struggles." PhD diss., Central European University.

——. 2015. "Speaking from the Margins." *Roma Rights* 2 (Nothing About Us Without Us? Roma Participation in Policy Making and Knowledge Production). European Roma Rights Centre. http://www.errc.org/cms/upload/file/roma-rights-2-2015-nothing-about-us-without-us.pdf.

——. 2018. "Race, Migration and Neoliberalism: Distorted Notions of Romani Migration in European Public Discourses." *Social Identities* 24 (4): 459–473.

——. 2020. "Gendered and Racialized Social Insecurity of Roma in East Central Europe." In *The Roma and Their Struggle for Identity in Contemporary Europe*, edited by Angéla Kóczé and Huub van Baar. Berghahn Books.

Kóczé, Angéla, and Márton Rövid. 2012. "Pro-Roma Global Civil Society: Acting for, with or Instead of Roma?" In *Global Civil Society 2012*, edited by Sabine Selchow, Mary Kaldor, and Henrietta L. Moore. Palgrave Macmillan.

Kóczé, Angéla, and Nidhi Trehan. 2020. "'When They Enter, We All Enter…': Envisioning a New Social Europe from a Romani Feminist Perspective." In *Romani Communities and Transformative Change: A New Social Europe*, edited by Andrew Ryder, Marius Taba, and Nidhi Trehan. Bristol University Press.

Kóczé, Angéla, Violetta Zentai, Jelena Jovanović, and Enikő Vincze, eds. 2018. *The Romani Women's Movement: Struggles and Debates in Central and Eastern Europe*. Routledge.

Kondo, Dorinne. 2018. *Worldmaking: Race, Performance, and the Work of Creativity*. Duke University Press.

Koycheva, Lora. 2016. "When the Radical Is Ordinary: Performance and the Everyday in Bulgaria's Protests of 2013." *Journal of Contemporary European Studies* 24 (2): 240–254.

Krastanova, Radosveta. 2019. "The Green Movement in Bulgaria. Actors, Generations, Challenges, Values." *Südosteuropa Mitteilungen* 59 (5/6): 112–123.

Krastev, Georgi, Evgenia Ivanova, and Velcho Krastev. 2020. *The Law Enforcement System and the Gypsies/Roma in Bulgaria (from 1878 to the Second Decade of the 21st Century)*. Avangard Prima.

Krasteva, Anna. 2016. "The Post-Communist Rise of National Populism: Bulgarian Paradoxes." In *The Rise of the Far Right in Europe: Populist Shifts and "Othering,"* edited by Gabriella Lazaridis, Giovanna Campani, and Annie Benveniste. Palgrave MacMillan.

Kristeva, Julia. 1982. "Approaching Abjection." *Oxford Literary Review* 5 (1/2): 125–149.

Kurtović, Larisa. 2019. "Interpellating the State: Activists Seek Political Authority in Postwar Bosnia and Herzegovina." *American Ethnologist* 46 (4): 444–456.

——. 2020. "When All That Is Solid Does Not Melt into Air: Labor, Politics and Materiality in a Bosnian Detergent Factory." *PoLAR: Political and Legal Anthropology Review* 43 (2): 228–246.

Lampland, Martha. 1995. *The Object of Labor: Commodification in Socialist Hungary.* University of Chicago Press.

la paperson. 2017. *A Third University Is Possible.* University of Minnesota Press.

Larkin, Brian. 2008. *Signal and Noise: Media, Infrastructure, and Urban Culture in Nigeria.* Duke University Press.

Lavergne, Dostena. 2010. *Expertite na Prehoda: Bulgarskite Think-tanks i Globalnite Mrezhi za Bliyanie* [The Experts of the Transition: The Bulgarian Think-Tanks and the Global Networks of Influence]. Iztok-Zapad.

Lecerf, Marie. 2024. "Understanding EU Action on Roma Inclusion." European Centre for Parliamentary Research and Documentation. https://www.europarl.europa.eu/RegData/etudes/BRIE/2021/690629/EPRS_BRI(2021)690629_EN.pdf.

Lemon, Alaina. 1995. "'What Are They Writing About Us Blacks?'—Roma and 'Race' in Russia." *Anthropology of East Europe Review* 13 (2): 34–40.

———. 1998. "'Your Eyes Are Green like Dollars': Counterfeit Cash, National Substance, and Currency Apartheid in 1990s Russia." *Cultural Anthropology* 13 (1): 22–55.

———. 2000. *Between Two Fires: Gypsy Performance and Romani Memory from Pushkin to Post-Socialism.* Duke University Press.

———. 2002. Without a "Concept"? Race as Discursive Practice. *Slavic Review* 61 (1): 54–61.

Lentin, Alana. 2004. *Racism and Anti-Racism in Europe.* Pluto Press.

———. 2011. "What Happens to Anti-Racism When We Are Post Race?" *Feminist Legal Studies* 19 (2): 159.

Lepawsky, Josh. 2018. *Reassembling Rubbish: Worlding Electronic Waste.* MIT Press.

Lewicki, Aleksandra. 2023. "East–West Inequalities and the Ambiguous Racialisation of 'Eastern Europeans'." *Journal of Ethnic and Migration Studies* 49 (6): 1481–1499.

Liboiron, Max. 2021. *Pollution is Colonialism.* Duke University Press.

Liboiron, Max, and Josh Lepawsky. 2022. *Discard Studies: Wasting, Systems, and Power.* MIT Press.

Lie, Siv B. 2021. *Django Generations: Hearing Ethnorace, Citizenship, and Jazz Manouche in France.* University of Chicago Press.

Lorde, Audre. 1988. *A Burst of Light: Essays.* Firebrand Books.

Lowe, Lisa. 2015. *The Intimacies of Four Continents.* Duke University Press.

MacBride, Samantha. 2011. *Recycling Reconsidered: The Present Failure and Future Promise of Environmental Action in the United States.* MIT Press.

Magazzini, Tina, and Stefano Piemontese. 2019. *Constructing Roma Migrants: European Narratives and Local Governance.* Springer Nature.

Mamdani, Mahmood. 2001. *When Victims Become Killers: Colonialism, Nativism, and the Genocide in Rwanda.* Princeton Publishing Press.

Mankekar, Purnima, and Akhil Gupta. 2016. "Intimate Encounters: Affective Labor in Call Centers." *Positions: East Asia Cultures Critique* 24 (1): 17–43.

REFERENCES

Manning, Paul. 2007. "Rose-Colored Glasses? Color Revolutions and Cartoon Chaos in Postsocialist Georgia." *Cultural Anthropology* 22 (2): 171–213.

Marche, Guillaume. 2012. "Why Infrapolitics Matters." *Revue Francaise d' Études Américaines* 1: 3–18.

Marinov, Aleksandar G. 2020. "Images of Roma Through the Language of Bulgarian State Archives." *Social Inclusion* 8 (2): 296–304.

Marushiakova, Elena, and Vesselin Popov. 1997. *Gypsies (Roma) in Bulgaria.* Peter Lang Publishing.

——. 2000. "The Bulgarian Gypsies–Searching Their Place in the Society." *Balkanologie: Revue d'études pluridisciplinaires* 4 (2): 1–16.

——. 2001. *Gypsies in the Ottoman Empire: A Contribution to the History of the Balkans.* University of Hertfordshire Press.

——. 2015. "The First Gypsy/Roma Organizations, Churches and Newspapers." In *From Dust to Digital: Ten Years of the Endangered Archives Programme*, edited by Maja Kominko. Open Book Publishers.

——. 2021. *Roma Voices in History: A Sourcebook.* Brill.

Matache, Margareta. 2017a. "Biased Elites, Unfit Policies: Reflections on the Lacunae of Roma Integration Strategies." *European Review* 25 (4): 58–607.

Matache, Margareta. 2017b. "Dear Gadjo (non-Romani) Scholar." *FXB Center for Health and Human Rights*, June 19. https://fxb.harvard.edu/2017/06/19/dear-gadje-non-romani-scholars/.

Matache, Margareta, and Jacqueline Bhabha. 2020. "Anti-Roma Racism is Spiraling During COVID-19 Pandemic." *Health and Human Rights*, April 7. https://www.hhrjournal.org/2020/04/anti-roma-racism-is-spiraling-during-covid-19-pandemic/.

Mattern, Shannon. 2018. "Maintenance and Care." *Places Journal*, November. https://doi.org/10.22269/181120.

Mauch, Christof, ed. 2016. "A Future Without Waste? Zero Waste in Theory and Practice." *RCC Perspectives: Transformations in Environment and Society* 3.

May, Antonia, and Christian Czymara. 2024. "Mainstream Parties Adopting Far-Right Rhetoric Simply Increases Votes for Far-Right Parties." *The Loop.* https://theloop.ecpr.eu/mainstream-parties-adopting-far-right-rhetoric-simply-increases-votes-for-far-right-parties/.

McKee, Emily. 2015. "Trash Talk: Interpreting Morality and Disorder in Negev/Naqab Landscapes." *Current Anthropology* 56 (5): 733–752.

Melamed, Jodi. 2015. "Racial Capitalism." *Critical Ethnic Studies* 1 (1): 76–85.

Melosi, Martin. 2004. *Garbage in the Cities: Refuse Reform and the Environment.* University of Pittsburgh Press.

Menninghaus, Winifried. 2003. *Disgust: The Theory and History of a Strong Sensation.* Translated by Howard Eiland and Joel Golb. State University of New York Press.

Methodieva, Milena B. 2021. *Between Empire and Nation: Muslim Reform in the Balkans.* Stanford University Press.

Millar, Kathleen M. 2018. *Reclaiming the Discarded: Life and Labor on Rio's Garbage Dump*. Duke University Press.

———. 2020. "Garbage as Racialization." *Anthropology and Humanism* 45 (1): 4–24.

Mills, Charles. 1997. *The Racial Contract*. Cornell University Press.

Ministry of the Environment and Water. 2009. "Natsionalna programa za upravlenie na deynostite po otpadatsite za perioda 2009–2013" [National Waste Management Programme (NWMP) for the Period 2009–2013].

Mirga-Kruszelnicka, Anna. 2015. "Romani Studies and Emerging Romani Scholarship." In "Nothing About Us Without Us? Roma Participation in Policy Making and Knowledge Production." Special issue, *Roma Rights: Journal of the European Roma Rights Centre* 2: 39–46.

———. 2018. "Challenging Anti-Gypsyism in Academia: The Role of Romani Scholars." *Critical Romani Studies* 1 (1): 8–28.

———. 2022. *Mobilizing Romani Ethnicity: Romani Political Activism in Argentina, Colombia and Spain*. Central European University Press.

Mirga-Kruszelnicka, Anna, and Jekatyerina Dunajeva. 2020. *Re-Thinking Roma Resistance Throughout History: Recounting Stories of Strength and Bravery*. European Roma Institute for Arts and Culture. https://eriac.org/wp-content/uploads/2021/03/Re-thinking_Roma_Resistance_throughout_History.epub.

Mishev, Mihail. 2023. "The Roma Don't Decide the Outcome of the Elections in Bulgaria." *Cross-Border Talks*, November 4. https://www.crossbordertalks.eu/2023/11/04/the-roma-dont-decide-the-outcome-of-the-elections-in-bulgaria/.

Mitrani, Leon. 1991. "Izvestija za naroda a ne za partija (nejuridičeska studija)" [News for the people, not for the party (non-legal study)]. *Evrejski Vesti*, January 9.

Moore, Sarah A. 2012. "Garbage Matters: Concepts in New Geographies of Waste." *Progress in Human Geography* 36 (6): 780–799.

Morris, Rosalind C. 1995. "All Made Up: Performance Theory and the New Anthropology of Sex and Gender." *Annual Review of Anthropology* 24 (1): 567–592.

Muehlebach, Andrea. 2012. *Moral Neoliberal: Welfare and Citizenship in Italy*. University of Chicago Press.

———. 2023. *A Vital Frontier: Water Insurgencies in Europe*. Duke University Press.

Murphy, Michelle. 2017. "Alterlife and Decolonial Chemical Relations." *Cultural Anthropology* 32 (4): 494–503.

Nadkarni, Maya. 2007. "The Master's Voice: Authenticity, Nostalgia, and the Refusal of Irony in Postsocialist Hungary." *Social Identities* 13 (5): 611–626.

Nadkarni, Maya, and Olga Shevchenko. 2004. "The Politics of Nostalgia: A Case for Comparative Analysis of Post-Socialist Practices." *Ab Imperio* 2: 487–519.

Nagle, Robin. 2013. *Picking Up: On the Streets and Behind the Trucks with the Sanitation Workers of New York City*. Farrar, Straus, and Giroux.

Neimanis, Astrida. 2017. *Bodies of Water: Posthuman Feminist Phenomenology*. Bloomsbury Publishing.

REFERENCES

Neuburger, Mary C. 2004. *The Orient Within: Muslim Minorities and the Negotiation of Nationhood in Modern Bulgaria.* Cornell University Press.

——. 2012. *Balkan Smoke: Tobacco and the Making of Modern Bulgaria.* Cornell University Press.

Nixon, Rob. 2011. *Slow Violence and the Environmentalism of the Poor.* Harvard University Press.

O'Brien, Thomas. 2019. "'Our Patience Has Run Out': Tracking the Anti-Government Protest Cycle in Bulgaria." *Journal of Contemporary European Studies* 27 (4): 515–528.

O'Higgins, Niall. 2012. "Roma and non-Roma in the Labour Market in Central and South Eastern Europe." *Roma Inclusion Working Papers.* United Nations Development Programme.

O'Neill, Kate. 2019. *Waste.* Polity Press.

Oprea, Alexandra. 2004. "Re-Envisioning Social Justice from the Ground Up: Including the Experiences of Romani Women." *Essex Human Rights Review* 1 (1): 29–39.

——. 2009. "Intersectionality Backlash: A Romani Feminist's Response." *Roma Rights Quarterly* (2): 21–23.

——. 2012. "Romani Feminism in Reactionary Times." *Signs: Journal of Women in Culture and Society* 38 (1): 11–21.

Owczarzak, Jill. 2009. "Introduction: Postcolonial Studies and Postsocialism in Eastern Europe." *Focaal* 53: 3–19.

Pandian, Anand. 2009. *Crooked Stalks: Cultivating Virtue in South India.* Duke University Press.

Park, Lisa Sun-Hee, and David Pellow. 2011. *The Slums of Aspen: Immigrants vs. the Environment in America's Eden.* New York University Press.

Parla, Ayşe. 2009. "Remembering Across the Border: Postsocialist Nostalgia Among Turkish Immigrants from Bulgaria." *American Ethnologist* 36 (4): 750–767.

——. 2019. *Precarious Hope: Migration and the Limits of Belonging in Turkey.* Stanford University Press.

Partridge, Damani James. 2008. "We Were Dancing in the Club, Not on the Berlin Wall: Black Bodies, Street Bureaucrats, and Exclusionary Incorporation into the New Europe." *Cultural Anthropology* 23 (4): 660–687.

——. 2022. *Blackness as a Universal Claim: Holocaust Heritage, Noncitizen Futures, and Black Power in Berlin.* University of California Press.

Pashov, Shakir. 2023. *Istoriya na Tsiganite v Balgariya i Evropa* [History of the Gypsies in Bulgaria and Europe]. Brill.

Pasieka, Agnieszka. 2017. "Taking Far-Right Claims Seriously and Literally: Anthropology and the Study of Right-Wing Radicalism." *Slavic Review* 76 (S1): S19–S29.

Patterson, Orlando. (1982) 2018. *Slavery and Social Death: A Comparative Study, with a New Preface.* Harvard University Press.

Pellow, David Naguib. 2017. *What Is Critical Environmental Justice?* John Wiley & Sons.

Petrova, Dimitrina. 1992. "Freedom Plus Three: Permanent Revolution in Bulgaria." *Peace Review* 4 (4): 35–39.

Pierre, Jemima. 2012. *The Predicament of Blackness: Postcolonial Ghana and the Politics of Race.* Duke University Press.

Popov, Metodii. 1938. *Bulgarskiat N arod mejdu Evropeiskite Rasi i Narodi* [The Bulgarian People Among the European Races and Peoples]. Pridvorna Pechatnitsa.

Potuoğlu Cook, Öykü. 2006. "Beyond the Glitter: Belly Dance and Neoliberal Gentrification in Istanbul." *Cultural Anthropology* 21 (4): 633–660.

Povinelli, Elizabeth A. 2002. *The Cunning of Recognition: Indigenous Alterities and the Making of Australian Multiculturalism.* Duke University Press.

——. 2011. *Economies of Abandonment: Social Belonging and Endurance in Late Liberalism.* Duke University Press.

——. 2016. *Geontologies: A Requiem to Late Liberalism.* Duke University Press.

Pulay, Gergő. 2018. "Crises, Securitizations and the Europeanization of Roma Representation." *Intersections. East European Journal of Society and Politics* 4 (3): 180–194.

Pulido, Laura. 2017. "Geographies of Race and Ethnicity II: Environmental Racism, Racial Capitalism and State-Sanctioned Violence." *Progress in Human Geography* 41 (4): 524–533.

Ragaru, Nadege. 2023. *Bulgaria, the Jews, and the Holocaust: On the Origins of a Heroic Narrative.* Boydell & Brewer.

Raffles, Hugh. 2007. "Jews, Lice, and History." *Public Culture* 19 (3): 521–566.

Rainbow, David, ed. 2019. *Ideologies of Race: Imperial Russia and the Soviet Union in Global Context.* McGill-Queen's University Press.

Ralph, Laurence. 2014. *Renegade Dreams: Living Through Injury in Gangland Chicago.* University of Chicago Press.

Rana, Junaid. 2011. *Terrifying Muslims: Race and Labor in the South Asian Diaspora.* Duke University Press.

Razsa, Maple. 2015. *Bastards of Utopia: Living Radical Politics After Socialism.* Indiana University Press.

Reeves, Madeleine. 2013. "Clean Fake: Authenticating Documents and Persons in Migrant Moscow." *American Ethnologist* 40 (3): 508–524.

Reno, Joshua. 2014. "Toward a New Theory of Waste: From 'Matter Out of Place' to Signs of Life." *Theory, Culture, and Society* 31 (6): 3–27.

——. 2015. "Waste and Waste Management." *Annual Review of Anthropology* 44 (1): 557–572.

——. 2016. *Waste Away: Working and Living with a North American Landfill.* University of California Press.

Reno, Joshua, and Britt Halvorson. 2021. "Waste and Whiteness." In *The Routledge Handbook of Waste Studies*, edited by Zsuzsa Gille and Josh Lepawsky. Routledge.

REFERENCES

Resnick, Elana. 2009. "Transnational Affiliations, Local Articulations: Consumption and Romani Publics in Bulgaria." *Anthropology of East Europe Review* 27 (2): 101–116.

———. 2011. "Using Ethnic Tensions for Political Games (and Gains): Anti-Roma Protests in Bulgaria." *Truthout*, October 8. https://truthout.org/articles/using-ethnic-tensions-for-political-games-and-gains-antiroma-protests-in-bulgaria/.

———. 2017. "Protest and the Practice of Normal Life in Bulgaria." *Lithuanian Ethnology: Studies in Social Anthropology and Ethnology* 17: 193–214.

———. 2018. "Durable Remains: Glass Reuse, Material Citizenship and Precarity in EU-era Bulgaria." *Journal of Contemporary Archaeology* 5 (1): 103–115.

———. 2020. "There Is Nothing Revelatory About It: Racialized Labor in the Age of COVID-19." *Exertions*, Society for the Anthropology of Work. https://saw.americananthro.org/pub/there-is-nothing-revelatory-about-it/release/1.

———. 2021. "The Limits of Resilience: Managing Waste in the Racialized Anthropocene." *American Anthropologist* 123 (2): 222–236.

———. 2023. "The Intimacy of Labor: Street Sweeping and the Pleasures of Anything Else." *Public Culture* 35 (2): 233–254.

———. 2024a. "The Determined Indeterminacy of White Supremacy: Strategies of Racial Disavowal in Bulgaria." *American Ethnologist* 51 (3): 433–447.

———. 2024b. "Sustaining Containability: Zero Waste and White Space." *Cultural Anthropology* 39 (2): 216–245.

Rexhepi, Piro. 2022. *White Enclosures: Racial Capitalism and Coloniality Along the Balkan Route*. Duke University Press.

Roberts, Elizabeth F. S. 2017. "What Gets Inside: Violent Entanglements and Toxic Boundaries in Mexico City." *Cultural Anthropology* 32 (4): 592–619.

Robertson, Jennifer. 1991. "Theatrical Resistance, Theatres of Restraint: The Takarazuka Revue and the 'State Theatre' Movement in Japan." *Anthropological Quarterly* 64 (4) 165–177.

Robinson, Cedric J. (1983) 2000. *Black Marxism: The Making of the Black Radical Tradition*. University of North Carolina Press.

Rorke, Bernard. 2023. "Bulgaria: Roma Inclusion and the Far-Right Threat in the EU's Own Absurdistan." *European Roma Rights Centre*, October 20. https://www.errc.org/news/bulgaria-roma-inclusion-and-the-far-right-threat-in-the-eus-own-absurdistan.

Rosa, Jonathan. 2019. *Looking Like a Language, Sounding Like a Race: Raciolinguistic Ideologies and the Learning of Latinidad*. Oxford University Press.

Rosa, Jonathan, and Vanessa Díaz. 2020. "Raciontologies: Rethinking Anthropological Accounts of Institutional Racism and Enactments of White Supremacy in the United States." *American Anthropologist* 122 (1): 120–132.

Rostas, Iulius, and Florin Moisă. 2023. "Romani People, Policing, and Penality in Europe." In *The Routledge International Handbook on Decolonizing Justice*, edited by Chris Cunneen, Antje Deckert, Amanda Porter, Juan Tauri, and Robert Webb. Routledge.

Rubin, Eli. 2008. *Synthetic Socialism: Plastics and Dictatorship in the German Democratic Republic*. University of North Carolina Press.

Rubin, Gayle S. 2011. *Deviations: A Gayle Rubin Reader*. Duke University Press.

Rucker-Chang, Sunnie. 2018. "Challenging Americanism and Europeanism: African-Americans and Roma in the American South and European Union 'South.'" *Journal of Transatlantic Studies* 16 (2): 181–199.

——. 2020. "Ideologies of Race: Imperial Russia and the Soviet Union in a Global Context." *Slavic Review* 79 (3): 636–642.

Rucker-Chang, Sunnie, and Chelsi West Ohueri. 2021. "A Moment of Reckoning: Transcending Bias, Engaging Race and Racial Formations in Slavic and East European Studies." *Slavic Review* 80 (2): 216–223.

Sarafian, Iliana. 2023. *Contesting Moralities: Roma Identities, State and Kinship*. Vol. 5 of *Romani Studies*, edited by Angéla Kócz and Huub van Baar. Berghahn Books.

Savić, Jelena M. 2018. "Heroines of Ours: Between Magnificence and Maleficence." In *The Romani Women's Movement: Struggles and Debates in Central and Eastern Europe*, edited by Angéla Kóczé, Violetta Zentai, Jelena Jovanović, and Enikő Vincze. Routledge.

——. 2022. "Gadjo Supremacy and Gadjo Privileges." Conference paper, Critical Approaches to Romani Studies Conference. https://www.academia .edu/82965318/Gadjo_supremacy_and_Gadjo_privileges

Schwenkel, Christina. 2015. "Spectacular Infrastructure and Its Breakdown in Socialist Vietnam." *American Ethnologist* 42 (3): 520–534.

——. 2018. "Governing Through Garbage: Waste Infrastructure Breakdown and Gendered Apathy in Vietnam." In *The Routledge Handbook of Anthropology and the City*, edited by Setha Low. Routledge.

——. 2020. *Building Socialism: The Afterlife of East German Architecture in Urban Vietnam*. Duke University Press.

Scott, James C. 1990. *Domination and the Arts of Resistance: Hidden Transcripts*. Yale University Press.

——. 2012. "Infrapolitics and Mobilizations: A Response by James C. Scott." *Revue Française d' Études Américaines* 1: 112–117.

Seigel, Jerrold. 1999. *Bohemian Paris: Culture, Politics, and the Boundaries of Bourgeois Life, 1830–1930*. Johns Hopkins University Press.

Seizer, Susan. 1997. "Jokes, Gender, and Discursive Distance on the Tamil Popular Stage." *American Ethnologist* 24 (1): 62–90.

Shange, Savannah. 2019. *Progressive Dystopia: Abolition, Antiblackness, and Schooling in San Francisco*. Duke University Press.

Sharpe, Christina. 2016. *In the Wake: On Blackness and Being*. Duke University Press.

Shoshan, Nitzan. 2016. *The Management of Hate: Nation, Affect, and the Governance of Right-Wing Extremism in Germany*. Princeton University Press.

Sigona, Nando, and Nidhi Trehan, eds. 2009. *Romani Politics in Contemporary Europe: Poverty, Ethnic Mobilization, and the Neoliberal Order*. Springer.

REFERENCES

Silverman, Carol. 2018. "From Reflexivity to Collaboration: Changing Roles of a Non-Romani Scholar, Activist, and Performer." *Critical Romani Studies* 1 (2): 76–97.

Simmons, Kimberly Eison. 2008. "Navigating the Racial Terrain: Blackness and Mixedness in the United States and the Dominican Republic." *Transforming Anthropology* 16 (2): 95–111.

Simpson, Audra. 2014. *Mohawk Interruptus: Political Life Across the Borders of Settler States.* Duke University Press.

———. 2016. "Consent's Revenge." *Cultural Anthropology* 31 (3): 326–333.

Sojoyner, Damien M. 2017. "Another Life Is Possible: Black Fugitivity and Enclosed Places." *Cultural Anthropology* 32 (4): 514–536.

Solomon, Marisa. 2019. "'The Ghetto Is a Gold Mine': The Racialized Temporality of Betterment." *International Labor and Working-Class History* 95: 76–94.

———. 2022. "Ecologies Elsewhere: Flyness, Fill, and Black Women's Fugitive Matter(s)." *GLQ* 28 (4): 567–587.

Solomon, Marisa, and Zoë Wool. 2021. "Waste Is Not a Metaphor for Racist Dispossession: The Black Feminist Marxism of Marisa Solomon." *Catalyst: Feminism, Theory, Technoscience* 7 (2): 1–5.

Sosna, Daniel. 2024. "The Inner Dynamics of Moral Economies: The Case of Waste Management." *East European Politics and Societies* 38 (1): 321–338.

Sosna, Daniel, Barbora Stehlíková, and Pavel Mašek. 2024. "Ecologies of Quantification in Waste Management: Landfilling, E-waste Recycling, and Car Breaking." *Critique of Anthropology* 44 (1): 42–63.

Speed, Shannon. 2005. "Dangerous Discourses: Human Rights and Multiculturalism in Neoliberal Mexico." *Political and Legal Anthropology Review* 28 (1): 29–51.

Stamatopoulou-Robbins, Sophia. 2019. *Waste Siege: The Life of Infrastructure in Palestine.* Stanford University Press.

Stanchev, Krasen. 2004. "Pouki ot Reformite ot 1990 do 2004" [Lessons from the Reforms from 1990 to 2004]. In *Anatomiya na Prehoda (Stopanskata Politika v Balgariya ot 1989 do 2004 g. prez Pogleda na Instituta za Pazarna Ikonomika)* [Anatomy of the Transition (Economic Policy in Bulgaria from 1989 to 2004 Through the Eyes of the Institute for Market Economics)], edited by Georgi Angelov, Lachezar Bogdanov, Martin Dimitrov, et al. https://www.easibulgaria.org/assets/var/docs/ANATOMIA_NA_PREHODA.pdf.

Stanoeva, Elitsa. 2010. "The Central City Square as a Legitimation Resource: The Main Square of Socialist Sofia." *Kritika i humanizam* [Critique and Humanism] 35: 285–320.

Stenroos, Marko. 2018. "Power and Hierarchy Among Finnish Kaale Roma: Insights on Integration and Inclusion Processes." *Critical Romani Studies* 1 (2): 6–23.

Stoler, Ann Laura. 2013. *Imperial Debris: On Ruins and Ruination.* Duke University Press.

Strasser, Susan. 1999. *Waste and Want: A Social History of Trash*. Macmillan Publishers.

Sudetic, Chuck. 2013. "Roma in Political Life: Bulgaria—Political Manipulation and the Damage Done." *Voices*, September 10. https://www.opensocietyfoundations.org/voices/roma-political-life-bulgaria-political-manipulation-and-damage-done.

Surdu, Mihai. 2019. "Why the 'Real' Numbers on Roma Are Fictitious: Revisiting Practices of Ethnic Quantification." *Ethnicities* 19 (3): 486–502.

Surdu, Mihai, and Martin Kovats. 2015. "Roma Identity as an Expert–Political Construction." *Social Inclusion* 3 (5): 5–18.

Sze, Julie. 2006. *Noxious New York: The Racial Politics of Urban Health and Environmental Justice*. MIT Press.

Szombati, Kristóf. 2018. *The Revolt of the Provinces: Anti-Gypsyism and Right-Wing Politics in Hungary*. Berghahn Books.

Tahir, Orhan. 2020. "122 Years Since the Birth of Shakir Pashov—the Apostle of the Roma Movement in Bulgaria." Paper presented at the Roma Standing Conference.

Thomas, Deborah A. 2004. *Modern Blackness: Nationalism, Globalization, and the Politics of Culture in Jamaica*. Duke University Press.

——. 2016. "Time and the Otherwise: Plantations, Garrisons and Being Human in the Caribbean." *Anthropological Theory* 16 (2–3): 177–200.

——. 2019. *Political Life in the Wake of the Plantation: Sovereignty, Witnessing, Repair*. Duke University Press.

Thomas, Deborah A., and Kamari Maxine Clarke, eds. 2006. *Globalization and Race: Transformations in the Cultural Production of Blackness*. Duke University Press.

——. 2013. "Globalization and Race: Structures of Inequality, New Sovereignties, and Citizenship in a Neoliberal Era." *Annual Review of Anthropology* 42: 305–325.

Tlostanova, Madina. 2010. *Gender Epistemologies and Eurasian Borderlands*. Palgrave Macmillan.

Todorova, Miglena. 2006. "Race Travels: Whiteness and Modernity Across National Borders." PhD diss., University of Minnesota.

——. 2018. "Race and Women of Color in Socialist/Postsocialist Transnational Feminisms in Central and Southeastern Europe." *Meridians: Feminism, Race, Transnationalism* 16 (1): 114–141.

——. 2021. *Unequal Under Socialism: Race, Women and Transnationalism in Bulgaria*. University of Toronto Press.

Trehan, Nidhi, and Angéla Kóczé. 2009. "Racism, (Neo-)Colonialism and Social Justice: The Struggle for the Soul of the Romani Movement in Post-Socialist Europe." In *Racism Postcolonialism Europe*, edited by Graham Huggan and Ian Law. Liverpool University Press.

Tronto, Joan, and Berenice Fisher. 1990. "Toward a Feminist Theory of Caring." In *Circles of Care: Work and Identity in Women's Lives*, edited by Emily K. Abel and Margaret K. Nelson. State University of New York Press.

REFERENCES

Tuck, Eve, and Wayne K. Yang. 2014. "R-Words: Refusing Research." In *Humanizing Research: Decolonizing Qualitative Inquiry with Youth and Communities*, edited by Django Paris and Maisha T. Winn. SAGE Publications.

Turda, Marius, and Paul Weindling, eds. 2007. *"Blood and Homeland": Eugenics and Racial Nationalism in Central and Southeast Europe, 1900–1940*. Central European University Press.

Tuvikene, Tauri, Wladimir Sgibnev, and Carola S. Neugebauer, eds. 2019. *Post-Socialist Urban Infrastructures*. Routledge.

van Baar, Huub. 2011. "The European Roma: Minority Representation, Memory and the Limits of Transnational Governmentality." PhD diss., University of Amsterdam.

———. 2019. "From 'Lagging Behind' to 'Being Beneath'? The De-Developmentalization of Time and Social Order in Contemporary Europe." In *The Securitization of the Roma in Europe,* edited by Huub van Baar, Ana Ivasiuc, and Regina Kreide. Palgrave Macmillan.

Vasudevan, Pavithra. 2019. "An Intimate Inventory of Race and Waste." *Antipode* 53 (3): 770–790.

Vaughn, Sarah E. 2022. *Engineering Vulnerability: In Pursuit of Climate Adaptation*. Duke University Press.

Velkova, Maria R. 2003. "Is the Proposed Bulgarian Government Strategy on Municipal Waste Separation Cost-Efficient?" MS thesis, University of Oxford.

Verdery, Katherine. 1996. *What Was Socialism, and What Comes Next?* Princeton University Press.

Vincze, Enikő. 2014. "The Racialization of Roma in the 'New' Europe and the Political Potential of Romani Women." *European Journal of Women's Studies* 21 (4): 435–442.

———. 2023. "The Making of a Racialized Surplus Population: Romania's Labor-Housing Nexus." *Focaal* 97: 63–78.

Vincze, Enikő, Norbert Petrovici, Cristina Raț, and Giovanni Picker, eds. 2018. *Racialized Labour in Romania: Spaces of Marginality at the Periphery of Global Capitalism*. Palgrave Macmillan.

von Schnitzler, Antina. 2016. *Democracy's Infrastructure: Techno-Politics and Protest After Apartheid*. Princeton University Press.

Voyles, Traci Brynne. 2015. *Wastelanding: Legacies of Uranium Mining in Navajo Country*. University of Minnesota Press.

Vukov, Nikolai. 2015. "Past Intransient/Transiting Past: Remembering the Victims and the Representation of Communist Past in Bulgaria." In *Remembrance, History, and Justice: Coming to Terms with Traumatic Pasts in Democratic Societies*, edited by Vladimir Tismaneanu and Bogdan C. Iacob. Central European University Press.

Waseem, Zoha. 2023. "Stateless and Vulnerable: Race, Policing, and Citizenship in Pakistan." *PoLAR: Political and Legal Anthropology Review* 46 (1): 128–134.

Weheliye, Alexander G. 2014. *Habeas Viscus: Racializing Assemblages, Biopolitics, and Black Feminist Theories of the Human.* Duke University Press.

Weinberg, Adam S., Allan Schnaiberg, and David N. Pellow. 2000. *Urban Recycling and the Search for Sustainable Community Development.* Princeton University Press.

Weiss, Erica. 2016. "Refusal as Act, Refusal as Abstention." *Cultural Anthropology* 31 (3): 351–358.

Weitz, Eric D. 2002. "Racial Politics Without the Concept of Race: Reevaluating Soviet Ethnic and National Purges." *Slavic Review* 61 (1): 1–29.

Wekker, Gloria. 2016. *White Innocence: Paradoxes of Colonialism and Race.* Duke University Press.

West Ohueri, Chelsi. 2021. "On Living and Moving with Zor: Exploring Racism, Embodiment, and Health in Albania." *Medical Anthropology* 40 (3): 241–253.

——. 2024. "Peripheral Whiteness and Racial Belonging and Non-Belonging: Accounts from Albania." In *Off White: Central and Eastern Europe and the Global History of Race,* edited by Catherine Baker, Bogdan C. Iacob, Anikó Imre, and James Mark. Manchester University Press.

Willen, Sarah S. 2019. *Fighting for Dignity: Migrant Lives at Israel's Margins.* University of Pennsylvania Press.

Winegar, Jessica. 2016. "A Civilized Revolution: Aesthetics and Political Action in Egypt." *American Ethnologist* 43 (4): 609–622.

Wolfe, Patrick. 2006. "Settler Colonialism and the Elimination of the Native." *Journal of Genocide Research* 8 (4): 387–409.

——. 2016. *Traces of History: Elementary Structures of Race.* Verso Books.

Wynter, Sylvia. 2003. "Unsettling the Coloniality of Being/Power/Truth/Freedom: Towards the Human, After Man, Its Overrepresentation—An Argument." *CR: The New Centennial Review* 3 (3): 257–337.

Yurchak, Alexei. 2005. *Everything Was Forever, Until It Was No More.* Princeton University Press.

Zhang, Amy. 2020. "Circularity and Enclosures: Metabolizing Waste with the Black Soldier Fly." *Cultural Anthropology* 35 (1): 74–103.

——. 2024. *Circular Ecologies: Environmentalism and Waste Politics in Urban China.* Stanford University Press.

Zimring, Carl A. 2016. *Clean and White: A History of Environmental Racism in the United States.* New York University Press.

Znepolski, Ivaylo, Mihail Gruev, Momtchil Metodiev, et al. 2018. *Bulgaria Under Communism.* Routledge.

INDEX

absurdity, 7, 14–15, 65, 99, 190, 213n112; of bureaucratic language, 102; of conferences, 96–97; and elections, 125–26, 128, 147, 189; of environmental sustainability initiatives, 177; of Europeanization, 182; of limiting water access, 187, 190; of racializing logics, 155, 163, 165, 182; of Roma "inclusion," 109; of right-wing anti-Roma claims, 130; of the status quo, 27; of sweepers' circumstances, 49; of the waste-race nexus, 200

acceptance: of bodily struggle, 54–55; and "moving on," 153, 173; and the waste-race nexus, 153; and water infrastructures, 192, 195. *See also* coping; futility

access: denied, 19; and disability, 157; to water, 184–93, 222n18, 232n13

Aenasoaie, Luciana: on Romani communities in Piatra Neamţ, Romania, 220n50. *See also* displacement

Anand, Nikhil: on hydraulic citizenship, 234n29. *See also* water

Andor, László, 121; on Roma integration, 106–7. *See also* integration, Roma

Ani (pseudonym), 41, 45, 48, 52–57, 156–57. *See also* sweeping, street

animals: disposal of dead, 36; dogs (as given more respect than Roma people), 23; dogs (stray), 55, 58–59, 66, 216n1; horse carts (for trash and recycling collection), 3, 77, 80, 86–88, 152, 199; mouse (dead in a dumpster), 1

Anton (pseudonym), 112, 114–16, 186. *See also* Romani Star NGO (pseudonym)

Arendt, Hannah: on race in Europe, 207n52. *See also* race

assimilation, 11; and labor, 21; racial, 58; socialist "total assimilation" policy, 10, 20–21

Ataka (political party), 92, 112, 136. *See also* far-right politics

INDEX

Atanasova, Maria: on Roma representation in European Parliament, 226n16. *See also* representation, Roma

Baka, 1–8, 14, 31, 77, 80, 109, 183, 188, 195, 199
bartering, 217n9
benefits, state: disability, 55, 57, 78, 167; employment, 160, 214n5; tax, 17; unemployment, 41–42, 214n5
Berlant, Lauren: on compromised conditions of possibility, 221n9; on "slow death," 177
Bhabha, Homi, 216n35
Bitaka (flea market), 23, 31, 182
Bițu, Nicoleta: on Roma history, 16
Blackness, 203n13, 204nn58–59, 206n40, 211n97, 227n35; and animalization, 231n27; and labor, 34, 231n32; and Roma, 22–23, 53, 144, 148, 164, 176–77, 180, 182. *See also* race
Bobi (pseudonym), 116, 194–95
boredom, 35, 164–65
Borisov, Boyko, 59, 110, 135–37
Boyan (pseudonym), 35–36, 52, 57, 158. *See also* sweeping, street
Browne, Simone: on racializing surveillance, 222n17. *See also* surveillance
bryukselski ("Brussels-speak"), 102, 110, 113, 189. *See also* language; obfuscation
Buchanan, Donna: on the location of Europe, 212n110
Buck-Morss, Susan: on slavery, 204n18
Bulgarian Communist Party, 19–20, 99–100, 173, 222n12
Bulgarian Helsinki Committee, 125, 222n21, 225n1, 229n2
Bulgarian Ministry of Environment and Water, 62, 74, 81, 86, 181

Bulgarian National Waste Management Programme (NWMP), 13–14, 206n43
Bulgarian Socialist Party (BSP) (political party), 135–36

Caldwell, Melissa: on Russian dachas, 232n14. *See also* labor
Campt, Tina: "living otherwise," 182; on refusal, 207n48, 208n58, 230n12. *See also* refusal
cash: potatoes as, 217n9; as preferred by street sweepers, 51–52, 160; trash as, 78. *See also* debt; sweeping, street
catharsis, 168, 178
Ceaușescu, Elena: execution of, 135
Ceaușescu, Nicolae: execution of, 135
census, 10, 20–21, 139, 165–66, 204n23
Césaire, Aimé: on colonization and "thingification," 202n7
Chang, Felix: on Roma integration initiatives, 223n30. *See also* integration, Roma
"changes, the" (*promenite*), 69, 128
charity, 66
Chistota (cleaning firm), 37–38, 58, 61, 213n4, 217n14; and Romani labor, 20–21, 128, 210n91; and worker value, 70
Citizens for European Development of Bulgaria (GERB) (political party), 136
citizenship, 234n29; vs. status, 16–17, 25, 68, 193, 201n1
Civil Society in Action, 227n37, 228n38
Clean Bulgaria in One Day (campaign), 218n21, 219n37
Cohen, Cathy: on leisure pursuits (as escape), 232n12; on nonnormative heterosexuality, 229n9; on political resistance, 228n44

INDEX

Collins, Patricia Hill, 208n59
consultants: environmental, 39; "experts," 29, 98, 105, 114, 221n8; waste management, 74
consumer waste, 70–74, 162–63
contagion: and COVID-19, 209n69; as racialized trope (against Roma), 18, 209n69
coping: of street sweepers, 49, 53–55, 153. *See also* acceptance
COVID-19, 179; and Romani containment, 209n69, 232n16. *See also* contagion
Cox, Aimee Meredith, 213n116
Creed, Gerald: on being Bulgarian (and whiteness), 205n29; on the criminalization of Roma, 219n36. *See also* criminalization; whiteness
criminalization, 230n14; of Black Brazilians, 227n35; of Roma, 76–90, 102, 106–11, 120–21, 130–33, 138, 146–47, 169, 195, 219n36, 221n54, 228n39; and waste, 67, 76–90, 147. *See also* recycling; theft
culture: and ideas of Europe, 5, 14; repression of, 19–20

DANS (Bulgarian State Agency for National Security), 135–36
Davcheva-Ilcheva, Nadezhda, 218n19
debt, 43–52, 56, 134, 157, 228n38; intergenerational, 34, 157, 214n7; and job security, 45; and shame/guilt, 47; and temporality, 63–64
dehumanization, 6, 12, 16, 155, 178, 182–83, 199, 207n50, 208n58; of waste workers, 23–24, 34, 50, 52–56, 60, 65, 161, 229n10. *See also* disposability, racial
denial: of racial hierarchy, 9–10, 20–23
depression: and the NGO sector, 114–16
Desi (pseudonym), 57, 161. *See also* sweeping, street

Deyanova Mahala (pseudonym), 151–53. *See also* displacement
Dimitrov, Georgi, 19; policy toward Roma, 210n75
discardability. *See* disposability, racial
displacement: of Romani communities, 5, 11, 17–18, 151–53, 195, 201n3, 229nn4–5. *See also* segregation
disposability, racial, 6–10, 12–13, 15–16, 23–24, 27, 34, 41, 60, 92, 108, 119–21, 126, 129, 134–35, 148, 161, 167, 181–83, 197, 199–200, 202n8, 207n47, 213n1. *See also* dehumanization
dispossession, 16. *See also* displacement
domestic: cleanliness, 146, 159, 167, 188; trash, 38–39, 206n38
Donchev, Tomislav: and the attempted pacification of protestors, 110. *See also* protest
Donka (pseudonym), 42, 47, 54, 153–56, 158, 161–68, 172, 178, 183, 185, 188, 199. *See also* humor; sweeping, street

Ecoglasnost: and human rights organizations, 222n21
education; and EU policies, 24, 110, 144–46, 203n10; and race, 11, 125, 148; and segregation, 20, 97, 101, 113–14, 118
elections. *See* voting
Emil (pseudonym), 87–88
endurance, 9, 55
ethnic cleansing, 20, 92
eugenics, 11, 62, 222n19. *See also* race: science
Europe. *See* Europeanness
Europeanization, 8–15, 17, 22–23, 27, 43, 51, 75, 91–92, 120, 149, 189, 196–98, 206n40, 212n106; and

Europeanization (*cont.*)
gatekeeping, 25; as racial project, 61–65, 205n29, 207n52, 216n36; refused, 182. *See also* Europeanness; European Union; integration, Roma

Europeanness, 11–17, 25, 61–65, 75, 82, 181, 216n36, 217n6. *See also* Europeanization; European Union

European Social Fund, 93–97

European Union, 212n107, 217n3, 212n103, 220nn45–46, 220n50, 221n5, 225n51; vs. Europe as "elsewhere," 25; mandates of, 7–9, 13–14, 24–25, 34–35, 56–57, 63, 67, 70, 72–75, 83–86, 90–91, 181–83, 203n10, 206n38, 215n18, 220n46

exoticism: and Blackness, 23; and Roma, 100

expendability. *See* disposability, racial

Fakulteta, 48, 54, 86–87, 111–13, 116, 123–27, 131, 147–48, 209n69, 211n101, 214n8, 218n21, 221n5; and infrastructure, 138, 186–88, 190–99, 232n13, 233n25. *See also* voting; water

family separation, 18, 195, 234n30

Fanon, Frantz: on racialization, 205n30

far-right politics, 128–38, 147, 166, 221n54; Ataka (political party), 92, 112, 136; National Front for the Salvation of Bulgaria (political party), 98; and Roma integration initiatives, 59, 93, 98, 101–2, 105–6, 117, 119–20, 133–34, 180; Revival (political party), 92; VMRO–Bulgarian National Movement (political party), 92. *See also* integration, Roma; neo-Nazi presence; voting; white supremacy

fear, 12, 15, 41–42, 172, 177, 195, 205n34, 228n38; of debt, 44; and far-right politics, 93, 116, 130; of Roma, 19–20, 44, 93, 98–100, 138, 163, 165, 167, 189; of violence, 173. *See also* white supremacy

Fehérváry, Krisztina, 226n21; on socialist ideas about labor, 216n27. *See also* labor

femininity, 173, 175, 177; and race, 59, 163. *See also* gender; International Women's Day

Fennell, Catherine: on bodily dispositions, 215n16. *See also* segregation

Fernando, Mayanthi, 216n38

Filipovtsi, 47, 161, 167, 197, 199

fire: neighborhood razing, 17, 128, 151, 195, 226n12; trash bins catching, 38, 40; waste-incineration, 73, 90, 197, 219n42, 234n32

Fischer, Eugen, 222n19. *See also* eugenics; Holocaust; race: science

Fotta, Martin, 203n13

Fredericks, Rosalind: on labor, waste, and the body, 219n33; on a trash-workers' union in Dakar, Senegal, 232n11. *See also* refusal

Freeman, Christina, 231n28

friendship: and street sweepers, 151–78, 198–99; and survival, 169–70. *See also* solidarity

futility, 115; of protest (seemingly), 103–5; of voting, 126–27, 134, 143, 146–50, 198. *See also* acceptance; protest; voting

gender: and intersections of race and class, 154–55, 163, 196, 230n19; and protest, 107; and waste work, 34, 38, 57, 70, 76–77, 157–59, 168, 173; and repair, 196. *See also* femininity; International Women's Day

INDEX

Georgiev, Kimon: and the banning of Pashov's work, 18. *See also* Pashov, Shakir

Ghodsee, Kristen, 215n24, 219n32

Gidwani, Vinay: on repair, 233n18; on the waste-value dialectic, 203n11

Gille, Zsuzsa: on the roots of ecological modernization, 71

Gilmore, Ruth Wilson: on premature death, 230n26

gold: and Roma stereotypes, 117; found in trash, 5–6

Graan, Andrew: on Europeanization, 206n40. *See also* Europeanization

Grant, Bruce, 204n18

graffiti, racist, 4, 25–26

Greenberg, Jack, 211n98

Greenberg, Jessica, 208n55

Grosz, Elizabeth, 230n12

Gupta, Akhil: on relationality, 229n10

harassment: and Blackness, 231n32; of waste workers, 3–4, 7, 31, 34, 59–61, 144, 154–55, 161, 174–75

hiding, 43, 51, 153, 155, 220n46; in plain sight, 129–30

Hill, Jane: on (racist) "real talk," 224n46

Hird, Myra, 202n6

Holocaust, 18–19, 209nn70–71

horse carts (for trash and recycling collection), 3–4, 77, 80, 86–88, 152, 199. *See also* animals; recycling; waste collectors (*kloshari*)

Hristina (pseudonym), 161–65, 178. *See also* sweeping, street

Hristo (pseudonym), 84, 88. *See also* recycling

Hristov, Anthony: and *WALL-E*, 91

Human Rights Project, 222n21, 229n2

Human Rights Watch, 224n40

humor, 4–5, 12, 14–15, 29, 36, 46, 49, 95–96, 99, 115, 138, 152, 159–65, 175, 178, 185, 190, 198, 200, 221n10; and conformity, 163; and

connection, 172; and insubordination, 27; and survival, 111

hygiene, 21, 186, 222n18; and COVID-19, 232n16; urban, 188; racial, 209n71. *See also* COVID-19; water

hyperinflation: in 1990s Bulgaria, 69–70, 159, 217n5

identification: for loans, 45–46, 214n10; for police-stops, 3; for selling metal at a collection site (*punkt*), 87. *See also* debt; recycling; surveillance

Imre, Anikó: on whiteness, 206n36. *See also* whiteness

infrapolitics, 149, 207nn48–49, 215n14

integration, Roma, 82, 93–111, 138, 144–46, 210n82, 212n106, 221n4, 224n41; and far-right politics, 59, 93, 98, 101–2, 106–7, 117, 119–20, 133–34, 180; "The National Strategy for the Integration of Roma," 119–20. *See also* Europeanization; far-right politics

International Day of Romani Resistance, 18. *See also* protest; resistance

International Waste Expo, 33–34

International Women's Day, 155, 173–78, 230n24. *See also* femininity; friendship; gender

intersectionality, 203n10. *See also* gender; race

Ivan (pseudonym), 83–85, 92. *See also* recycling

Ivanka (pseudonym), 169–72, 188, 199. *See also* sweeping, street

Ivanova, Izabela, 3, 94, 96, 105, 124, 156, 196

Jackson, Stephen, 234n29. *See also* repair

Jackson, Zakiyyah Iman: on animalization, 231n27. *See also* dehumanization jokes. *See* humor

Jung, Yuson, 211n101, 216n6, 219n30, 221n8, 226n21

Justin, Eva, 100–101, 209n71, 222n19. *See also* Holocaust; race: science; surveillance

Jesus (pseudonym), 43, 161. *See also* sweeping, street

Kanev, Krassimir, 222n21

Karakachanov, Krasimir: and Roma integration strategy, 101–2. *See also* far-right politics; VMRO–Bulgarian National Movement (political party)

Katunitsa, 131–32, 227n37, 228n38. *See also* Rashkov, Kiril; voting

Kelley, Robin D. G., 207n53, 228n44; on the racialized workplace, 231n32; on infrapolitics, 207n49; on politics from below, 149; on racialization and the European project, 15–16. *See also* infrapolitics

King, Tiffany Lethabo: on decolonization, 232n10

Kóczé, Angela: on Romani feminism and Black feminist epistemologies, 208n59

Komicite (The Comedians), 139, 163, 165–66

Kremikovtsi (metallurgy plant), 76–77. *See also* metal

labor: and assimilation, 21; and Blackness, 34; and the body, 53–55, 158–59, 168, 172, 178, 198; escaping, 232n14; forced, 19, 209n71; and gender, 34, 38, 57, 70, 76–77, 157–59, 168, 173; informal, 63, 224n34; intimacy of, 229n7; and race, 34, 48, 57, 61, 70, 144, 148, 180, 189, 207n53, 213n1; as (potentially) transformative, 216n27

language, 223n22; *bryukselski* ("Brussels-speak"), 102, 110, 113, 189; and

discrimination, 103; and identity, 210n83, 216n31; and politics, 201n1; repression/suppression of, 19, 134

Larkin, Brian: on urban space and infrastructure, 28

leftover food: as waste, 1, 6, 199

Lemon, Alaina: on the racialization of Roma, 216n31. *See also* race; racialization

Lepawsky, Josh, 234n29

Liboiron, Max: on transforming Land into resource, 13

Lie, Siv: on a "raciosemiotic" approach, 216n31

loans. *See* debt

londzha system, 44, 214n8. *See also* mutual aid

Lora (pseudonym), 57–61. *See also* animals: dogs (stray); sweeping, street

Lowe, Lisa: on inequity and conceptions of the "human," 214n12

Lyuba (TV character on *Komicite*), 139, 163, 165–66

MacBride, Samantha: on the original Zero Waste approach, 73. *See also* recycling; Zero Waste programs

mafia, 109, 128, 131, 133, 143, 228n42

Mankekar, Purnima: on relationality, 229n10

Maria (pseudonym), 23, 93–94, 97–99, 104, 107–11, 114, 120–22, 133, 149, 183. *See also* protest

Maringanti, Anant: on the waste-value dialectic, 203n11

Martin (pseudonym), 111–17, 121, 186. *See also* Romani Star NGO (pseudonym)

Mattern, Shannon, 234n29. *See also* repair

Maya (pseudonym), 45–46, 53–54, 160–61, 178, 183, 188, 199. *See also* sweeping, street

INDEX

memes, 135–36
Mengele, Josef, 209n71. *See also* eugenics; Holocaust; race: science
metal: scrap, 2, 38, 71–72, 77–78, 86–87, 193, 218n22. *See also* Kremikovtsi; recycling
Mihaylova, Daniela, 220n43
Millar, Kathleen: on form, 212n108
Mimi (pseudonym), 45, 48, 54, 56–57, 156–57, 174–75. *See also* debt; sweeping, street
Mitrani, Leon: on Jews in Bulgaria, 209n72
mockery, 57; of absurdity, 15; refusal of, 141; of Roma, 24, 96, 166; of white womanhood, 162–63, 165
modernization: and race, 9, 14, 17; and recycling, 71
Morris, Rosalind, 230n19
Movement for Rights and Freedoms (DPS) (political party), 136
Murphy, Michelle: on alterlife, 230n11
mutual aid, 44, 214n8. *See also londzha* system

Nadka (pseudonym), 54–55, 64. *See also* sweeping, street
names: and forced "integration," 210n82; and race, 11, 20; of waste companies 24; street (and postsocialism), 223n28; and Bulgaria's "total assimilation" policy 10, 20
National Front for the Salvation of Bulgaria (political party), 98. *See also* far-right politics; Simeonov, Valeri
Neimanis, Astrida: on water and connection, 232n13. *See also* water
neo-Nazi presence, 3–4, 25, 174. *See also* far-right politics; violence; white supremacy
Nixon, Rob: on slow violence, 177. *See also* violence

"no life" (*nyama zhivot*), 5, 9, 115–16, 120, 153, 184; refusal of, 155, 172–73, 184, 194, 197–200
normalcy, 188–89, 218n30

obfuscation: vs. incompetence, 48–49. *See also bryukselski* ("Brussels-speak")
Open Society Institute, 97, 111, 118, 212n106, 223n22, 224n25, 225n49, 227n37. *See also* Soros, George
Organisation Istikbal, 214n8. *See also* Pashov, Shakir
Organization for Security and Co-operation in Europe (OSCE), 125–26, 225n1, 227n37
overpopulation: as racialized trope (against Roma), 39–40, 93–95, 102, 111, 130, 154, 163, 165, 167. *See also* sterilization, forced

Palmer, Paul: and the term "Zero Waste," 73. *See also* recycling; Zero Waste programs
Panayotova, Bojina, 30, 171
Pandian, Anand: 232n8, 232n13
Pashov, Shakir, 18, 209n68, 210n75. *See also Organisation Istikbal*
Petrova, Dimitrina, 222n21
Petko (pseudonym), 77–81, 86, 92, 199. *See also* recycling; waste collectors (*kloshari*)
Petar (pseudonym), 139–49, 189, 194, 227n29. *See also* voting
Petya (pseudonym), 54–55, 170–72. *See also* sweeping, street
Phoenix Resource, 72. *See also* metal; recycling
pipes. *See* water
Plevneliev, Rosen, 119
polluter pays principle, 56–57, 65, 91, 203n10
Popov, Metodii, 205n27

Povinelli, Elizabeth: on alternative worlds and the otherwise, 231n31. *See also* friendship; solidarity

power: perpetuation of, 104, 137; and race, 11

pressure: blood (of street sweepers), 50, 53–55, 178

protest, 99, 103–11, 182, 224n39, 226n8, 227n22, 227n24, 231n2; anticommunist, 227n24; anti-Roma, 128–38, 147, 166, 221n53, 229n4; at French embassy, 181; seen as futile, 103–5; and gender, 107; at Sheraton Hotel, 93–99, 105–14, 116, 120–21, 129, 133, 149, 179, 181; strikes, 51–52, 135–37; year of, 135

public: bathhouses, 187; bathrooms, 161; cleaning (voluntary), 72, 217n21; discomfort/embarrassment, 46, 153, 164–65, 168, 178, 185; vs. private relations, 230n323

purity, 58; notions of Bulgarian, 19; refusing racial, 188. *See also* Chistota (cleaning firm)

race, 10–12; colorization, 22–23, 164, 211n99, 230n20; denial/disavowal of, 9–10, 20–23; and education, 11, 148; and the European project, 15–16, 207n52; and gender, 163; and labor, 34, 48, 57, 61, 70, 144, 148, 180, 189, 207n53, 213n1, 224n34, 231n32; and language, 216n31; and modernization, 9, 14, 17; and recycling, 218n18; science, 11, 18, 62, 222n19; and value, 16. *See also* disposability, racial; racial capitalism; racialization; racial sustainability

racial capitalism, 13, 16, 24, 34, 49, 55, 75, 193, 198, 202n9, 206n39, 207n53. *See also* race; racialization; racial sustainability

racialization, 7, 9–16, 27–28, 61, 82, 92, 100, 117, 134, 138, 149, 155, 164, 180–82, 184, 187, 201n1, 202n8, 204n16, 205nn30–31, 207n53, 208n59, 210n83, 212n102, 216n36, 224n34, 231n32; of repair work, 196; of Roma, 10–12, 16, 19–23, 50, 68, 147, 149, 154–55, 182, 216n31, 222n17, 231n27; of waste work, 21, 24–25, 29, 34, 41, 50–51, 53–54, 58, 65, 70, 79, 90–92, 96–97, 110, 177–78, 181, 205n30, 213n1, 231n27. *See also* disposability, racial; race; racial sustainability

racial sustainability, 13–16, 25–27, 68, 76, 92, 138, 184, 200, 202n9. *See also* race; racialization

Rada (pseudonym), 42, 44, 46–49, 54, 153–56, 167, 174–75, 183, 188, 199. *See also* debt; sweeping, street

Rafiev, Ali, 222n12

Ralph, Laurence, 203n13

Rashkov, Kiril, 131–33. *See also* Katunitsa

Raya (pseudonym), 161–62, 165. *See also* sweeping, street

recycling, 8–9, 66–92, 152, 218n18, 218n20; bins, 66–67, 72, 82–83; and cynicism, 8; decline of, 72; and education, 88–89; of politicians, 135–37; producer responsibility organizations, 67, 84; *punktove* (collection points), 67–68, 71, 76–80, 83–85, 87, 89–91, 220n45; and state pride, 71–72; and trust, 72, 75; Zero Waste programs, 72–75, 86, 91–92, 197, 218nn26–27, 220n51. *See also* reuse; waste collectors (*kloshari*); Zero Waste programs

red: cards, 104, 109, 116; national football team uniforms, 49; trash (and communism), 135, 227n24; waste-worker uniforms, 7, 35–36, 49, 152, 160, 163. *See also* protest; uniforms

refusal, 207n48, 226n6, 226n9, 230n12, 232n11; to dance, 170; of

INDEX

the death paradigm, 178; of Europeanization, 182; of funding, 127; generative, 215n14; and lasting change, 104; to mock, 141; of personhood-denial, 99; play as, 154–55, 162–63; of racial disposability, 167, 182; to be refuse, 231n11; of the status quo, 15, 27, 31, 104, 109, 135, 147, 150, 178, 182, 194, 198, 200, 207n48; of the sustainability paradigm, 183; to vote, 126–27, 134, 143, 146–50, 198
refuse-derived fuel (RDF), 73, 90, 197, 234n32. *See also* fire
reign of terror (surveillance campaign), 117, 121. *See also* surveillance
repair, 207n48, 233n26, 234n29, 234n31; and care, 193–97; infrastructure, 188–91, 193–99
replaceability, 42–43. *See also* disposability, racial
representation, Roma political, 118, 130–33, 135, 226n16, 228n40
resistance, 15, 18, 60, 207nn48–49, 228n44, 230n12, 231n32, 232n12; abstention as, 126–27; play as, 154–55, 162–63. *See also* refusal; retreat; protest
retreat, 104, 122, 126–27, 150, 207n48, 226n6. *See also* refusal
reuse, 70, 72, 76–77, 220n50; and race, 218n18. *See also* recycling
Revival (political party), 92. *See also* far-right politics
risk: of government assistance, 195; of street sweeping, 171, 174, 178; of trash collecting, 2
Robertson, Jennifer: on gender subversion among Takarazuka performers, 230n19. *See also* gender
Robinson, Cedric, 202n9, 206n39, 207n53, 208n55; on retreat, 104, 122, 126–27, 207n48, 226n6

Romani Star NGO (pseudonym), 86, 111–17, 186, 221n5. *See also* Fakulteta
romanticization: of Roma, 205n24; of Turkish Bulgarians, 11
Rosa, Jonathan: on the workings of race, 11. *See also* race; racialization
Rosa (pseudonym), 126, 128, 132–34, 147–50, 183, 187–88, 190, 192, 195. *See also* voting; water
Rucker-Chang, Sunnie T.: on the conflation of whiteness with European, 202n5. *See also* whiteness

Sadinata (waste facility), 197–98. *See also* Valentina (pseudonym)
Sara (pseudonym), 143–50. *See also* refusal; voting
Sarafian, Iliana: on the politics of childbearing, 221n1
Sarkozy, Nicolas: and deportation/ expulsion of Romani citizens, 106, 127, 181
Savić, Jelena, 208n59
Schengen Zone, 12, 205n34
Schwenkel, Christina, 234n29; on traveling technologies, 218n27; on waste accumulation in Vietnam, 219n30; on water relations in Vietnam, 233n23. *See also* water
Scott, James, 149, 228n41, 228n44. *See also* infrapolitics
segregation: and the body, 214n16; of communities, 20, 25, 29, 140; and education, 20, 97, 101, 113–14, 118. *See also* displacement
Shange, Savannah, 206n40, 216n37; on the rhetoric of the liberal state, 139; on the term "progressive," 202n4
Simeon II, King, 137
Simeonov, Valeri: and (improbably) the Council on Ethnic Minority

Simeonov, Valeri (*cont.*)
  Integration, 98. *See also* far-right
    politics; National Front for the Sal-
    vation of Bulgaria (political party)
Simmons, Kimberly: on colorization,
  211n99, 230n20. *See also* race
Simon (pseudonym), 93–99, 102–11,
  114, 118, 120–22, 129–31, 133, 137,
  149, 152, 179–83, 188, 198. *See also*
  protest
Simpson, Audra, 147, 228n41; on the
  political, 207n48. *See also* refusal
sink (dumping ground): locating a,
  13, 73, 90–91, 183, 199, 220n46,
  232n8
slavery, 16, 204n18, 208n54, 216n36,
  22n17; of Roma, 16, 209n61
Sofka (pseudonym), 44, 48–54,
  115–16, 154, 167, 183, 188, 199–200.
  See also sweeping, street
solidarity, 182, 202n7; and dignity,
  188; and street sweepers, 151–78,
  198–99, 229n10; and survival,
  169–70, 183; as threat, 44, 99–100.
  See also friendship; mutual aid
Solomon, Marisa, 219n31; on race and
  waste, 203n13
"something else" (*neshto drugo*), 9,
  128, 203n13
Soros, George, 97–98, 223n22. *See
  also* Open Society Institute
Sosna, Daniel: on waste management
  and the EU, 215n22
Stamatopoulou-Robbins, Sophia: on
  the need to constantly manage
  waste, 231n15
Stefan (pseudonym), 117–18, 225n51
sterilization, forced, 18, 102. *See also*
  overpopulation
Stoyanova, Iskra: on recycling and
  Romani labor, 86. *See also* recycling; waste collectors (*kloshari*);
  Zero Waste programs
Sudetic, Chuck, 225n49

surveillance, 93–122, 195, 221n11; and
  anthropology, 100–101; and (Roma)
  integration, 100, 102; and pride, 51;
  and protest, 111; and recycling, 85,
  87–88; racializing, 222n17; reign of
  terror, 117, 121; of street sweepers,
  35, 43, 45, 51, 56, 153, 155–58, 161,
  165, 174
survival: and humor, 111; and sol-
  idarity/friendship, 169–70, 183,
  231n30. *See also* acceptance;
  coping
sweeping, street, 7–8, 28–65, 109;
  vs. automation/machines, 42–43,
  62–64; as catharsis, 168; firings,
  30–31, 41–42, 45; and friendship/
  solidarity, 151–78, 198–99, 229n10,
  231n30; as compared to prostitution, 159–61; and resistance,
  15; and risk, 171, 174, 178; and
  surveillance, 35, 43, 45, 51, 56,
  153, 155–58, 161, 165, 174; and the
  weather, 36, 41. *See also* uniforms

Tahir, Orhan, 208n56
Tanya (pseudonym), 31–32, 109. *See
  also* Baka
taxes, 17, 133, 193; waste, 39–41, 57,
  215n22
temporality: and sustainability, 13–14;
  and waste, 63–64
theft, 202n7, 217n11; car, 69; child,
  195, 234n30; of funds, 117; waste,
  31, 38, 81–82, 84, 86, 89, 130.
  See also criminalization, Roma;
  recycling
Thomas, Deborah, 204n17; on the
  objectification of workers, 215n14
Thurnwald, Richard, 222n19. *See also*
  eugenics; Holocaust; race: science
Todor (pseudonym), 116, 121–22
Todorova, Miglena, 205n27
tools, waste work, 2, 37. *See also*
  sweeping, street

INDEX

Tosen (pseudonym), 174–75. *See also* sweeping, street

Trayanka (pseudonym), 188–89, 191, 194. *See also* voting; water

Treaty on European Union, 217n3

Trehan, Nidhi: on Romani feminism and Black feminist epistemologies, 208n59

trust: and recycling, 72, 75; and voting, 125

Tsvetanov, Tsvetan: and the criminalization of Roma, 107–10, 116. *See also* criminalization, Roma

Turkish Bulgarians, 10–11, 19–22, 99, 204n23, 210n84, 214n13; romanticization of, 11

Tyson, Mike: product-shilling of, 23. *See also* Blackness

uniforms, 7, 33, 35–36, 152; and aesthetic standards, 62; as changing colors, 24, 148; flammable, 7; partial, 55; racialization of, 29, 34, 61, 96–97; and status (with the company), 41–42, 45; unofficial, 3. *See also* sweeping, street

United States, 22, 31, 58, 60, 69, 180, 202n4, 211n97; civil rights movement in, 122; Embassy, 28, 110–11, 224n47, 229n5; racialization in, 208n58, 211n99, 230n20; and Romani communities, 224n47

Vabrava (pseudonym), 139–40, 189. *See also* voting

Valentina (pseudonym), 197–98. *See also* Sadinata (waste facility)

Verdery, Katherine: on the meaning of "Europe" in postsocialist Romania, 212n110

Veronika (pseudonym), 49, 52, 57. *See also* sweeping, street

Viktor (pseudonym), 174–75. *See also* sweeping, street

violence, 3–4, 23, 69, 98–99, 124, 128–31, 148, 153, 173–74, 178, 228n39, 229n4; slow, 177

Violeta (pseudonym), 184–85, 188. *See also* sweeping, street; water

visibility/hypervisibility: of protestors, 105–6; of waste workers, 64, 97, 109, 154–55, 161, 177. *See also* protest; surveillance; sweeping, street

vivification, 190. *See also* water

VMRO–Bulgarian National Movement (political party), 92. *See also* far-right politics

Voix des Rroms, La, 18

voting, 123–50; buying and selling votes, 123–27, 138–42, 144–45, 147, 188, 225n1, 227n37; and propaganda, 127, 128–33, 138, 165; and refusal, 126–27, 134, 143, 146–50, 198; rights, 17; suppression of, 124, 128, 139, 141, 147

waste collectors (*kloshari*), 67–68, 83, 85–86, 91, 219nn39–40, 220n45. *See also* recycling

waste-race nexus, 13–15, 23, 34, 41–42, 46, 56–61, 64, 68, 79–80, 153, 155, 183–84, 193, 200, 232n13. *See also* race; racialization

waste-value dialectic, 203n11

water, 216n29, 222n18, 233n23, 233n25; and connection, 232n13, 233n22; and dignity, 185, 189; as harassment tool, 7; infrastructures (decaying), 9, 184–96, 211n101; and normalcy, 188–89; pressure, 191–92; and socializing, 187; and vivification, 190; and waste, 219n37; well-digging, 17

Weiss, Erica: on a politics of abstention, 126. *See also* refusal

West Ohueri, Chelsi, 9; on embodied racism, 215n16; on peripheral whiteness, 206n35 whiteness, 218n21, 220n51, 221n8, 226n17, 228n40; as default/Bulgarianness, 59, 129, 201n1, 205n27, 205n29, 212n102; denaturalizing, 177, 182; and Europe, 5, 12, 25, 213n1; as excluded from waste work, 34; and humanness, 11–12; and "innocence," 206n36

white privilege, 28–29

white supremacy, 3–4, 25–26, 76, 98–99, 104, 155, 208n58, 224n46; and anthropology, 28; normalization of, 127

Willen, Sarah: on dignity (despite criminalization), 230n14. *See also* criminalization

witnessing, 4

Wonder Clean Sofia (WCS) (pseudonym), 35, 37–38, 41, 153, 160. *See also* sweeping, street

work. *See* labor

Zero Waste programs, 72–75, 86, 91–92, 197, 218nn26–27. *See also* recycling

Zhivkov, Todor, 19–20, 137. *See also* Bulgarian Communist Party

Zlatna (pseudonym), 44–45, 151, 153, 159–61. *See also* sweeping, street

Zoellick, Robert: and the (attempted) donation of funds to Romani communities, 113–14